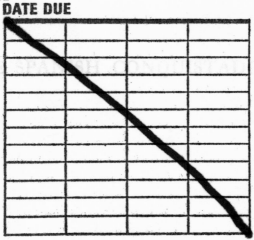

THE
SPANISH
CONQUISTADORES

by

F. A. KIRKPATRICK

Meridian Books

THE WORLD PUBLISHING COMPANY

CLEVELAND AND NEW YORK

A MERIDIAN BOOK

Published by The World Publishing Company
2231 West 110th Street, Cleveland 2, Ohio
Published simultaneously in Canada by
Nelson, Foster & Scott Ltd.
Third Printing, April 1968

INTRODUCTION

APART from some contact with Creole life through travel and sojourn in lands of Spanish speech, the materials for this volume are derived entirely from printed pages to be found on the shelves of the British Museum. Yet the volume aims at supplying a need; for the work of Spanish-American historians remains in great part unknown to English readers, notably the vast, varied and illuminating work of the Chilian historian, the late José Toribio Medina, the greatest authority on the history of Spanish America. Moreover the story of the Spanish conquests in America has never yet been told as one great movement within the space of a single volume. That limitation of space has meant much compression and many omissions, some of them regrettable but unavoidable.

A question occurs whether in printing proper names the accentuation now prescribed by the Spanish Academy should be used. In the many English works concerning the Conquest it is hard to find any consistency except in those books which omit accents altogether. Some accents, as on Cortés, Colón, Córdoba, Cumaná, Belalcázar, are helpful; others, as on Díaz, Velásquez, López, are probably only disturbing to the English reader. Seeing that the accents of to-day were unknown to the Conquistadores and to writers of their age, it has been decided to print them only in the Index and on the first appearance of any name, omitting them elsewhere.

As a matter of convenience, the usual English custom has been followed of anglicising the name of King Ferdinand V of Aragon: in other cases the Spanish form of the name has been preserved—Fernando or Hernando.

Since the testimony of Las Casas concerning the treatment of the Indians is suspect to some Spaniards and since his numbers are certainly exaggerated, no use has been made in this volume of that part of the writings of Las Casas.

Acknowledgment is here made to the Syndics of the Cambridge University Press for permission to reproduce in Chapter XXVI two or three paragraphs from *A History of the Argentine Republic* published by the University Press.

One point deserves emphasis: whatever be the standpoint of time or place from which the work of the Spanish Conquistadores should be judged, their work should first be viewed from the Golden Tower by the water-side at Seville and through the eyes of the generation which saw the cross raised on the towers of the Alhambra and, twenty-seven years later, the accession of the King of Spain to the imperial throne.

F. A. K.

CONTENTS

MAPS

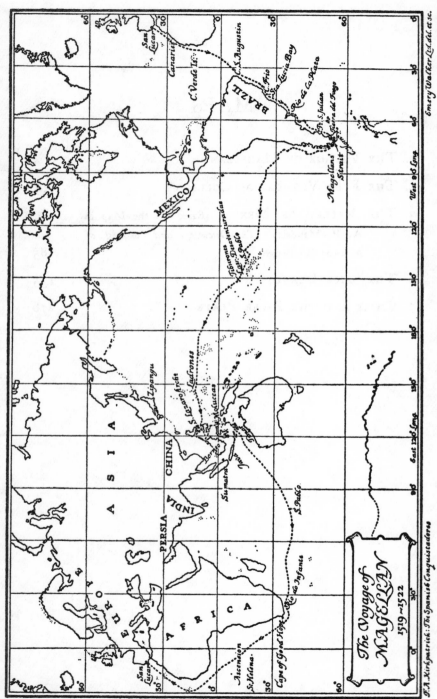

The Voyage of
MAGELLAN
1519~1522

F. A. Kirkpatrick: The Spanish Conquistadores

Emery Walker Ltd del. et sc.

THE SPANISH CONQUISTADORES

CHAPTER I

COLUMBUS

He accomplished a thing of the greatest glory and such that his name will never be forgotten. GÓMARA

THERE is one historical event which everybody knows. Even those whose predilections do not turn towards history know that Christopher Columbus discovered America. This general knowledge of one fact indicates how that singular achievement, the discovery of a New World, has captivated the sentiment of all Europe and all America as the most notable event in secular history. But Columbus chiefly concerns us here as the man who gave to Spain a vast and opulent dominion beyond the Ocean, as the first of the Conquistadores. He found the way for those Spanish explorers, discoverers, conquerors and settlers who in the course of a marvellous half-century penetrated a world of novel and fantastic pattern, subdued two extensive monarchies rich in hoarded treasures and in unworked veins of precious metals, traversed forests, deserts, mountains, plains and rivers of a magnitude hitherto unknown, and marked out the limits of an empire nearly twice the size of Europe with an audacious and almost careless rapidity, lavish of effort, suffering, violence and human life.

In picturing those who came after Columbus early biographies concern us little. We see these men step upon the scene as captains leading their followers to effort and to victory. But the quality of the man who opened the way for their work and reserved that work for Spaniards and for Spain demands fuller enquiry. His setting out with three little ships on his westward oceanic quest was not the beginning of his work, but rather the culmination of efforts pursued through long years, whereby an obscure foreigner, seemingly the projector of a chimerical scheme, won the support of the most sagacious sovereigns who ever ruled Spain; so that by their favour and his own prowess he became 'Admiral of the lands and islands of the Ocean Sea' and Viceroy of all lands discovered by him.

Columbus, though prolific of speech and writing, was reticent about his early life. So also was his eulogistic biographer, his son Fernando. But both father and son abound in anecdotes and allusions, which are amplified by Las Casas, his second admiring biographer—allusions to noble ancestors, to imaginary university studies, to service under an 'illustrious kinsman' admiral of France, to Columbus as commander of a fighting ship, leading a timorous crew into action by an extraordinary feat of navigation, to Columbus leaping from a burning pirate ship ('which perhaps he commanded,' says Las Casas) and swimming two leagues ashore ('exhausted by wounds,' adds Las Casas).

When Columbus, writing his own testimonial, talks of forty years at sea, of voyages wherever ships had sailed, of scientific learning and of intercourse with learned men, we must remember that the man who thus viewed his early life through a coloured and magnifying haze was the same man who later suggested that the Orinoco was one of the four rivers flowing from the Earthly Paradise, and promised to fit out, with the gold of the Indies, 100,000 foot and 10,000 horse to recover the Holy Sepulchre.

The adventurous career of Columbus, at once tragic and triumphant, is more strange than all invention and needs no embellishment.

He was born in 1451, the son of a weaver in Genoa, who for a time kept a wine-shop. He followed his father's trade, but also made some Mediterranean voyages from the busy port of Genoa, either as a seaman or in charge of merchandise. At the age of twenty-five he joined a longer and more venturesome expedition, bound for England. Hardly had the five Genoese ships passed westward through the Straits of Gibraltar, when they were attacked off Cape St. Vincent by a French corsair: two Genoese ships were burnt: three escaped to Cadiz; men leaping from the burning ships were rescued by Portuguese shore-boats. Columbus was one of the Genoese who escaped: whether he was one of the swimmers cannot be known: but when, shortly before his death, he spoke of his 'miraculous' arrival in the Peninsula, he was recalling the strange adventure which brought him thither and which was the first unpremeditated step towards his conception of a westward voyage across the Atlantic.

After completing early in 1477 on board a Genoese ship the interrupted voyage to England, Columbus settled in Lisbon and joined his younger brother Bartolomé in his business of making mariners' charts: but he was also engaged in trade and in seafaring, making a voyage to Genoa and one or more to Portuguese Guinea, where he came into contact with the dusky inhabitants of strange lands, with profitable trade by barter and with the lucrative slave trade.

Through attendance at the same church, he met and

finally married a Portuguese lady, Isabel de Moñiz, whose father, the first Governor of the island of Porto Santo, near Madeira, had left records of Atlantic voyages, eagerly perused by Columbus. In Lisbon and in Madeira, where he lived for a time, he was caught up into the movement of oceanic discovery which for sixty years had flowed from Portugal. Year by year the Portuguese were pushing their way southwards along the west coast of Africa. Towards the west they had occupied the distant Azores and had made efforts towards yet more remote Atlantic discovery. 'Columbus concluded', says his son, 'that there must be many lands to the west. . . . He hoped to find on the way to India some beneficial island or land whence he might pursue his main design. He concluded that between the coast of Spain and the known boundary of India there must be many other islands and lands.' He heard of carved wood floating in the Ocean, of huge canes and strange trees drifting ashore in Porto Santo or the Azores, boats also, and once even two dead bodies having broad faces different from the aspect of Christians. There were tales of Antilia, of St. Brandon's Isle, of the Island of Seven Cities, of islands intermittently descried by mariners gazing westward.

Later, in the convent of La Rábida, he listened to sailors' talk about signs of land and even about land seen to the west of Ireland. Indeed many maps showed islands lying far west in the unexplored Ocean.

Fernando and Las Casas both relate that Columbus, through a Florentine living in Lisbon, consulted Toscanelli, a famous Florentine geographer. Toscanelli replied by sending a copy of a Latin letter which he had written to a Portuguese priest in 1474. This letter, which has been preserved, speaks of a 'short (westward) route to the Indies where the spices grow', and to Cathay (Northern China), the abode of the Great Khan. A map, which was enclosed with the letter, does not exist: but the notes on the map which are appended to the existing letter add that from Lisbon due west to the city of Quinsay (Kwang Chow) are 1625 leagues; 'and from the island of Antilia, which is known to you, as far as the island of Cipango (Japan) are . . . 2500 miles. . . . That island is rich in gold, pearls, and gems: the temples and palaces are roofed with solid gold.' Toscanelli's figures reduce the circumference of the earth by one-third and exaggerate the eastward extent of Asia.

Las Casas, without vouching for its truth, tells, as probable, a story which he found believed both by Columbus' first companions and by the inhabitants of Haiti (Española) generally when Las Casas settled there ten years after Columbus' discovery of the island. A ship, he says, sailing from the Peninsula for England or Flanders, driven westward by storms, came upon 'these islands' (the Antilles): after a disastrous homeward voyage, she reached Madeira with a few dying survivors. The pilot, being received and tended in Columbus' house, before his death revealed to his host, in writing and with a chart, the position of the newly found island.

Oviedo (1478–1557) tells the story independently, but disbelieves it. Gómara (1510–60), an honest but uncritical historian, whose book appeared in 1552, relates the story as a fact, adding that, although the details were differently related, 'all agree that the pilot died in Columbus' house' and left him the account of the voyage and the situation of the 'lands newly seen and found'. The story has not won general credence.

About the end of 1483 Columbus petitioned King John II of Portugal for three caravels provisioned for a year and furnished with trifling objects for barter, 'hawks'-bells, small brass bowls, thin sheets of brass, strings of beads, coloured glass, small mirrors, scissors, knives, needles, pins, shirts, coarse coloured cloth, red caps and other such things. . . . things of little value but much esteemed by people ignorant of them.' So says Las Casas, apparently copying from a document. He is not likely to have invented the list, especially as it tells against his view that Columbus' main design was to reach 'the rich lands of Cathay'.

It has been much debated whether Fernando and Las Casas were right in saying that Columbus' main design was, by sailing west, to reach the Far East, vaguely designated by the word 'India', or whether he rather expected to find unknown lands. His two biographers clearly state that he had both designs. He was certain of finding land: but it would be unreasonable to attribute to Columbus, alone among all discoverers, unvarying certainty as to the character of the lands to be found. Moreover, 'Cipango', so prominent in his search, was a link between the two designs. Barros, the Portuguese chronicler, says, 'Columbus hoped to find Cipango and other unknown lands'. Cipango, never subdued by the Great Khan, unvisited by any European, and said by Marco Polo to lie 375 leagues from the Asiatic Continent, was remotely connected with the Far East, but was also an 'unknown land' to be found somewhere in the Ocean. Fernando, writing after the event, implicitly claims success for his father by declaring that Española (Haiti) is 'Antilia and Cipango'. And in his preface he speaks of Columbus' discovery 'of the New World and of the Indies' as if both designs had succeeded, although Fernando knew that his father had not reached the Far East. The matter is confused by the fact that down to the nineteenth century the Spaniards gave the name *Las Indias*, 'the Indies', to Spanish America. Since Columbus concerns us here as a Conquistador, a man of action, not as a theorist, this brief paragraph may suffice.

In his application to the Portuguese King, Columbus demanded for himself, if successful in his western search, extraordinary dignities, power and emolument. The Portuguese King, after consulting experts, declined the proposal.

By this rebuff and by the death of his wife Columbus was cut loose from Portugal. His brother Bartolome, a sturdy, determined and energetic sailor, took ship for England, was taken by pirates, escaped, and in February 1488 submitted the scheme to Henry VII, who rejected it. Bartolome then passed to the Court of France, to find no better success. Bartolome's movements are not quite certain, and do not concern the present narrative. There is some evidence that he was with the Portuguese expedition which discovered the Cape of Good Hope in 1487. He did not return from France to the Peninsula till the end of 1493, when Christopher had departed on his second voyage. Meantime Christopher, about the end of 1484, sailed secretly from Lisbon to the port of Palos, in south-west Spain. He found hospitality in the neighbouring monastery of La Rábida, where the friars took charge of his little son Diego, while he departed for Seville to seek support, without success at first. But the Count (afterwards Duke) of Medina Celi, a man of princely wealth and authority, feudal lord of the Port of Santa María near Cadiz, listened to the poor foreigner, lodged him in his own house for over a year, and prepared to supply him with ships. However, judging upon reflection that such an enterprise was for royalty alone, the Count wrote to Queen Isabel, who in May 1486 summoned Columbus to Córdoba, received him in audience and delivered him to the charge of Quintanilla, Treasurer of Castile, who befriended him. Gradually he obtained the countenance of other magnates of the Court, particularly of Sant-ángel, a Valencian of Jewish descent, joint-Treasurer of the Santa Hermandad, and also Controller and Account-ant of the Royal Household, a post which brought him into close intercourse with Isabel. Santangel had served Ferdinand in various financial affairs, including loans of money. It says much for Columbus that he won the effective support of this practical calculating business man.

But to ask for ships, men and money seemed madness when Ferdinand and Isabel, whose marriage had united the crowns of Castile and Aragon, were striving to regulate a land distracted by misrule and were devoting all resources to the War of Granada, which was to end Moorish dominion in Spain. This poor foreign sup-pliant had nothing in his favour but his strength of char-acter, his tenacious ambition, the impressive force of his personality and his faith in his idea, a faith which grew into the consciousness of a manifest divine mission and found persuasive expression in imaginative and some-times inventive talk and writing. 'He was a man', says Oviedo, who knew him, 'of good stature and aspect, above the middle height and strong-limbed: vivid eyes and well-proportioned features; fair-haired; his face high-coloured and somewhat freckled. . . . pleasant in speech when he chose, angry when he was annoyed'. 'An aquiline nose', says his son, 'and hair, which had been fair, snow-white at the age of thirty'; a man whose bearing, dignified and impressive except for occasional bursts of passion, helped to win for him the scarcely deserved reputation of a scholar and a geographer.

For five years, while a Royal Commission examined the project, Columbus lived the wearisome humiliating life of the poor suitor at Court. 'Since his cloak was threadbare, all held him to be a fabulous dreamer', offering, as he did, dominion and glory to the Crown, spiritual conquests to the Church, and demanding for himself unheard-of dignity, power and emolument.[1]

Early in 1491 he emerges from this dim time of expectancy in Santa Fe, half military camp, half hastily constructed city, set up by the Catholic Sovereigns in sight of the Moorish towers of the Alhambra. Here the Commission gave their decision—against Columbus. He departed from Santa Fe, determined to carry his proposal to France.

In a legal deposition twenty-three years later, Maldonado, one of the Commission, declared that they had discussed with scholars, learned councillors and mariners about the admiral's 'going to the said islands (no mention of the Far East) and all agreed that what the admiral said was impossible'. Columbus himself may perhaps be held partly responsible for his disappointment; for according to the testimony of his own son he

---

[1] The story that Columbus argued for his proposal before the dullard Doctors of the University of Salamanca is a fable. The Commission sat for a time at Salamanca, when the Court was there; and Columbus secured the favour of the excellent and learned Deza, afterwards Archbishop of Seville, tutor to Prince John and a powerful advocate of Columbus at Court. The Archbishop's secretary, Bernáldez, in his Chronicle of the Catholic Sovereigns, gives a valuable account of Columbus' doings.

only gave feeble arguments to the Commission, not wishing to give away his design lest he should be anticipated in the execution of it. A man who always keeps something back can hardly expect complete confidence.

On his way to take ship for France, Columbus revisited La Rábida. Here he found a warm advocate in the friar Juan Pérez, who had been confessor to Queen Isabel: after due consultation, Perez wrote a letter to the Queen: in a fortnight his messenger returned with a summons to Court: Perez borrowed a mule and set out at midnight for Santa Fe: he returned in due course with good news. The Queen sent money to Columbus to provide suitable apparel for appearance at Court and a mule for the journey. Full of hope, he travelled to Santa Fe, where the proposal was submitted to a committee of great Councillors. They were divided in opinion but rejected the proposal, and Columbus again departed.

He had barely gone two leagues when a royal messenger, riding hard, overtook him and called him back. Queen Isabel had decided to grant all his demands, Santangel having promised to lend the necessary funds and having urged acceptance, pointing out that Columbus was to get nothing in case of failure.

The decisive intervention of Juan Perez and of Santangel has been questioned as improbable. But all notions of probability must be discarded in dealing with Spanish history, which constantly startles one with surprises. 'In Spain everything happens by accident', wrote Richard Ford. Columbus had other advocates, but the intervention of these two is well authenticated and is explained by the intimate relations of both men with the Sovereigns and by their firm faith in Columbus' proposal. Santangel, who should be conspicuous in history, since he played a determining part at the crisis of Columbus' life, was rather a dim and enigmatic figure until Señor Serrano y Sanz traced and illustrated by documents his biography and family history in a book entitled *Orígenes de la dominación española en América*. It is the biography of an astute and successful business man: Santangel had been Receiver of the Royal Dues in his native city of Valencia, had farmed the Customs in the same busy port, and had lent money to King Ferdinand. These and other financial transactions brought him into close touch with the King, while his position as a sort of glorified royal housekeeper meant frequent business with the Queen. Serrano y Sanz expounds the mode in which Santangel raised the funds: but to a layman unacquainted with finance the details are difficult to follow. It is clear, however, that the money did not come out of Santangel's own pocket, but from the finances of the Santa Hermandad: although entitled joint-Treasurer of the Santa Hermandad, he seems to have been in fact joint-Farmer of the Revenues of the Santa Hermandad.

The moment was propitious. 'I saw', wrote Columbus a year later, 'the royal banners of your Highnesses on the towers of the Alhambra; and I saw the Moorish King come out to the city gates and kiss your royal hands.' Granada had capitulated: the long adventurous epic of the Reconquista had ended in triumph; and Spain was ready to launch out upon her second epic, an adventure which should circle the globe and make her the envy of all nations. It is no mere fancy to view the conquest of America as a continuation of the *Reconquista* of Spain, as a fresh adventure of expanding dominion, of crusading zeal and of lucrative enterprise. The royal banners now hoisted on the towers of the Alhambra were within half a century to wave over the palaces of Montezuma and Atahualpa: the long war against the infidel in the Peninsula was to continue in war against the gentile beyond the Ocean. But the issue could not be foretold. The enterprise sanctioned by Isabel within sight of the towers of the Alhambra was a great act of faith on the part of the Queen of Castile and her people.

An agreement or 'capitulation' was drawn up which granted, in case of success, noble rank, the title of Admiral, with all the prerogatives enjoyed by the Admiral of Castile, to Cristóbal Colón and to his heirs for ever in all these islands and mainlands,[1] which should be discovered or won by his hand and industry, also that he and his heirs for ever should have the office of Viceroy and Governor in the islands and mainlands discovered or won by him, with power to judge in all cases pertaining to these offices and to inflict punishments, and with power to name three persons for every vacant magistracy, of whom the Crown should choose one; that the Admiral should have one-tenth of all profits obtained by the Crown within his jurisdiction; that in every expedition sent to those lands the Admiral might contribute one-eighth of the cost and receive one-eighth of the profit. There is no mention of Asia, India or the Far East. But, in addition to a passport or open letter addressed to 'all Kings and Princes', Columbus was furnished with a letter from the Catholic Sovereigns addressed to the

[1] The plural is used, *tierras firmes*. In the 'title' issued a few days later the singular is used, *tierra firme*. In a later paragraph of the capitulation and also in the subsequent title the words are 'discovered *and* won.' The privileges of the Admiral of Castile were to hold civil and criminal jurisdiction at sea and in navigable rivers and all ports, to decide all litigation, to appoint Magistrates, Constables, Notaries and officials, and to grant Letters of Reprisal.

Great Khan, 'for he always believed' says Las Casas 'that beyond the finding of mainlands and islands, he was to come upon the kingdoms of the Great Khan and the rich lands of Cathay'.

It should be noted that colonisation—the provision of homes overseas for emigrant Spanish families in empty or unclaimed lands—was not the intention. The objects were commerce, especially the lucrative trade in spices, with rich civilised countries, and the acquisition of lands where the discoverer might reign as Viceroy over newly won vassals of the Castilian Crown and neophytes of the Catholic Church. But obviously these matters could not be clearly defined until the issue of the enterprise should be known. Columbus was not only a seafaring trader and a determined vigorous adventurer, but also a dreamer and a visionary. Exact precision in defining his objects and forecasting the issue was not to be expected of him. In any case his hopes, his ambition and his promises were grandiose, and they were justified by results which he did not live to see.

NOTE.—A much-debated question concerning the authenticity of Toscanelli's letter need not be examined here, since Professor Prestage in *The Portuguese Pioneers* (p. 189) discusses both its authenticity and the value of its contents. To justify the statement on page 3 that Columbus discovered America, the definition of the word 'discover' in the Concise Oxford Dictionary may be quoted,—'to disclose, expose to view, reveal.' Thus the statement is not a denial of any earlier contact with the Western Hemisphere, but an assertion that Columbus opened the gate of the New World.

CHAPTER II

THE FOUR VOYAGES, 1492–1504

I think that in future times the Spaniards who discovered this empire
will be much esteemed and their names will be more talked of than in
these present times. . . . that which I esteem most is not the conquests
nor battles with the Indians, but the labour of discovery.

CIEZA DE LEÓN

THE decision was now taken. The town of Palos was
commanded by the Crown to equip three ships.
But their equipment in fact was mainly due to the three
brothers Pinzón, 'rich mariners and principal persons'
of Palos, particularly the eldest, Martín Alonso, a man
'very spirited and an experienced mariner', who believed in success as firmly as Columbus himself and
was bent on finding Cipango. Martin Alonso swept in
recruits, evidently with hope of great profits for himself,
although it is not known what agreement or promises
were made by Columbus. Without the aid of Pinzon,
Columbus could never have found in Palos crews who
would have crossed the Atlantic. Yet neither Columbus
nor his son mention this indispensable help, which is
fully attested from other sources. Las Casas believes,
although without certain proof, that Pinzon lent the
money which Columbus was bound to supply towards
the cost of the expedition.

On Friday, 2 August 1492, three little ships,
'very suitable for the service' says Columbus, crossed

the bar of Palos (or Saltes). The crews numbered ninety: there were about thirty others: servants, officials and other landsmen. Columbus sailed in the largest but slowest ship, the *Santa María*, with the famous navigator Juan de la Cosa as master. Martin Alonso Pinzon commanded the *Pinta*, with his brother Francisco as master. The third Pinzon brother, Vicente Yáñez commanded the little *Niña*, with her owner, Pedro Alonso ('Peralonso') Niño, as master. At first they traversed familiar seas; for a course was set for the Canary Islands, most of which had lately been subjected to the Crown of Castile. The real enterprise was begun when on 6 September the little squadron set sail from Gomera, the most westerly of those islands, upon the voyage which was to set the history of the world upon a new course. Orders were given that after sailing 700 leagues the ships should lie-to at night-time, since they would then be approaching land.

'For thirty-three days I never knew sleep', wrote Columbus years afterwards, recalling the intense anxiety of those weeks. They sailed steadily westward before the perennial north-east trade wind, 'through temperate airs' and on a calm sea—a most prosperous voyage. But the suspense; the alarm caused by the variation of the compass; the supposed signs of nearing land, repeatedly found deceptive; murmuring among the crew; even mutterings of mutiny lest there be no return home—all this is pictured in the log or journal kept by Columbus daily until his return home. This survives only in an abridgment by Las Casas, which preserves, however, the direct personal touch of Columbus and often gives his words.

After a fortnight—400 leagues from the Canaries—

Columbus and Pinzon agreed that they were approaching islands marked on Columbus' chart, which was passed on a cord from ship to ship and eagerly scrutinised. But in reality they were still sixteen days from land. On 7 October the course was altered to southwest, since birds were flying in that direction, apparently to land. On the 10th the crew, alarmed at the increasing distance from home, refused to go farther: but Columbus, promising great rewards, insisted. Next day signs of land were certain. Columbus, after the customary evening prayer, 'spoke pleasant and joyous words to the men'. At dawn of Friday, 12 October 1492, they anchored off the shore of a small island, one of the Bahamas: Columbus rowed ashore with the other two captains and a notary: displaying the royal banner, while the naked and beardless islanders gathered round, he called his companions to witness that he took possession of that island for Ferdinand and Isabel; an island of green trees, many waters and various fruits, 'marvellous woods, climate and foliage like an Andalucian spring, songs of birds so that a man might never wish to depart, flocks of parrots obscuring the sky, fruits and perfumes from the trees'. The inhabitants, 'poor in everything'—though some wore pieces of gold in their pierced nostrils—brought parrots and balls of cotton in exchange for beads and hawks'-bells—gentle people, says Columbus, ignorant of arms; easy to subjugate and carry to Castile or make captive in their own land; would make good servants and easy converts.

As he cruises among the Bahamas and coasts along the larger islands, everything has the freshness of novelty; the boats, which they call *canoas*, hollowed from a tree-trunk, some carrying forty men, who row with a thing like a baker's shovel and travel with incredible

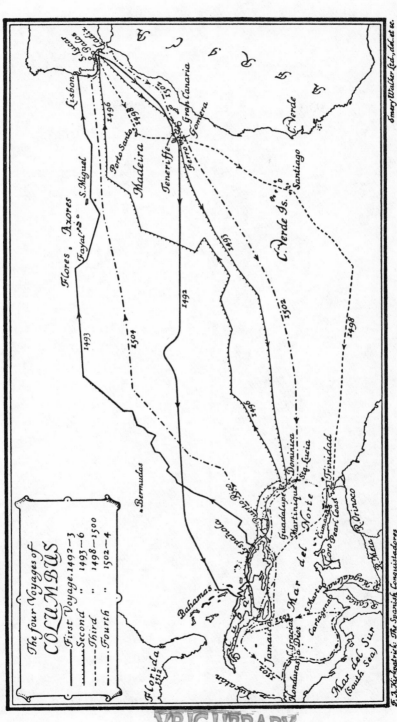

The four Voyages of
COLUMBUS

First Voyage, 1492-3
Second   "   1493-6
Third   "   1498-1500
Fourth   "   1502-4

Emery Walker Ltd. del. et sc.

F. A. Kirkpatrick: The Spanish Conquistadores

speed: if they upset, they swim and right the boat and
bale the water with calabashes: their hanging netted
beds they call *hamacas*. Men and women walk carrying
a lighted brand (a cigar) and fumigate themselves: a
naked 'king' is vastly delighted with the gift of a pair of
gloves.

Having forcibly seized six Bahama islanders to carry
to Spain, Columbus sailed for Cuba, hoping for Cipango, and spent six weeks exploring the northern coast
—a coast so long that he fancied it might be a projection
of the Asiatic Continent. Delighted with the harbours,
the climate, beauty and fertility, but finding only naked
dwellers in huts, he sent two men inland to search for
'a king and great cities'. They found small villages,
'nothing civilised'. But, still thinking of Asia, Columbus
called the people Indians, a name which has stuck; and
the trans-Atlantic dependencies of the Spanish Crown
were known thenceforth as *Las Indias*, 'The Indies.'

On 21 November Martin Alonso in the fast *Pinta*
sailed away to the east 'from covetousness', says Columbus, 'thinking that an Indian on board would give him
much gold'.

On 6 December the two remaining ships reached the
north-western projection of Haiti, which Columbus
named *Isla Española*, finding fresh and greater delight
in the wooded mountains and the fertile beauty. Here
the people brought pieces of gold and masks with
golden eyes and ears, begging for *chug-chug* (bells).
Columbus, intent upon his Oriental fantasies, pictures
to himself vast undiscovered treasures of gold, besides
mastic and spices, although these islands produced no
mastic and no spices except pepper. He hears of an interior province called Cibao: it sounds like Cipango.
He prays that he may find a gold mine; 'may Our

Lord in His mercy guide me that I may find this gold' are his words.

On a calm night, Christmas Night, while Columbus took some much-needed rest, the *Santa María* grounded on a sandbank and was wrecked. Columbus, always full of his divine mission, declares that the wreck was the work of the Lord and a happy event, since it led him to make a settlement. The contents of the ship were saved and with her timbers a fort was built, named *Navidad*, where thirty-nine men were left to hold the land. On 6 January Martin Alonso with the *Pinta* reappeared, with profuse explanations: 'all lies', says Columbus . . . 'but for his defection we might have brought a ton of gold'.

A few days later the two ships sailed north-eastward for home through the region of prevalent south-west winds. They separated in stormy weather. The *Niña*, after touching at the Azores, entered the harbour of Lisbon, driven by a gale from S.S.W., on 4 March 1493, and ten days later sailed into the port of Palos after an absence of seven months. On the same day the *Pinta*, which had first put into Bayona in north-west Spain, reached Palos. Martin Alonso landed, took to his bed and died a few days later. He had had his share in giving the New World to Spain.

In a letter written at the Azores and sent to Santangel from Lisbon, Columbus announces 'the great victory which our Lord has given me': he extols the beauty and fertility of Española, the 'many mines, great rivers and good waters', many of which contain gold. He promises to the Crown 'all the gold which they may need', spices, cotton and mastic and 'as many slaves as they shall command to be sent . . . our Redeemer gave this victory to our illustrious King and Queen . . .

whence all Christendom should rejoice for the winning of so many peoples to our Holy Faith and also for temporal benefits, not only for Spain. All Christians shall find here refreshment and gain.'

The words were prophetic. Columbus had not found what he sought. But he had found regions of a beauty and fertility beyond description, gorgeous islands set in tropical seas, lands which, notwithstanding earthquakes and furious hurricanes, were for many generations the envy and the prize of warring nations, lands which inspired a stirring literature and gave to sober history a tinge of romance.[1]

As Columbus journeyed north-eastward, traversing the whole Peninsula of Spain, in every place where he passed the people flocked to see the nuggets of gold, the belts and grotesque masks and the red-skinned Indians themselves. In April 1493 he was received in Barcelona with great state and honour by the Sovereigns, who confirmed to him the title and prerogatives of Admiral and Viceroy with all the privileges set forth in the Capitulation, and granted him the castles of Castile and the lions of León to be quartered in his arms. The news of his discovery spread through Italy and elsewhere, and his account of it was published at Rome in Latin prose and at Florence in Italian verse. It was the most glorious moment of his career.

The Sovereigns, in order to obviate possible Portuguese claims, hastened to procure papal sanction for these western conquests. This was readily granted by the Spanish Pope, Alexander VI,[2] with the proviso that

---

[1] Charles Kingsley's book *At Last* brings out this tinge of romance. The international bearings of this story are treated in another volume of this series, *The European Nations in the West Indies*, by Professor A. P. Newton.

[2] In order to satisfy the Portuguese and obviate some ambiguity in the Papal Bulls—for there were several Bulls—the Spanish and Portuguese

the inhabitants of those lands should be brought to the Catholic faith. A great expedition was now prepared. Adventurers eager for gold and rapid fortune crowded to join. Horses, cattle and swine—animals unknown to the New World—were embarked, also seeds and farming implements. In September 1493 the Admiral sailed from Cadiz for the Canaries with seventeen ships carrying 1200 armed men, besides artisans, officials and some priests, headed by the Benedictine, Fray Bernardo Buil—1400 or 1500 men in all, but no women. The Admiral had a retinue of ten personal attendants (*escuderos*) and twenty servants. Nearly 100 stowaways contrived to hide on board the ships.

From the Canaries the Admiral steered farther south than in the previous year, and after a prosperous voyage, reached an island which he named Dominica but found no harbour. He landed on a neighbouring island, which was named Guadalupe after a famous Spanish shrine. Here the sight of fragments of human bodies in the native huts horrified the Spaniards. They had come into contact with the Caribs (whence the word *Cannibal*), the fierce man-eating inhabitants of the southern West Indian Islands, whose fleets of war-canoes were the terror of the timid and unwarlike

Crowns agreed by the Treaty of Tordesillas in 1494 that a line drawn from North to South 370 leagues west of the Cape Verde Islands should divide the western discoveries and conquests of the Spaniards from those of the Portuguese to the east. This line gave the eastern part of Brazil to the Portuguese. The Treaty was not meant to supersede Papal sanction but to give it a practical interpretation by the removal of ambiguities and by direct agreement between the two Powers concerned. The story of the Papal Bulls and the Treaty of Tordesillas has been clearly related in another volume of this series, *The Portuguese Pioneers*, by Professor Edgar Prestage (pp. 238-44), and need not be here retold. It may be added that during the period of conquest both the Spanish Crown and the Conquistadores acted on the assumption that it was not only a right but a duty to subjugate the heathen—by peaceable means if possible, by force if not.

dwellers in the northern islands, swooping down upon the coasts to carry off captives, the men to be eaten, the women to be concubines and slaves.

The Admiral's passage along the lovely chain of tropical islands which fringe the Caribbean Sea is recorded in the Spanish names Montserrat, Santa María la Antigua, Santa María la Redonda, Santa Cruz. Steering westward, he discovered the large island of Puerto Rico and finally reached Española—to find the fort of Navidad burnt and not one survivor of its occupants, a fate which they had brought on themselves by throwing off discipline and wandering about the land 'doing much evil to the Indians. . . . They took their wives and daughters and all that they had, at their own pleasure': so says Oviedo, who believed the probable testimony of the Indians, the only surviving witnesses.

Columbus dissembled his chagrin, in order to maintain friendly relations with the neighbouring Indians, and proceeded to take formal possession by tracing the rectangular plan of a city, which he named Isabela, nominating town councillors (*regidores*) and two magistrates (*alcaldes*). Municipal institutions had secured the Reconquista in Spain, and were now to be the foundation of Conquest in America. Every later conqueror was careful to secure his footing in the land by setting up a city which, even if it only contained a score of householders living in wooden huts, nevertheless had all the character of an organised civic community claiming jurisdiction over all the surrounding country.

An exploring party started for Cibao under Alonso de Ojeda, a typical Conquistador, small in stature, but spirited, resourceful, jovial, valiant and not too scrupulous, strong and expert in all athletic and martial exercises, delighting in dare-devil feats of strength and nerve, always in the thick of every fight and never wounded until his last disastrous combat. The Admiral himself, to impress the Indians, marched through the land in military array with all the sound men, the few horsemen riding in front. The natives gazed at these in astounded terror, taking horse and man to be one monstrous creature, until the sight of a man dismounting renewed their amazement. But many sick men were left behind at Isabela, for the site proved pestilential: fever broke out and many died. All the men, including priests and gentlemen-adventurers reared in luxury, were put upon scanty rations and compelled to labour even when weak from hunger and fever. Already there was much discontent among the Spaniards and increasing trouble with the natives when Columbus sailed away in the *Niña* on a voyage of discovery, leaving his brother Diego as his deputy in Isabela, and placing one Margarit, an Aragonese gentleman, in command of a sufficient force to explore and subjugate the interior, with orders to treat the Indians well, but to cut off the ears and nose of any caught thieving, 'since those members could not be concealed'. The Admiral was absent five months. He discovered the fertile and beautiful land of Jamaica, and explored the south coast of Cuba, striving to prove its continuity or connection with the Asiatic realms of the Great Khan. But, assailed by bad weather and entangled in shallows and among the islets which he named the Queen's Garden, he had to content himself with forcing all his crew to swear to their opinion concerning Cuba, on pain of having their tongues slit, besides other penalties, if ever they denied it. Their opinion, for the moment, necessarily coincided with his own hope that Cuba was part of a continent.

Worn by anxiety and fatigue, the Admiral returned

to Isabela in a deathlike stupor and was ill for months. During his absence his brother Bartolome, henceforth his right-hand man, had arrived from Spain; the Admiral now appointed him Adelantado or Governor of the Indies: but government was difficult. Margarit, instead of exploring and subjugating the interior, had sat idle in his fort, ill-treating the Indians and their women; and finally, afflicted with a contagious disease which spread among the Spaniards both now and later, had slipped away to Spain in company with the priest Buil, to spread damaging reports and deride the tales of gold. The history of Isabela was one of sickness, mortality, scarcity and threatened mutiny. The natives were killing every stray Spaniard and finally broke out in revolt: but a crowd of naked men with their clubs and pointed stakes were helpless against the cross-bows, muskets, spears and swords of Columbus' little army of 200 men. The fight was a slaughter, and savage dogs were let loose on the helpless fugitives—an episode in the sufferings of the native population, doomed to disappear in these islands in little more than one generation. Columbus now imposed a poll-tax of gold dust, which his subjects could not pay, and shipped 500 of them to be sold as slaves in Spain, most of whom died. His later efforts to make his dominions profitable by the slave-trade were frustrated by Isabel's decision that her subjects must not be enslaved.[1]

The natives, weary of feeding these voracious guests, ceased to till the ground; famine followed, grievous to the Spaniards but destructive to the natives. Disheartened adventurers returned to Spain without gold but

[1] Later it was ruled that cannibals might be enslaved and also enemies captured in war. The Spanish adventurers gave a liberal interpretation to this concession; and slave-hunting on the Spanish Main became a lucrative business.

'as yellow as gold'. In October 1495 a Royal Commissioner arrived, who assumed arrogant authority. Six months later Columbus, accompanied by the Commissioner, sailed for Spain, leaving his brother Bartolome as deputy, and afterwards sending him orders to make a settlement on the south coast where there was more gold. The city of Isabela was abandoned to the jungle and, so it was said, to phantom hidalgos who stalked about the deserted streets. The newly founded city of Nueva Isabela, afterwards known as Santo Domingo, was for half a century the chief seat of Government for the Spanish Indies. Meantime the Admiral, having brought to Spain some specimens of gold and presenting at Court an Indian 'king' decorated with a heavy gold chain, announced that he had discovered Solomon's Ophir. He received a generous welcome from the Sovereigns, fresh confirmation of privileges and additional marks of honour.

But there was no crowd of eager volunteers to accompany the Admiral on his return to Española. The talk was 'much cost and little profit'. Recruiting was so slow and difficult that pardon was offered to criminals volunteering to go to the Indies. After a year some supplies were sent to Española, and after two anxious and laborious years Columbus sailed with six ships. At the moment of embarkation the Viceroy-Admiral knocked down and heartily kicked an official who had exasperated him—an incident not quite trivial, for it contributed, says Las Casas, to the disgrace of Columbus two years later.

Sending half his fleet direct to Española, the Admiral himself took a more southerly course than before, and, exactly reaching his object, sailed between the island, named by him Trinidad, and the mainland, through the straits which he called Serpent's Mouth and Dragon's Mouth in astonishment at the conflict between the salt water and the vast volume of fresh water flowing from the mouths of the Orinoco. He rightly judged that so great a river must flow through a great continent extending southwards, but adds that the said river flows from the Earthly Paradise. He explains that the earth is not quite spherical but is pear-shaped, that a projection resembling the tail of a pear rises towards Heaven at the Equator, and the Earthly Paradise lies on the top of this projection. He claims to have reached the 'end of the East', but adds with truth, 'your Highnesses have here another world where our holy faith may be spread and great profits won'. There was indeed something fantastic about this land; for the dusky inhabitants, clad in nothing else, were wearing great ropes of pearls. The Spaniards had found the pearl fisheries of Paria, and acquired pearls by the pound either for nothing or in exchange for glass beads.

The Admiral's lieutenants cut boughs from trees in token of taking possession; for Columbus himself, prostrated by illness and temporarily blind, was unable to land on the Continent now discovered by him (August 1498). Nor was he able to pursue the westward voyage which might have solved his geographical perplexities, for the provisions, much needed in Española, were already perishing in the tropical climate.

Arrived at Española, he found that his brother, a foreigner among adventurous gold-hunters, had failed to govern. Food was scarce. 'All their principal evils were from hunger', says Las Casas; the native population, suppressed in repeated revolts, was much diminished; and the Spaniards were in two camps, fighting one another. Roldán, whom the Admiral had left as judge in the island, withdrew to the interior, assumed supreme authority, intercepted supplies coming from Spain and drew to himself all the unruly and dissatisfied men. Columbus was obliged to make two humiliating agreements with him, which the Admiral afterwards advised the Sovereigns to repudiate. Columbus then by force of arms and summary hangings restored some kind of order. In order to satisfy the Spaniards and to encourage economic settlement he assigned to every settler a group of Indians as servants and labourers[1]— an institution of serfdom which hastened the rapid extermination of the natives through mortality caused by unaccustomed labour on meagre diet and through the break-up of family life and fall in the birth-rate. Suicide became common among these forlorn people. But the most sweeping and irresistible destroyers were the plagues of smallpox and measles, newly imported from Europe.

The news which reached Spain moved the Sovereigns to send out a Visitor, one Bobadilla, a knight of the Order of Alcántara and a man of reputation, with full authority to regulate affairs. Bobadilla arrived in August 1500, occupied the house of Columbus, seized his property and papers, put the three brothers in irons —the Admiral submitting with quiet dignity—and after hearing the charges of oppression, injustice and the keeping back of treasures due to the Crown, sent them fettered on board ship for Spain.

'Whither are you taking me, Vallejo?' asked the Admiral of the officer sent to the prison to convey him on board.

---

[1] These *repartimientos* were afterwards developed into the system of *encomiendas,* fiefs of vassal Indians granted to the Conquistadores throughout the Spanish Indies.

'Your worship is going to the ship, to embark', said Vallejo.

'Is it true, Vallejo?' asked the Admiral.

'By the life of your worship it is true', said Vallejo, who was an honourable hidalgo. Whereupon the Admiral took comfort, seeing that he was not going to death.

He refused to have the irons removed during the voyage and reached Cadiz in fetters. The Sovereigns, on hearing it, ordered his release, sent him a handsome gift of money, received him at Granada in an emotional interview and ordered the restoration of his property in Española. But so far from reinstating him as Governor, they sent out to supersede Bobadilla, whose conduct they disapproved, one Ovando, who held high office in the Order of Alcantara, a prudent, just, dignified and honourable man, says Las Casas, 'worthy to govern many people, but not Indians'. A single sentence of Gomara illustrates this remark: 'Ovando pacified the Province of Xaragua by burning forty Indian chiefs and by hanging the cacique Guaorocuya and his aunt Anacoana . . . a woman absolute and dissolute in that island'. In fact the Crown was taking over the administration of the new lands: a Colonial Office was taking shape, afterwards formed into the famous 'Council of the Indies', under Juan de Fonseca, later Bishop of Burgos, a public servant of tried prudence and capacity; and the Casa de Contratación, or Board of Trade to deal with trans-Atlantic commerce, was established at Seville soon after Columbus' departure on his last voyage. The hindering animosity which Fonseca showed towards Columbus was partly due, Las Casas thinks, to the Admiral's independent ways and indiscreet impatience of tedious officialdom. This animosity was probably exaggerated by Columbus' friends: but the later proceedings of Fonseca, particularly his antagonism to Balboa and to Cortés, show him to have been a bureaucrat wanting in imaginative enthusiasm and helpful sympathy; it must, however, be admitted that the Conquistadores were not easy people to deal with.

Other explorers were now putting to sea. A royal decree of 4 April 1495 permitted any subject to solicit, under strict conditions, royal licence for western exploration. A protest from Columbus produced not a revocation of the decree but only an order (June 1497) that if it contained any infringement of the Admiral's rights, such infringement should be revoked. Columbus afterwards modified his claims, merely insisting that any royal licence should be countersigned by his agents at Seville. In 1499–1500 five expeditions, commanded or accompanied by former companions of Columbus and following up his discoveries, ranged along 3000 miles of coast from 7° south latitude to the Isthmus. Ojeda, accompanied by two famous navigators, Juan de la Cosa and Amerigo Vespucci, explored the coast of Guiana and of the country which he humorously called Venezuela ('a queer little Venice'), finding Indian huts on piles above the water in the Gulf of Maracaibo: his methods were combative rather than diplomatic and his frequent fights with the natives were an unfortunate introduction of European civilisation to that region.

Bastidas, a notary of Seville, continued the exploration up to the Isthmus of Panamá. Although on his return voyage he lost both his worm-eaten ships on the coast of Española, Bastidas and his men carried away, travelling on foot, enough treasure to make the voyage most profitable. Meantime Vicente Yañez Pinzon passed the Equator, found the mouth of the huge Amazon and coasted the shore of Brazil; but having lost all that he risked upon the venture, Pinzon led back to Spain a few exhausted survivors of tempest and ship-wreck.

Lepe, a pilot of Palos, pushed still farther south along the Brazilian coast. But the richest venture was that of Peralonso Niño who sailed for the Pearl Coast in a fifty-ton ship with thirty-three men, and on his return after eleven months raised a sensation by producing pearls 'as if they were chaff', besides gold and valuable log-wood: the crew were suspected of concealing many pearls, besides those which paid the royal dues. There are some indications of other voyages, not distinctly recorded. The Admiral protested in vain against the grant of licences without his concurrence, and also against the senseless cruelties perpetrated upon the Indians by some of these adventurers, to the discredit of all white men and the detriment of later enterprises.

So far the Crown had derived little profit from these western discoveries. But there were clear indications of possible wide dominion and of future revenues. No wonder then that the Admiral, who had shown the way for all this, was despatched upon another royal quest to win dominion and treasure (1502-4): he received civil and criminal jurisdiction over 140 men, paid by the Crown, which also paid for the hire and equipment of four ships. The course to be taken was prescribed, with orders not to touch at the island of Española except on the homeward voyage; directions were also given con-cerning the search for treasure and the establishment of a settlement in newly found lands. The Admiral was accompanied by his brother Bartolome and also by his illegitimate son Fernando, aged fourteen years, who drew the King's pay as a member of the expedition. That the Admiral was in command of an armed royal fleet and was treated with signal confidence by the Sovereigns is proved by the fact that just before sailing he received orders from the Crown to divert his course in order to bring aid to a Portuguese post in Africa which was besieged by Moors. The documents which testify to these preliminaries and to the history of this voyage are printed by Navarrete whose *Colección de viajes* (Madrid 1823–37) is still the principal and indispensable authority for the voyages of Columbus and forms the most valuable part of the Raccolta published in 1892. The Admiral duly carried out the last commission, only to find that the siege of the place had been raised and the succour which he brought was not needed by the Portuguese garrison.

This last voyage of Columbus in command of a royal fleet is notable in the history of exploration and conquest: for just as Columbus had been the first to discover the Antilles and the mainland, so now he was the first to explore the coast of the region now known as Central America, to search for a strait and to attempt a settlement on the mainland. He was also the first to come into contact—a contact brief and slight, it is true —with the remarkable civilisation or semi-civilisation of Yucatán and the Mexican region. His enterprise was marked by a characteristic persistence of endeavour in spite of accumulating disasters and prostrating sickness.

Before his departure he wrote to the Pope, 'I gained 1400 islands and 333 leagues of the Continent of Asia, besides many other great and famous islands. . . . This island (Española) is Tarsis, is Scythia, is Ophir and Ophaz and Cipanga.' His voyage was an attempt to justify such claims by finding rich lands farther to the west and by finding more gold and yet more gold. 'Gold is most excellent', he wrote; 'of gold is treasure made; with gold the possessor of it does all that he desires in the world and arrives at sending souls to Paradise.'

Before leaving Spain, the Admiral completed his *Book of Privileges*, that is to say Privileges granted to him, and also his strange *Book of the Prophecies*, wherein he seeks to prove that Old Testament prophecies foretold the discoveries which he had accomplished and the reconquest of the Holy Sepulchre which he hoped to accomplish. Columbus' belief and his desire to persuade others that there was something mysterious, something marked out by Divine ordinance, in his name and person find expression in his customary symbolical signature, which has been variously interpreted by conjecture, but never with certainty.

.·S.   S̊.
  ·S·   Å   S̊·
    X M y
  X P͞O FERENS //

At last, in May 1502, he sailed from Cadiz. The needs of his fleet brought him, notwithstanding royal prohibition, to Santo Domingo, the only Spanish base in the New World, where thirty ships were about to sail for Spain. They put to sea, disregarding Columbus' forecast of a hurricane; twenty ships sank with all hands, among them Bobadilla and Roldan, and with much treasure, including a gold nugget said to weigh thirty-six pounds, 3600 pesos de oro; one ship reached Spain: the rest put back, much shattered. Among the countless tragedies of the Conquest this disaster stands out owing to its dramatic personal appeal.

Meantime Columbus' four ships, although refused

entrance to the harbour, rode out the storm, made for Jamaica and southern Cuba and thence steered west-south-west across the Caribbean Sea. A notable episode is recorded by his son Fernando. At the island of Bonaca (Guanaca) off the north coast of Honduras, they came upon a great canoe, loaded with merchandise and manned by twenty-five men: a cabin of palm-leaves, impervious to rain, sheltered the women and children and the goods—garments and sheets of dyed cotton, hatchets and other articles made of copper, and weapons such as were afterwards found in Mexico. The people in the canoe declared that they had brought these things from the west, that is to say from Yucatan. But instead of being drawn westward by this certain evidence of 'wealth, politeness and ingenuity', the Admiral stuck to his original design. Sailing eastwards to the point which he named Cape Gracias a Dios, and thence southwards, he explored the coasts of Honduras, Nicaragua and Costa Rica (to use the modern names) as far as the Isthmus. Gold was found, and evidence of much gold, especially in Veragua. But the people of the coast, although somewhat more advanced in the arts of life than the islanders of the Antilles, were less amenable than the islanders. However, hearing, as he believed, of a rich and civilised country lying nine days' march overland to the west and washed by the sea, Columbus sought a passage whereby ('just as one sails from Catalonia to Biscay or from Venice to Pisa') he might sail round to that land lying on the opposite shore: this most interesting and apposite observation shows that Columbus had succeeded in getting from the natives a tolerable notion about the form of the land which he was coasting; but the further remark that the Indians reported the opposite coast to be 'ten days' journey from the Ganges' shows that Columbus knew no more than anybody else what might be on the other side and, like other eager explorers, interpreted the signs and utterances of the Indians according to his own wishes and hopes, clinging to the notion of the proximity or contact of the Asiatic continent. Continuing his voyage eastward he reached the point which had been recently touched by Bastidas sailing in the opposite direction; and there was no strait. The point reached by Bastidas was probably known to Columbus and his men; for Bastidas had reached Santo Domingo on his return before Columbus touched there on his outward voyage; it is almost certain that the men of the out-going and of the home-coming expeditions met and talked; for every fresh voyage was always eagerly discussed by sailors and charts passed from hand to hand among them.

In accordance with royal command, an attempt was made to establish a settlement under Bartolome as Governor. But the natives were very different from those of Española: they fell furiously upon detached parties of these intruders: several Spaniards were killed: others, among them Bartolome, were wounded. After much danger and suffering and after anxious delay owing to stormy weather on the surf-beaten coast, the survivors were taken on board the ships and the settlement was abandoned.

Having suffered even more than the common hazards of travel in uncharted seas and savage lands—tempest, torrential rains, shipwreck, fights with savages and loss of men, sickness, hunger—Columbus was stranded for a year in Jamaica, his two remaining worm-eaten ships beached. He was rescued through the devotion of Diego Méndez, a valiant gentleman, who made a long sea-voyage in an Indian dug-out canoe to Santo Domingo and sent a ship to the Admiral at Jamaica. In his will Mendez directed that a canoe should be carved on his tombstone.

Columbus reached Spain for the last time about the time of Queen Isabel's death in 1504. He survived her eighteen months, afflicted by gout and premature old age, and importuning Ferdinand in vain for the full restoration of his rights and authority. Technically he was treated with gross injustice and faithlessness, and undoubtedly he was unfairly deprived of rights which could have been reasonably granted. But reinstatement in full vice-regal authority would have been mistaken justice, for experience showed that he could not have maintained that authority. The establishment in the Indies of hereditary personal despotism and nepotism, without effective control by the Crown, would have plunged every island and every coast into strife such as afterwards destroyed Pizarro and his men in Peru. But, although disappointed in his grandiose ambitions and in respect of promises unfulfilled, the Admiral was not indigent nor derelict. The Crown now drew some revenue from Española owing to the royal dues on gold produced by private enterprise with Indian forced labour, as well as dues on pearls and on the lucrative trade in log-wood. Columbus regularly received one-tenth of these royal dues. His testament is that of a man in easy circumstances, and he left a *mayorazgo* or noble entailed estate to his heir. His sons Diego and Fernando were both educated as pages at Court. Diego, the second Admiral and Viceroy, married the niece of the King's first cousin, the Duke of Alba, bringing, as he declares, to the House of Toledo 'revenue and lordships of which all the grandees of Spain have much envy'.

During the past forty years—ever since in 1892 the celebration of the fourth centenary of his great voyage drew the attention of the world—much controversy in several languages has gathered about the name of Columbus. These endless questionings are in part due to the circumstance that Columbus himself was seldom content with bare facts: nor can his divagations and contradictions always be entirely attributed to the pleasant impulses of an uncontrollable imagination. But the laborious investigations of critics and the voluminous literature concerning the man and his work are in themselves evidence of greatness. The fame of Columbus is mainly posthumous: but those who knew him and speak of him to us knew him as a great man. To Mendez, who loved him, he is the 'great Admiral— the Admiral of glorious memory'. The chronicler Bernáldez, in whose house he was a guest, speaks of 'Cristobal Colon, of wonderful and honoured memory'. Las Casas, who, although condemning much that Columbus did, yet cannot withhold enthusiastic admiration, declares that no other subject ever rendered such service to any sovereign. That service is expressed in the motto which his family added to their arms:

A Castilla y a León
Nuevo Mundo dió Colón.

('To Castile and to Leon Columbus gave a New World.')

CHAPTER III

THE ISLANDS

AFTER Columbus' last voyage and the death of the Queen there was a lull of some five years in exploration and attempts at settlement. The Crown was absorbed in home affairs, and the few hundreds of Spaniards who were dropped down in the New World found room enough in the great island of Española and in the neighbouring island of Puerto Rico, which was entered in 1508. During this interval of comparative quiescence the coasts of the Antilles were explored and were raided for captives to replace the dwindling serf population of Española; and the amphibious islanders of the Bahamas, whose gentle innocence had so impressed Columbus, were kidnapped to dive for pearls at Paria, 1000 miles from their homes. Meantime Ojeda, Juan de la Cosa and others gathered pearls and gold by barter or by force along the Venezuelan coast and shipped slaves thence to Española or occasionally even to Spain.

These were merely passing voyages. But the years 1509–12 brought a double movement of expansion from Española, the comparatively easy enterprise of occupying the neighbouring islands, and the perilous enterprise of distant settlement on the Spanish Main or Mainland (*Tierra Firme*), that is to say the Caribbean coasts, whither the more adventurous spirits sailed, risking their lives in the quest for gold and dominion.

The occupation of the islands, inhabited by naked and unwarlike people, may be briefly told. One Ponce de León, 'an honourable caballero', had gone out with Columbus in 1493 and during fifteen years had proved his quality as a capable and trustworthy man. Under Columbus and his successors he distinguished himself in the conquest or pacification of the eastern part of Española: that district was placed in his charge: there his Indian subjects told him of much gold to be found in the island of Puerto Rico, lying almost within sight. In order to win this rich prize, he passed thither with Indian guides and a few Spaniards. The principal cacique of the island received him amicably, exchanged names with him in token of affection, led him to gold-bearing rivers and gave his own sister to the Spaniard: but this amity was brief: the Indians were assigned (*repartidos*) by Ponce de Leon to Spanish masters, whom they served perforce in gathering gold dust and cultivating land: the friendly chief died: his successor planned with other chiefs the extermination of these troublesome guests. The revolt was sudden and unexpected: the Spanish settlements were set on fire and the Christians had to fight their way out through crowds bent upon their destruction; above seventy Spaniards, half the total number in the island, perished. Fierce retribution followed — burning, hanging, casting to savage dogs, complete enslavement, diminution and, later, disappearance of the native population.

Two stories told by Oviedo illustrate the circumstances of the conquest. A certain Diego de Salazar, whose name was a proverb among the Indians for irresistible valour, learnt from a weeping Indian slave that the slave had left his master, one Juárez, bound by a crowd of Indians who were celebrating a joyous and triumphant feast, to be followed by a ball game which was a kind of religious exercise among the natives. On this occasion it was also to be a gamble or competition for a prize: the victors in the game were to win the prize of killing their Christian captive. Salazar, on hearing of the imminent tragedy, forced the terrified fugitive slave, much against his will, to guide him to the scene, made his way to the hut where Juarez was lying and cut his bonds, exclaiming, 'Be a man and follow me'. The two Spaniards, sword in hand, burst through 300 unsuspecting Indians and escaped. The Indian chief, wounded in the scuffle, sent messengers after Salazar, invited him to return, offered perpetual friendship and begged that he, the Indian, might bear the name of Salazar. The Spaniard agreed; and the Indian chief, while his subjects saluted him with cries of 'Salazar, Salazar', gave to the Spaniard four slaves and some jewels in token of amity.

The other story concerns a dog named Becerillo, who for his skill in war against Indians earned a crossbowman's share of all booty, half as much again as that of a common soldier; at every distribution of the spoil, this share was duly paid to the owner of Becerillo: ten Spaniards with the dog were more feared than 100 without him: Becerillo could pick out a wild Indian (*Indio bravo*) among a crowd of tame Indians (*Indios mansos*): if sent after a fugitive, the dog would follow the trail, take the Indian by the arm and lead him back or, in case of resistance, tear him to pieces. On one occasion Salazar, after a fight, determined to throw one of his captives, an old woman, to Becerillo: he ordered the woman to take a letter to some Christians who were about a league distant: when she had carried the letter half a stone's-throw, the dog was loosed upon her, whereupon she sat down, showed the letter to the dog and addressing him in the Indian tongue said, '*Señor perro*, I am taking this letter to the Governor; do not hurt me': the dog quietly sniffed at her and left her alone: the Governor, when he arrived, in order not to be less merciful than the dog, set her free. Becerillo was often wounded and in the end he was fatally hurt by an arrow as he was swimming after a fugitive Indian.

The second Admiral, Diego Colón,[1]—to give him the Spanish name which he always bore—came out to Española accompanied by his noble wife, María de Toledo, in 1509, with the partial restoration of his inherited privileges, and resided in the island as Governor for six years, although the real authority was transferred to the Audiencia, a tribunal and administrative council consisting of four magistrates (*oidores*) which was established in 1511. The arrival of the Admiral and his household 'much ennobled the city', and the ladies who accompanied his wife as maids of honour found husbands among the principal people of the island, thus introducing an element of high-bred Castilian culture. At this time the hardier negroes imported from Africa were replacing the dwindling Indian population. The sugar-cane, introduced from Spain, flourished exceedingly and the quest for gold was already giving place to the sober industry of the cane-field and the sugar-mill— the true source of wealth for the settlers and of revenue for the Crown. The swine, first introduced in 1493, had increased enormously; and, since bacon was a big element in the provisioning of every ship and every expedi-

---

[1] Diego Colon departed for Spain in 1515, and after pressing his hereditary claims at Court for five years came back to Santo Domingo as Governor (although the Audiencia ruled in fact) until 1523: he then returned to Spain and spent two years following the itinerant Court and pressing his claims in vain until his death in 1526.

tion, pig-farming was profitable.[1] Española was becoming a field for the industrious planter and stock-farmer: it was no longer a place for the adventurer in search of golden fortune and possibly of conquest: such unquiet and ambitious spirits must now range farther afield. Diego Colon claimed that all the Antilles, having been discovered by his father, were under his dominion—a claim which was not entirely countenanced by the Crown. The result was that the conquest or 'pacification' of Puerto Rico was delayed and disturbed by frequent changes of governors and disputes concerning authority. But the issue was inevitable—Spanish dominion over the island.

Puerto Rico, now 'pacified', was the base for a fantastic but typical enterprise worthy of Columbus himself. Ponce de Leon and his men had suffered in Puerto Rico 'many labours in war, in sickness, in scarcity of provisions and of all other things necessary to life'. But the veteran had the spirit of the Conquistador, and in 1512 he set out with two caravels northward to discover 'the island of Bimini', said to contain a spring of water which gave back youth to old men. For six months they cruised among the Bahamas and in the neighbouring seas: in the course of these wanderings they came on Easter Day (*Pascua Florida*) to a land which he named La Florida, a name which it still bears. The end, which came nine years later, may be told here. Ponce de Leon returned to Spain, told his story, was appointed by the Crown 'Adelantado of Bimini', renewed his quest to the coast of Florida in 1521, was struck by an Indian arrow and made his way to Cuba to die. 'Nor was he the only one', says Oviedo, 'who lost his life and

[1] The great increase of horned cattle which fed wild upon the plains was somewhat later.

his time and his goods in that quest; for many others who came after him died on the voyage, or after their arrival thither, some at the hands of the Indians and some of sickness; and thus ended the Governor and the Government.'

The Admiral Diego Colon, residing in his tropical palace in Santo Domingo, boasted that through his deputies he had occupied and pacified the islands of Jamaica and Cuba without bloodshed. 'Without bloodshed of Spaniards' was what he meant, for the chief defence of the naked and timid Indians was not the use of their feeble weapons but flight to the thick forests and abrupt mountains of their native islands. Thither they were gradually pursued and the survivors were assigned as serfs to the Spaniards. The conqueror of Jamaica (1509) was Juan de Esquivel of Seville, a prudent man, who ruled the island until his death three years later.

In these island expeditions the trials of the invaders were not the hazards of battle, but fatigue, exposure, sickness, and worst of all, hunger. Near the coasts a man could eat enough, for the natives were expert fishermen: apart from this they produced only enough food for their own immediate need. And as the Spaniards penetrated the inland parts of the great Antilles, scanty rations of cassava bread and sweet potatoes, when these were obtainable, were poor sustenance for a European soldier.

The enterprise of the great and fertile island of Cuba was more notable; for, just as Cuba drew adventurous and ambitious spirits from Española, so in turn Cuba became the starting-point for more famous enterprises. Here the Viceroy's deputy was one Velásquez, a rich man of good repute, one of the early companions of

Columbus. The cacique of the eastern part of the island offered resistance, but his people were scattered; he was pursued, captured and burnt alive as a rebel or traitor. The island, 700 miles long, was gradually subdued in successive expeditions without serious fighting, chiefly by a lieutenant of Velasquez named Pánfilo de Narváez, whose name will recur in the story of continental conquest. Spanish towns were founded in Cuba and the natives were distributed or allotted (*repartidos*) among the settlers, who thus became *encomenderos*, feudal lords of Indian vassals. On the islands these *encomiendas* or feudal fiefs, more commonly known by the less technical and simpler word *repartimientos* (allotments), had a brief history: they shrank to nothing with the disappearing native population, and negro slaves were imported to take the place of the vanished Indian serfs.

Two of the early settlers in Cuba demand mention, the priest Bartolomé de Las Casas, afterwards the champion and Protector of the Indians, who at this time, as he tells us, lived thoughtlessly, like the other *encomenderos*, on the labour of his Indian serfs; and Hernán (Fernando or Hernando) Cortés, whose doings are related in four later chapters of this volume (Chapters V to VIII).

CHAPTER IV

THE SOUTH SEA

To the South! To the South! PETER MARTYR

THE strange and moving story of the first discovery of these great islands, endowed with fantastic beauty and marvellous fertility, must always stir
the imagination: yet the history of the islands is almost
prosaic compared with the vicissitudes and achievements of adventure on the mainland. In 1509 two
licences were granted by the Crown: Ojeda was to settle
what is now the north coast of Colombia: from the
Isthmus to Cape Gracias a Dios (that is to say approximately the present territories of Panama, Costa Rica
and Nicaragua) the land was assigned to Diego de
Nicuesa, notwithstanding the protests of the Admiral
Diego Colon who claimed all that land, discovered by
his father, as belonging to his jurisdiction. Nicuesa was
an hidalgo enriched by the gold-mines of Española: he
had been brought up as a page to the King's uncle; was
'a prudent person,' says Las Casas, 'a courtier, pleasant
in speech, a skilful player of the *vihuela* and above all an
accomplished horseman, who did wonders upon a mare
which he rode, a man as well gifted with human graces
and perfections as any in Castile; of middle height, but
so strong that when he played at *las cañas* his stroke
upon his adversary's shield pounded the very bones'. He
staked his whole fortune on this enterprise, besides

47

much that he borrowed. Ojeda sailed in November 1509 with 300 men and twelve mares. Nicuesa sailed a few days later with six horses and above 700 men, since his charming personality, together with the golden fame of Veragua since Columbus' last voyage, attracted many recruits to the second enterprise. The horse was still unknown on the Continent and a monstrous terror to the inhabitants. Of the thousand men and more who thus set out in two companies in quest of fortune, there survived after a few months less than a hundred. Some fell in fight or by shipwreck or by poisoned arrows shot by lurking savages from ambush in the forest. But the greater number simply died of starvation and hardship. This tragedy was the prologue to the discovery of the South Sea and to the conquest of half a Continent.

Ojeda anchored in the wide bay where afterwards stood the city of Cartagena: he at once landed with seventy men to attack the Indians: but his careless confidence received a rude shock; he himself, flying with his men, only escaped death, with one companion, by his speed of foot and by skill in using his shield, which showed the marks of twenty-three arrows, while the rest of his company, including Juan de la Cosa, Chief Pilot of the Crown of Spain, were struck by poisoned arrows and died raving. After taking fierce vengeance on the inhabitants, Ojeda made a settlement farther west on the Gulf of Uraba: but his men were dying of hunger, besides losses by poisoned arrows. He himself, with careless audacity, fell into an ambush, was pierced through the thigh by a poisoned arrow and saved his life by binding two red-hot iron plates to the wound, threatening to hang the surgeon unless he applied this fearsome cautery. The company, daily diminished by death, were only saved from total extinction through

the chance arrival of a stolen pirate ship manned by
runaways from Española. Ojeda departed with the
pirates to seek help, leaving a stout soldier named
Francisco de Pizarro in charge until the second-in-command, the lawyer Enciso, should come with reinforcements. After extraordinary hardships Ojeda reached
Española, where he lived about a year longer in poverty
but still full of indomitable spirit and the terror of any
cloak-and-sword assailant.

Enciso, arriving with reinforcements and provisions,
at first took Pizarro and his surviving companions to be
merely a few deserters from the main body. Among the
newcomers was a stowaway, one Vasco Nuñez de Balboa
who, to escape creditors in Española, had hidden on
board Enciso's ships in an empty cask. He was a man
of about thirty-five years, tall, well-built, strong, intelligent, impatient of repose and idleness, strong in the endurance of fatigue and labour. His energy, capacity and
local knowledge—for he had visited this coast with
Bastidas—brought him to the front; for the Bachelor
Enciso, although an estimable law-abiding official and
notable later as the author of a valuable work on the
geography of the Indies, proved unequal to the task of
commanding, in a savage country, a company of starving and desperate adventurers, themselves almost reduced to savagery by want, hardship, danger and primitive surroundings.

Balboa led his companions by sea to a site in Darien
where food existed, but no poisoned arrows. Here by
general consent Balboa became Alcalde of a newly
founded 'city' which received, in fulfilment of a vow,
the name of Santa María la Antigua, but was generally
and more conveniently known as Darien. It was not
long before a pretext was found to disavow the authority

of the protesting but impotent Enciso, to arrest him and dismiss him to Spain—there to tell his story at Court: an incident which later had a tragic issue for Balboa.

Meantime to Nicuesa and his men 'no kind of tribulation and adversity was wanting'—dissension, shipwreck, exhaustion, sickness, starvation. A captain, sent with a ship to rescue Nicuesa, found him 'dried up with extreme hunger, filthy and horrible to behold'. He was conveyed with his forty surviving men to Darien, which lay within his jurisdiction as defined by the royal licence. Here, being accused of asserting his authority with covetous arrogance, he was put with a few companions on board a rotten ship with scanty provisions and was never heard of again.

Balboa, now seated in command and receiving soon afterwards a welcome commission as Captain-General and Governor *ad interim* pending the King's pleasure, showed signal qualities as a leader. From his headquarters at Darien he ranged the coast in his brigantines twenty-five leagues westward, subjugating or conciliating the coastal tribes and making incursions inland or up the rivers in quest of food, gold, slaves, and conquest. He appeased the stirrings against his authority among the Spaniards by quiet astuteness, by leading the way in every toil and danger, by fairness in dividing spoil and by solicitous care of his men. 'I have always gone in front as guide, opening the road with my own hand', said Balboa in a letter to the King. 'If one of his men wearied or fell sick in any expedition', says Oviedo, who knew him well, 'Balboa did not desert him. Rather . . . he went with a crossbow to shoot a bird and bring it to the sick man, whom he tended like a son or a brother and encouraged. No other Captain in the Indies has equalled him in this.' Balboa, says Peter Martyr, 'was turned from a rash roysterer to a politic and discreet captain'.

Over the Indians he gained ascendancy by a combination of force, terror, conciliation and diplomacy. It is typical of his methods that, like Cortes ten years later at Cholula, he was warned by an Indian girl named Fulvia, whom he had in his house, of a native conspiracy to exterminate the Spaniards. He married or accepted the daughter of a native chief named Careta, whom he had first defeated in battle and then aided in his tribal wars, thus securing valuable allies and subjugating the country with the help of the inhabitants themselves. His father-in-law Careta and another notable chief named Comogre even accepted baptism and received Spanish names at the font. More rigorous methods with others brought him submissive subjects and slaves. Supplies of food came in; maize was sown, and his men, now reinforced to 450 by fresh arrivals from Española and from Spain, became inured to the life of the pioneer in the tropical wilderness. Much gold was collected, chiefly hoarded gold in the form of ornaments, by free gift or barter from friendly Indians, by force and by torture from others. Balboa owned a dog named Leoncillo, son of the famous Becerillo and endowed with the same sagacity in tracking a fugitive, whom he would lead back gently by the hand or tear in pieces in case of resistance: Leoncillo received an archer's share of all spoil and won for his master much treasure in gold and slaves.

In a long letter to the King, an able and characteristic document, dated January 1513, Balboa tells of the 'great secrets of marvellous riches' which he has discovered (although they had more gold than health and sometimes a basket of maize was worth more to them than a basket of gold), ' . . . many rich mines . . . gold and wealth with which great part of the world can be conquered. I have learnt it in various ways, putting some to the torture, treating some with love and giving Spanish things to some'. He asks for 1000 acclimatised men from Española, arms, provisions, shipwrights and materials for constructing river craft. Finally he begs that no lawyers may be sent 'because every lawyer who comes here is a devil . . . they have ways of bringing about a thousand lawsuits and wickednesses'.

Balboa, probably with justice, speaks of his own politic humanity towards the Indians, and in a later letter (October 1515) contrasts it with the senseless, brutal and impolitic cruelties of other captains, which later stirred the whole country into revolt. But his claim demands some qualification: he advises that a tribe of cannibals or reputed cannibals, unfit even to be made slaves, should be burnt, both old and young: and in order to avoid the loss of runaway slaves, he suggests that Indians be sent from Darien to the Antilles, and others brought thence to Darien, since they could not escape if they were removed from their own country. The compassion of an adventurous stowaway, perhaps never very susceptible, is apt to be blunted by constant suffering and danger and by seeing his companions daily perishing of hunger. Burning, mutilation, quartering, flogging to death—all in public—were familiar punishments in Europe: and Balboa could without a qualm burn or torture an Indian, or throw him to the savage dogs which accompanied the Spaniards in all their enterprises. 'The Spanish adventurers in America', says John Fiske, 'need all the allowances that charity can make for them', and Helps tells the reader to picture to himself 'what his own nature might become if he formed one of such a band toiling in a new fierce clime, enduring miseries unimagined by him before, gradually giving up all civilised ways, growing more and more indifferent to the destruction of life—the life of animals, of his adversaries, of his companions, even his own—retaining the adroitness and sagacity of man and becoming fell, reckless, and rapacious as the fiercest brute of the forest'.

A dramatic incident led to a fresh advance. As the Spaniards were weighing gifts of gold at the door of Comogre's house, the son of the Indian chief suddenly struck at the scales, scattered the gold and pointing to the south exclaimed that in that direction lay a sea and a province more rich in gold than Spain was rich in iron; but the conquest of that land he declared would need 1000 men. Balboa determined to reach that 'other sea' of which he had heard. Having accurate information from his Indian friends, he took ship from Darien westward to the narrowest part of the Isthmus, here barely sixty miles wide (or less, were it possible to travel in a straight line), but sixty miles of broken hilly country, obstructed by rivers and swamps, covered with dense matted tropical forest, remote from food supplies and harbouring hostile Indian tribes. Balboa set out southwards with Indian guides and attendants and with 190 Spaniards. Twice at least the way was barred by hostile Indian tribes: but the explorer's object was peace, and by a combination of force and diplomacy he cleared the way or turned his enemies into friends.

Upon nearing the summit whence the sea, as his Indian guides assured him, would be visible, he advanced alone. From the height he looked down upon another Ocean spread before him: falling upon his knees he raised his hands in thankfulness: he then beckoned to his companions and, after a second act of devotion in common, spoke of the end and accomplishment of all their labours. He had solved the main secret of the new lands, and the date, 25 September 1513, just twenty-one years after Columbus' first landfall, is the second great landmark in the story of the Conquistadores.

After cutting boughs in token of possession, setting up a cross and a pile of stones and carving the King's name upon the trees, Balboa descended southwards. Reaching the shore of the Gulf of San Miguel some days later, he waded into the salt water armed with drawn sword and shield. Standing breast-deep amid the waves of the newly discovered sea, he raised aloft the banner of Castile and called his companions to witness that he took possession of that sea and all provinces and kingdoms adjacent thereto for the sovereigns of Castile. That sea was the Pacific Ocean.

At the risk of his life Balboa embarked upon the stormy waters in frail canoes. He found a rich pearl fishery and reserved the best pearls to be sent to the King with a store of gold and the news of his discovery. After nearly five months' absence he returned to Darien with much treasure 'proud and full of spirit': he had left none but friendly or pacified Indians in the country which he traversed. Oviedo, who knew him and his work, gives the names of twenty Indian chiefs whom Balboa won over as allies in the course of his government: the total number of these allied kinglets was about thirty.

The messengers whom Balboa despatched to Spain bearing gold and pearls in evidence of his services and his great discovery, arrived at Court too late to avert a gathering tragedy. The King, on receiving Enciso's damaging account of Balboa's early proceedings, had nominated as Governor of Darien Pedro Arias de Avila, usually called Pedrarias, nicknamed 'The Jouster', an elderly man trusted for his prudence and his loyal service in many wars. Unlimited power in savage surroundings must have roughened his character, for he was later known as *furor domini*. When Balboa's messengers came with their eloquent offerings, the King was disposed to cancel the appointment of Pedrarias but was dissuaded by Fonseca. However, in response to Balboa's appeal for men, Ferdinand ordered that 1200 paid soldiers should accompany the new Governor; but the stories of gold—gold said to be fished from the water in nets—attracted so many volunteers, besides the 1200 paid men, that it was necessary to limit Pedrarias' total company to 1500 men, 'the most brilliant company that ever left Spain'. More than 500 of these died of starvation or of '*modorra*', an overpowering depression or lethargy, soon after reaching the land of promise: so says the historian Oviedo, who accompanied the expedition as a royal official. Gentlemen arrayed in silks and brocade, purchased as gay equipment for the Italian wars and incongruously worn in the savage surroundings of these strange lands, were daily dying of hunger.

The messengers who were sent to announce Pedrarias' approach expected to find Balboa attended by official state. They found him dressed as a labourer and helping his Indians to thatch his house.

Although superseded in the general government, Balboa was appointed by the King to be Adelantado of the South Sea and Governor of two provinces bordering that sea. For five years outwardly amicable relations subsisted between the two men: Pedrarias, in token of jealousies healed and forces united, even betrothed his daughter, who was absent in Spain, to Balboa, whom he thenceforth addressed as 'son', using the accustomed language of an affectionate father-in-law: but the position was difficult. Sixteen months after Pedrarias' arrival Balboa wrote to the King with vehement indignation about the undoing of his work through the desolating cruelties perpetrated upon loyal allies by Pedrarias' captains. Meantime Balboa himself was determined to continue that work by navigating the South Sea and finding the rich lands bordering its coasts. From Acla, the settlement made by Pedrarias on the north coast at the narrowest part of the Isthmus, Balboa conveyed to the South Sea the materials for four brigantines—a labour which cost the lives of many Indians. The four brigantines were built: Balboa was only waiting for some pitch and iron to be brought across the Isthmus from Acla when he received a summons from Pedrarias: he obeyed at once: half-way upon his northward journey he was met by Pizarro, sent to arrest him. 'What is this, Francisco Pizarro?' he exclaimed, 'You were not wont to receive me thus?' Pedrarias believed or alleged that Balboa, in an indiscreet conversation overheard and reported by an informer, had proposed treasonable designs. The discoverer of the South Sea was tried, condemned to death and beheaded, with four others. Pedrarias did not himself sit in judgement on his 'son-in-law', but committed that task, in due form, to the *alcalde* or judge of the settlement, Gaspar de Espinosa, a man who distinguished himself by shocking barbarity in hunting, killing and enslaving Indians. By a strange turn of fortune, the ships which Balboa had built upon the Pacific were now taken over by Espinosa, who set sail upon an expedition westward to explore the coasts of lands yet awaiting conquest.

The death of Balboa was a disaster. Though far from tender towards the Indians, he desired, after inflicting the first cruel lesson, contented and friendly subjects. He was made of other and nobler stuff than Pizarro: and had he been allowed to carry out the discovery and conquest of Peru, that conquest might have had a happier issue. 'From the school of Vasco Nuñez,' says Oviedo, 'there issued notable men and captains for those things which happened afterwards'. In any case he stands second among the four great leaders who gave the New World to Spain—Columbus, Balboa, Cortes, Pizarro.

The appointment of Pedrarias in 1513 is in one way a landmark in the history of the Conquest; for an attempt was now made to define royal policy towards the Indians both for him and for future governors. He received written instructions concerning the humane and politic treatment of the natives, who were never to be attacked unless they were the aggressors and unless they refused to submit peaceably. Only cannibals and inveterate enemies might be enslaved. The Indians must indeed be *repartidos* or *encomendados* (the words are synonymous in use), that is to say assigned as serfs to Spanish Conquistadores, but with careful regard to good treatment and the regulation of moderate labour, without disturbing their domestic life and the tillage of their own ground. Every effort must be made for their conversion, for which purpose a bishop was appointed to the See of Darien, accompanied by a group of clergy.

Pedrarias was also furnished with a 'requisition', which was to be read aloud and interpreted to any party of opposing Indians. This was a theological exposition of the Creation, the authority granted to St. Peter and to his successors, the donation made by the Pontiff to the Castilian sovereigns 'of the islands and mainlands of the Ocean Sea', whose inhabitants were bound to recognise these authorities. 'If thus you do, you will do well. .... But if you do not thus ... I will invade your lands ... and I will take your persons ... and make them slaves.'

This discourse, unintelligible to the Indians even if it had been possible to interpret it in their various tongues, soon became a mockery to those entrusted with it. The royal injunctions concerning humane and discreet treatment of Indians meant nothing to the captains sent out by Pedrarias to explore and to gather gold. Concerning one of them named Ayora, who was not the worst destroyer, Oviedo writes, 'He committed extreme cruelties and killings upon the Indians without cause, although they came to him with offers of peace: he tormented and robbed them. He left the whole land in revolt and war ... in profound enmity.'

Pedrarias, with all his faults, was not wanting in energy. In obedience to the behest of the King, who hoped that the spices from the Moluccas might find a way to Europe across the Isthmus, he secured the passage from Acla to the town of Panama which he founded in 1519 at some distance to the west of the gulf where Balboa had reached the South Sea. Ships sent out by him from Acla and from Panama explored both coasts of his dominions. Explorers and conquerors advanced by both seas and also overland north-westward, meeting perils, privations, losses and hardships. Some of these were captains sent out by Pedrarias, some claimed or assumed separate authority. They pushed onwards fighting and slaying Indians and sometimes fighting one another for mastery. In the western part of Nicaragua they came upon tribes of vigorous and determined warriors armed with no despicable weapons: here there was hard fighting and serious loss, but no more than a temporary set-back. Their way was too often marked by the atrocious cruelties inseparable from the names of Pedrarias and his men. Finally, penetrating Nicaragua and Honduras, they came into contact with men sent thither by Cortes after the conquest of Mexico in such a way that two streams of conquest from north and south met, spreading Spanish dominion over the whole Isthmian region.

When in due course Pedrarias was superseded in the Government of Darien, the opportune death of his successor left him in command of that province for seven years longer. At the end of that time he contrived to acquire the Government of Nicaragua. There the terrible old man died in 1530 after sixteen years of tyrannical rule in the Indies. Oviedo, who, it is fair to say, hated him, declares that Pedrarias was responsible for the death or enslavement of two million Indians. Although obviously not statistically accurate, it is a significant epitaph.

CHAPTER V

NEW SPAIN, 1517–1519

The Story of the fall of Aztec civilization before the Spanish invaders has deservedly won a great hold upon popular imagination; for every page is redolent of romance, and indeed few, if any, writers of fiction have conceived a tale so full of incident or have brought their heroes to victory in the face of greater odds. Moreover the existence of Aztec civilization, an organized empire with cities built of stone and rich in gold and gems, burst upon the Old World as a thing almost beyond belief.   T. A. JOYCE

THE passage quoted above occurs not in some decorative historical divagation, but in a sober scientific exposition of Mexican archæology. Prescott began his famous narrative, now a century old but ever fresh, by remarking that 'the subversion of a great empire by a handful of adventurers, taken with all its strange and picturesque accompaniments, has the air of romance rather than of sober history'. In attempting to trace 'this daring plunge into the unknown and the triumphant struggle of an isolated handful of Spaniards against a powerful and warlike race',[1] the narrator is almost checked at the outset by a sense of amazement.

Yet no part of the conquest is so well known. Cortes himself tells his story in five despatches[2] addressed to

[1] A. P. Maudslay.

[2] The first of these despatches is from the municipality of Vera Cruz, but was obviously written by Cortes, who accompanied it by a personal letter from himself to the Emperor which has been lost. Between the first and the second despatch there is a gap, which is supplied by other narratives.

the Emperor Charles V. There are other narratives either contemporary or founded on contemporary records. Then in 1552, five years after the death of Cortes, his chaplain Gomara published his *History of the Conquest of Mexico*. This book, inspired by Cortes, roused vehement indignation in an old soldier of the Conquest, Bernal Díaz del Castillo, because Gomara, though he told the story clearly and well, gave the credit of every decision and every success to his patron Cortes. Bernal Diaz, now an old man and a Town Councillor of the city of Guatemala, had been living there for many years in peace supported by his Indian vassals when he sat down to write or to resume the writing of *True History of the Conquest of Mexico*. This intimate straightforward story, vivid and convincing from its very simplicity, is one of the finest narratives to be found in any language. The veteran had the faithful memory of one not dependent on written records: he still, so he tells us, saw before his eyes the things through which he had passed. Of his comrades he says, 'We lived like brothers. . . . I remember all of them so well that I could paint all their faces if I knew how to draw', and he describes the colour and the qualities of every one of the sixteen horses, strange monsters to the Mexicans, which repeatedly by the terror of their onslaught turned imminent defeat into victory. To read Bernal Diaz is like listening to the talk of one who, without any elaborate literary art or studied eloquence, possesses the natural art of the born story-teller, the power to create a living sense of all that he relates—the hardships of fatigue, hunger, wounds, fever, danger and watching, the array of Aztec warriors gorgeous with feathered head-dress, the fantastic magnificence of Montezuma's court, the horror of human sacrifices, the confused and fatal nightmare of the *noche triste*, the booming of the great serpent-skin drum as Christian captives were driven up the stairs of the pyramid to be stretched upon the sacrificial stone, and the final victory, which is told without a word of rhetoric or triumph, but with all the more telling force.

Diaz says plainly what he thinks about Cortes, criticises the commander's occasional rashness or stubbornness of opinion, and complains that Cortes was unfair in the distribution of booty and of pretty women and in writing to the Emperor 'I did this, I ordered one of my captains to do that' instead of giving due credit to his valiant companions. But in general Diaz speaks with loyal and affectionate admiration of 'the stout and valiant captain Hernan Cortes', who was the first to set his hand to any laborious task, 'who was careful in everything . . . and always used great care and forethought and let nothing escape him to be put right'. And the old soldier closes his 'true History' with a vivid and sympathetic portrait of the captain and companion whom he had loved and followed.

The story of New Spain begins when some of the men of Darien, among them Bernal Diaz, wearied by profitless and inglorious endurance of hunger and pestilence, procured a ship and left Pedrarias, sailing for Cuba. Failing of fortune there, they joined with other disappointed or ambitious men—above 100 in all—and, with licence and aid from Velasquez, sailed with three vessels in search of new lands, choosing as commander one Córdoba, a spirited and capable leader, says his friend Las Casas. Departing from the western point of Cuba they came in February 1517 to the coast of Yucatan. Here everything was new to them. They were astonished to find people clothed in dyed cotton and cultivating maize-fields; monstrous idols elaborately carved; a towered city of masonry so strange and imposing to their unaccustomed eyes that they called it Gran Cairo. There was reason for their wonder. They had come into contact with an elaborate and artistic culture, separate and distinct from anything existing in the Old World.[1]

But wherever they landed or tried to fill their water-casks, they were assailed, after a brief show of amity and some barter for gold, with showers of arrows and stones; for the vigorous and intelligent Maya people, though ignorant of iron or bronze and still living in the stone age, were not only expert bowmen and slingers, but also determined warriors, never subjugated by the Aztecs of Mexico, who had mastered the neighbouring peoples. In this first expedition less than half of the Spaniards survived wounds and thirst to return to Cuba, where Cordoba, after ten days, died of his many hurts.

Velasquez, at sight of their specimens of gold, despatched a second expedition, thrice as numerous, under his cousin Grijalva, a man of tried prudence and loyalty, to open trade with the new lands. At Campeche there was a fight and thirteen Spaniards fell. Elsewhere, in his long coasting voyage from Cape Catoche to Tampico—along half of the Caribbean shore of the

---

[1] It is strange that before this date nothing was known in Cuba or Santo Domingo of the Yucatan coast; if any unknown explorer had brought news thence, his report made no impression and has left no record. Señor J. T. Medina in his biography of Solís has proved that a supposed voyage of Pinzon and Solis along that coast in 1506 is a myth. A ship conveying an emissary from Balboa on his way to Santo Domingo and to Spain was wrecked on the Yucatan coast in 1513, but no news of the wreck reached the Spanish settlements. The first news of that coast reached Spain at the end of 1517; and one of Charles' Flemish Ministers at once solicited a grant of the newly discovered land. Charles promised the grant, but upon the protest of Diego Colon, who was then at Court, rescinded his verbal promise.

present Mexican Republic—Grijalva found the natives friendly, offering food to the Spaniards and bartering golden jewels for glass beads; for such were the commands of the Aztec potentate Montezuma who reigned in a great city surrounded by salt water in a lofty valley or plain beyond the western mountains and claimed the allegiance of all these lands. Pictured records painted by trained scribes on sisal cloth and carried to his palace by swift runners had made known to Montezuma the arrival and all the doings of the bearded white men in the previous year; and now Grijalva's movements were quickly reported to him. The people of the coast, pointing towards the sunset, told the Spaniards that gold abounded there. Grijalva, having thus established contact with the natives of the coast, returned to Cuba, bringing not only specimens of gold but also a description of the ghastly blood-stained shrine on the 'Isle of Sacrifices', where five human victims had just been offered to the idols, their hearts torn from their living bodies.

Velasquez, mortified that Grijalva, too obedient to his instructions, had attempted nothing more, prepared a third expedition, choosing as commander Hernan (Hernando or Fernando) Cortes, Alcalde of the City of Santiago. Cortes had passed a gay and lively youth in the University of Salamanca and in his native city of Medellín, where he narrowly escaped being run through the body in an amorous adventure. In 1504 he sailed to the Indies in quest of fortune. Marked out by effective service in the 'pacification' of Española and by the gallant audacity of his love affairs, he accompanied Velasquez to Cuba as Secretary: but being a pleasant sociable person and a welcome companion, he left most of the dull work to a colleague and plunged into sensational adventure which brought him on one occasion to prison, on another to a swim for his life and finally to unintended matrimony, although, when once married, he declared to Las Casas that he was as pleased with his bride as if she had been a duke's daughter. Velasquez, who had imprisoned him, was reconciled to this spirited and pleasant person, stood godfather to Cortes' child and now placed him in command. Cortes possessed all the qualities of a commander, including discreet but uncompromising independence. A typical Spanish cavalier, he was unswerving in loyalty to the King: but, also a typical Conquistador, he was determined to obey none beneath the King.

Velasquez received a hint of this danger and revoked the appointment: but it was too late. Cortes had sailed from Santiago and was at the other end of the island gathering recruits and collecting stores, for which he could not pay. 'I played the gentle corsair', he remarked later to Las Casas. His men were already devoted to him: 'we would have died for our leader Cortes', says Bernal Diaz. In order to buy a horse for one of his captains named Puerto Carrero, Cortes cut the gold buttons from his cloak; for, now that he was a commander, he wore fine clothes and a feathered hat. Other captains were the headstrong and ambitious Pedro de Alvarado, who had commanded a ship under Grijalva and now brought his four brothers to follow Cortes, called by the Mexicans *Tonatiuh*, 'the Sun', for his valour, beauty and gracious manners, afterwards conqueror of Guatemala, and destined to a tragic end; Cristóbal de Olid, Camp-master, 'a Hector in single combat', whose valour would have availed more if accompanied by equal prudence, who was afterwards beheaded for rebellion in the conquest of Honduras; Gonzalo de Sandoval, *alguacil mayor*, a 'pre-eminent captain', youngest of them all, most trusted and beloved by Cortes: he died, still young, at Palos on accompanying Cortes to Spain.

In February 1519 the fleet of eleven ships sailed to the island of Cozumel, carrying, besides 100 sailors, about 500 volunteers, including thirty-two crossbowmen and thirteen musketeers, also some negro and Cuban slaves: there were seven small cannon. Pedro de Alvarado, reaching the island first in a fast ship, had frightened away the natives with characteristic recklessness by petty plunder and by making a few captives. Cortes sternly rebuked him and restored the stolen property, adding gifts besides. Next day 'they went about among us as though they had been used to us all their lives, and Cortes ordered us not to annoy them'. A strange but welcome recruit joined them here, who came from the mainland in an Indian canoe—a man blackened by the sun, half naked, carrying a paddle on his shoulder, to all appearance an Indian slave. He presented himself with the words *Dios y Santa María de Sevilla*. This was a Spanish priest named Aguilar who seven years earlier had escaped from the cage where he and his shipwrecked companions were being fattened for the cannibal feast following sacrifice: he had since been slave to a chief and, since he spoke the Maya language, he was able to serve Cortes as interpreter. After expounding to the friendly islanders a summary of the Christian religion, Cortes sailed along the mainland coast, taking with him this valuable companion.

Landing at Tabasco, he found the natives hostile: accordingly the 'requisition' was duly read thrice and interpreted by Aguilar—to no purpose. After several skirmishes a massed host of many thousand Indians advanced to the attack. They were armed with slings, bows, lances, javelins hurled from 'throwers', and a weapon which the Spaniards called *montante*, 'two-handed sword'. This was formed of a blade nearly four feet long having on each side a groove set with hard obsidian stones sharp as a razor, though blunted after a few formidable blows. All the tribes of New Spain—Tlaxcalans, Aztecs, Guatemalans and others—were expert in the use of these weapons and hurled their missiles, round stones, javelins and arrows, with accurate aim. Most of the javelins, arrows and lances were merely of pointed wood hardened in the fire; but some were tipped with bone or sharp stone. For defensive armour the Indians carried round shields of wood or hide and wore jackets of quilted cotton: these last adopted by the Spaniards, few of whom had coats of mail. The Spaniards suffered many wounds in fight, chiefly from stones hurled from slings with great force and precision: but in the long campaigns which followed not many Spaniards fell in battle in the open field; and it is evident that the native weapons were no match for the steel of swords, spears and crossbow bolts, besides the few muskets and the round stones shot from the cannon. Moreover the Indians did not know how to use their numbers: if a chieftain fell, his followers usually dispersed; and Indian warriors, when it came to fighting at close quarters, were not so eager to slay their enemies as to take them alive for ceremonial sacrifice.

Diaz, describing this first battle at Tabasco, tells of great squadrons which covered the plain. 'They come on like mad dogs and surround us on all sides and hurl so many arrows, javelins and stones that at the first onslaught they wounded more than seventy of us . . . and they kept on shooting and wounding. With our artillery and muskets and crossbows we fought hard. . . . Mesa, our gunner, killed many of them because they were dense squadrons . . . but with all the hurts and wounds we gave them, we could not drive them away. . . . All this time Cortes with the horsemen did not appear . . . and we feared some disaster had happened to them. . . . When we fired, the Indians raised loud shouts and whistling and threw dust and grass in the air that we might not see their losses; and they sounded their trumpets and drums and whistlings and shouts and cried *Ala Lala.*

'At this, we saw the horsemen appear; and since these dense squadrons were heedlessly intent on attacking us, they did not at once perceive the horsemen who attacked them in the rear: and since the ground was level and the horsemen were good riders and some of the horses handy and swift, they deal with them so well, spearing them as they pleased . . . and we went so hard at them, the horsemen on one side and we on the other, that they soon turned their backs. The Indians thought the horse and rider were one creature, for they had never seen horses till then . . . they took refuge in some woods that were there. . . . We buried two men who had been killed and we seared the wounds of the men and the horses with fat from a dead Indian, and we set guards and sentinels and supped and went to rest.'

Cortes followed up his victory with amicable overtures and thus by a combination of firmness and conciliation induced the Indian chiefs to make the best of their defeat, to accept peace and to bring supplies of food: peace was sealed by an exposition of the Christian faith, by the setting up of an altar with cross and image of Virgin and Child, by the public celebration of Palm Sunday and by gifts from the submissive Indians—

golden ornaments and twenty Indian women, who duly received baptism. One of these women, called by the Spaniards Doña Marina, a lady of noble Aztec birth, had been sold in youth by a cruel mother into slavery among the Mayas. Finding that she spoke both the Maya tongue and the Aztec, Cortes took charge of her: Aguilar interpreted Cortes' words to her, and she in turn interpreted them to the Aztecs. Deserting her own people—if indeed she owed any allegiance to the Aztecs who sold her or to the Mayas who enslaved her—this spirited and intelligent woman served her lord and lover Cortes with devoted loyalty and in time bore him a son.

Following the coast westward and north-westward, the fleet anchored in the harbour of San Juan de Ulloa. On Good Friday 1519 the men encamped on shore, and there the ceremonies of Easter Day were performed by the two chaplains, Padre Olmedo and Padre Diaz, in the presence of native onlookers. Four months were spent in the neighbourhood of the coast—not on the same spot, for in the first camp thirty-five men died of fever. During those four months two extensive provinces were won to Spanish allegiance without a blow struck, and a fortified city was set up to hold the land.

CHAPTER VI

THE MARCH TO MEXICO, 1519–1520

And Cortes said, 'Señores, let us follow our banner, which is the sign of the Holy Cross, for with it we shall conquer'. BERNAL DIAZ

THAT a party of armed adventurers, men only, should initiate an audacious enterprise by the ceremonial foundation of an organised municipality may seem a whimsical proceeding. But to the Spaniard, imbued with the great tradition of the medieval Spanish municipality, the regular constitutional method of securing permanence for his work was the establishment of a city at the outset. Cortes' men, however, were not unanimous: the adherents of Velasquez were for returning to Cuba, whereas his own captains and partisans were resolute to follow him anywhere: these presented a demand, concerted with Cortes himself, that a city should be founded to take possession of so rich a land. Having gravely received this petition, Cortes, after a discreet show of deference to Velasquez' adherents, went through the comedy of allowing himself to be coerced by his own men, and accordingly nominated the town councillors (*regidores*) and two magistrates (*alcaldes*). The municipality thus constituted, assuming jurisdiction over the whole country, nominated Cortes himself to be Governor and Commander of New Spain.

This astute arrangement looks like a farcical vicious circle, Cortes being nominated by his own nominees:

but the people concerned saw nothing anomalous in the assumption of comprehensive authority by a civic body, however nominated; and the municipality of the city of Villa Rica de la Vera Cruz narrated the whole proceeding in a despatch[1] sent to the King by the hand of two *procuradores*, deputies representing the newly constituted city. Cortes had in a manner regularised his position, which now, so it was claimed, was independent of Velasquez and dependent solely on the Crown. He showed his peculiar power of leadership by persuading all the men to surrender their booty, to be sent to the King as the most telling argument in support of this claim.

The central plaza and rectangular plan of the city were now ceremoniously traced out. The rollo or pillar which symbolised justice was set up in the plaza and a gallows erected outside. Sites were marked for the church, the *cabildo* or town-hall and the prison. Cortes himself was the first to carry stone for the walls and to dig at the foundations. But the work was mainly done by Indian labourers from the neighbourhood.

For meantime intercourse with the coastal natives was friendly; and from the 'great Montezuma' (as Diaz always calls him) came messengers who fumigated the strangers with copal incense and offered gifts—cotton cloth, mantles of gorgeous iridescent feathers, beautifully worked golden ornaments, a golden disk 'as large as a cart-wheel, with many pictures on it' representing the sun and a larger disk of silver for the moon. This sensational evidence of treasure, to be gained by advance, did not reinforce Montezuma's repeated messages that they should not come to Mexico.

Conditions favoured the invaders; for a tradition was

[1] See note on p. 60.

current among the Aztecs that their beneficent tutelary god Quetzalcoatl, after teaching their ancestors the arts of life, had departed to the east, promising to return one day. The god was represented as a tall bearded man of fair complexion: thus when—at a time which fitted in with the prophecy[1]—there arrived in floating houses bearded white men who could tame giant deer (horses) and wielded thunder and lightning, Montezuma, who was priest and augur as well as King, feared or half believed that the god, accompanied by other *teules* (superhuman beings) had come to claim dominion over the land and that his own throne was doomed. Hence his vacillation between submissive dread and indignant alarm: hence the propitiatory gifts and the urgent messages not to come to Mexico.

Moreover the dominion of the Aztecs, who from their home in the lofty valley of Mexico had conquered the land down to both oceans, was an oppressive and hated tyranny. The tribes of the Caribbean coast, smarting under recent subjugation and remembering their freedom, complained that Montezuma's tax-gatherers seized all their goods and took their youths and maidens for sacrifice to the Aztec gods. And indeed the tribute, paid in kind, must have been an intolerable burden in a country possessing no beasts of burden or draught, where the wheel was unknown until Cortes' cannon appeared. Thus all tillage was gardening by hand with tools of stone or wood or soft copper. The backs of men took the place of farm-carts, and the crops exacted by Montezuma were carried by porters through tropical heat and alpine cold for many days' journey. The subjugated tribes toiled and denied themselves in order to support three luxurious royal courts and an idle warrior

[1] See *Mexican Archæology*, by T. A. Joyce, p. 47.

aristocracy; for the Aztec polity consisted of three federated kings, ruling in three cities, namely the island city of Tenochtitlan-Mexico[1] and the two cities lying east and west on the adjoining mainland, Tezcuco and Tacuba. Each king held sway in his own city and in the neighbourhood, but Montezuma, lord of the island city, was paramount: he was supreme military chief and was sovereign over the subject lands, which paid him tribute. Particularly grievous must have been the tribute of cacao, which only grew on the tropical coast and was carried in great quantities to Mexico in order to provide a beverage reserved for nobles and priests: cacao beans, which were used as currency, filled a great storehouse in the imperial city.

Cortes, delighted to hear of these grievances, visited the city of Cempoala, capital of the Totonac tribe: the chieftain of the city was too fat to go outside the city to greet him; but the Spanish commander was met by festive crowds who led him through streets decked with flowers to the spot where the chief stood, supported by two attendants, to welcome the mysterious and powerful strangers. In Cempoala and in a neighbouring city Cortes found his opportunity: five Aztec lords magnificently clad, arrogantly smelling roses which they carried in their hands, accompanied by a troop of attendants and by fan-bearers to brush away the flies, came to demand tribute and also twenty youths and maidens for sacrifice in expiation of the welcome given to the strangers without Montezuma's commands. Cortes persuaded his new friends, at first quaking with fright, to refuse payment and imprison the tax-gatherers:

[1] The double name is due to the fact that the island originally contained two cities, which afterwards became the two parts of a single city. At the time of the conquest Tenochtitlan was the northern part and Mexico (or Tlateluco) was the southern.

he restrained them, however, from the further logical step of sacrificing and devouring the five Aztec lords, and himself secretly released the prisoners—first two and then the remaining three—bidding them go and tell their lord Montezuma that Cortes was his friend, the saviour and liberator of his servants. The whole province of the Totonac tribe, containing a score of 'cities', was thus committed to revolt against Montezuma and depended on the wisdom and power of those godlike beings to save them from destruction: Cortes by his astute management had secured active and submissive allies who readily provided food and servants as well as a troop of porters who were urgently needed to carry the baggage, guns and munitions.

The 'fat cacique' attempted to lead his new Spanish allies against a hostile tribe; for hereditary feuds and intermittent warfare were the normal condition of the whole country: Cortes, however, insisted on reconciling the enemies and thus added another province and another score of 'cities' to those who disavowed Montezuma and accepted the lordship of the great Emperor Carlos. The fat cacique of Cempoala, in sign of closer amity, presented eight damsels, chieftains' daughters, beautifully arrayed and attended by servant maids, to the Spanish captains. The women were duly baptized: but Cortes, presuming too much upon this amity, risked his whole enterprise by violently overthrowing, in sight of the weeping and menacing chiefs and people, the hideous idols to which human sacrifices were daily offered. On every possible occasion he showed the same crusading zeal, which was sometimes checked by the prudent counsel of the chaplain, Father Olmedo: throughout the whole expedition mass was celebrated whenever wine could be obtained: in his stirring addresses to the soldiery, Cortes always reminded them that they were champions of the Cross. None had any doubt that the subjugation of the heathen and the spread of Christianity were meritorious duties; and Cortes, although he sincerely disliked slaughter and destruction, did not shrink from them when they seemed necessary in so sacred a cause.

Having won the coastal region, Cortes was now ready to march to Mexico, and to win the whole country by means of the inhabitants: but all retreat was first cut off by an act of audacious confidence which has stirred the imagination of the Spanish people more than all his other exploits. He ordered all the ships to be destroyed. This spectacular and decisive stroke not only compelled the reluctant to go forward but also added to the little army, as volunteer soldiers, the 100 sailors who had manned the ships—a welcome reinforcement. The rigging, sails and metal-work were stored on land, to prove most valuable later.

One hundred and fifty men were left to garrison Vera Cruz: and in mid-August 1519 the Spanish army of fifteen horse and about 400 infantry set out westward, accompanied by 200 Indian porters to drag the six little guns and by 40 Cempoalan nobles with their retainers— above 1000 Cempoalans in all.[1] Nearly three months were spent on the march to Mexico, distant about 200 miles over a lofty mountain pass overtopped by towering

[1] Gomara, whose information came from Cortes or his papers, says they were accompanied by 1300 Indians, of whom 1000 were porters, including some Cubans. Diaz says there were 200 porters and 40 Cempoalan chiefs, but does not mention their attendant warriors. Cortes, in describing an incident of the fighting in Tlaxcala, says, 'I took with me 400 of the Indians whom I brought with me from Cempoala', implying that 400 were only part. Gomara's statement that all the auxiliaries and porters, including Cubans, together numbered about 1300, seems probable.

volcanoes: during those twelve weeks the tribes through which they passed were left friendly or submissive to the Spaniards by means of fighting, diplomacy and the singular personal qualities of Cortes. As they mounted from the torrid tropical coast to the higher temperate region, they were received with amity in the places which they passed and were provided with food until, after a fortnight's march, they came to the strong and solid wall which guarded the frontier of the little independent state of Tlaxcala, whose warrior people had never accepted Aztec sovereignty; although, being hemmed in by Montezuma's vassals, they had neither salt, a product of the salt lake of Mexico, nor cotton, which grew only in the hot coastal region. Montezuma hardly desired their complete submission, since the chronic warfare with Tlaxcala provided training for his soldiers and victims for sacrifice to his gods.

The brief but hot Tlaxcalan campaign, with its startling perils and its strange issue, which gave to Cortes the means of winning all New Spain, would in itself furnish a moving narrative; but a mere summary of this crucial matter must here suffice. The narrow passage through the frontier wall was undefended, and Cortes, hoping for free passage through Tlaxcalan territory, sent messages of peace. The reply was, 'We will kill those *teules* and eat their flesh'. The reading of the 'requisition' was ineffective; and after some skirmishing, the little body of Spaniards found themselves immovably surrounded by a great host armed with slings, bows, lances, javelins hurled from 'throwers' and, for hand-to-hand fighting, the *montantes* which have already been described on page 67. But every Spanish bolt and shot told on the dense masses, and, although two horses were killed, the remaining thirteen horsemen did their work:

when eight Indian captains had fallen, the attack slackened and the enemy drew off.

Cortes' fresh offers of peace received the same reply as before; and a greater army, in five divisions,[1] wearing the insignia of five chiefs, under the Tlaxcalan banner, a white bird with outstretched wings, surrounded the invaders. The Spaniards, under stress of numbers, fell into some confusion, but were saved by sword-play and by the fact that the enemy, says Diaz, were so heaped together that the shots did them much hurt: moreover they were badly commanded, and their captains, jealous and quarrelling about the previous defeat, failed to support one another. 'Above all the great mercy of God gave us strength': upon the fall of 'a very principal captain, not counting others', the enemy drew off, pursued by the few horsemen as far as their tired horses could carry them.

Fifty Tlaxcalan emissaries now came offering peace. Cortes, having questioned some of them and found them to be spies, cut off their hands and sent them back to their own people. Nevertheless the Tlaxcalans made yet one more effort by the advice of their wizards, who declared that these *teules* lost their strange power after nightfall. Accordingly the Tlaxcalan captains broke all the traditions of Indian warfare—to their own undoing

---

[1] Diaz says that each division contained 10,000 men—50,000 in all. Cortes says there were more than 149,000. Similar huge estimates of numbers constantly recur and obviously cannot be accepted. They are not entirely due to the desire to exalt Spanish valour, for Cortes exaggerates equally the numbers of his Indian allies: for example he says that 100,000 Tlaxcalans accompanied him from Tlaxcala and were with difficulty persuaded to return home on approaching Cholula: 5000 remained with him and encamped outside Cholula. Although the Spaniards were astonished at the abstemious diet of the Indians, these many thousands could not have found food on the march. The excessive statements may be partly due to exaggerated or ill-understood reports received from the Indians themselves.

—by attempting a night attack. They found the Spaniards vigilant: 'we slept ready shod and armed, with the horses saddled and bridled'. Cortes retaliated by a night attack upon two towns, meeting no resistance from the terrified and unsuspecting inhabitants. Meantime the Cempoalan auxiliaries who had accompanied the Spanish march from the coast, 'very cruel people', were burning villages and slaughtering the inhabitants.[1]

The Tlaxcalans now offered peace, 'preferring to be vassals of your Highness', says Cortes, 'rather than to die and have their houses, wives and children destroyed'. They welcomed Cortes with festivities into their capital, accepting him now as their champion against the hated Aztecs. Thenceforth the Tlaxcalans were the devoted allies of Cortes, working and fighting side by side with the Spaniards with mingled cries of 'Castile, Castile; Tlaxcala, Tlaxcala', and in fact enabling him to conquer Mexico.

It is time to turn for a moment to the imperial city of Mexico: it is easy to imagine the growing alarm of the Aztec monarch when he heard that these audacious and mysterious strangers, after detaching the tributary tribes of the coast from their allegiance, had first vanquished and then bound in close alliance the inveterate and untameable enemies of his house and people. In his perplexity Montezuma sent fresh emissaries to the city of Tlaxcala, urging Cortes not to come to Mexico. But the magnificent gifts which these messengers brought were stronger arguments in favour of advance. Accordingly after three weeks' rest in Tlaxcala, Cortes, followed by a host of Tlaxcalan warriors, took the road

---

[1] There is no mention of food supply. Obviously for the Spaniards it meant forcible foraging, so also for the Cempoalans; but these were able to supplement their commissariat by killing the inhabitants.

for Mexico through Cholula, a city allied with the Aztecs and marked out by its great temple-crowned pyramid as the holy place of all that region. Here they were festively received and well fed at first: but the demeanour of their hosts soon changed: an ambush was suspected, and this apprehension was confirmed when Marina, who told Cortes everything, heard from a friendly Cholulan woman of a plot to destroy the Spaniards. Cortes struck first. At a given signal his men fell upon a crowd of unarmed Cholulans 'so that in two hours more than three thousand perished. . . . They are, since that affair, secure vassals to your Majesty', says Cortes. Having released all the captives who were being fattened for sacrifice in Cholula, having denounced the idols and commended the Christian religion to the Cholulans, Cortes led his men, attended by 4000 Indian allies, over the mountains towards Mexico. From the towns near their march they received gifts—gold, cotton, mantles and Indian women—and heard bitter complaints of Aztec tyranny wherever they passed.

Always watchful, they descended into the valley and slept at a town half on land and half in the water. Next day the Lord of Tezcuco, a nephew of Montezuma, came borne in a magnificent litter by eight chieftains who swept the ground before him as he alighted to greet Cortes. Next day they advanced as far as the city of Iztapalapa, marching upon a broad causeway raised above the water. 'When we saw', says Diaz, 'so many cities and towns set in the water and others on dry land and that causeway which went straight and level to Mexico, we were astonished and kept saying it was like the enchanted things which they tell of in the book of Amadis, for the great towers and temples and buildings in the water all of solid masonry; some of our soldiers were asking whether that which they saw was not in dreams. . . . I know not how to relate the seeing things never seen nor heard nor even dreamt . . . and in the town of Istapalapa how great and well-built were the palaces where they lodged us . . . and the gardens, diversities of trees . . . and paths full of roses and flowers. . . . Now all that town is levelled with the ground and destroyed, nothing left standing.'

Thence they marched along a causeway wide enough for eight horsemen to ride abreast and pierced at intervals by gaps which were spanned by movable wooden bridges . . . 'in front of us the great city of Mexico, and we were barely 450 soldiers', says Diaz. Next day Montezuma himself, borne in a gorgeous litter, attended by 400 barefooted nobles, himself magnificently clad and wearing sandals with golden soles, came to meet them. They were led through gazing throngs which filled the streets, the housetops and canoes crowded on the lake, to the palace which had belonged to Montezuma's predecessor. In a neighbouring palace lived the Emperor himself, 'surrounded with a semi-divine state . . . the rich tribute which poured into Tenochtitlan (the city of Mexico) enabled him to model his personal service on a scale which surpasses the Arabian nights'.[1] At every meal countless dishes were served on lighted braziers, no utensil being used a second time. The greatest nobles approached him with downcast eyes and wearing a humble dress: dancers, acrobats and buffoons enlivened his court. His armoury and rich storehouses, his aviary and collection of caged wild animals, his gardens of flowers and fragrant trees, astonished the visitors. Finding in their quarters signs of a concealed door, they opened it and found a chamber piled up with the vast

[1] T. A. Joyce.

treasure left by Montezuma's predecessor. Mounting the great temple-pyramid they viewed the city with its crowded market and straight clean streets not soiled by the passage of any animal, the causeways leading to the mainland, the aqueduct which brought fresh water, the crowds of canoes bringing food and merchandise. But upon entering the sanctuaries which crowned the pyramid, they were appalled by the stench and bloody horror of human sacrifices. The victim was driven up the stairway, was held down upon the convex sacrificial stone by five priests, while a sixth opened the breast with a stone knife and plucked out the heart, which was burnt before the idol. The body was thrown down the steps, the limbs cut off for the ceremonial banquet of the priests, and the trunk thrown to the caged wild beasts. Cortes' fervid denunciation of the idols left Montezuma unmoved.

CHAPTER VII

VICISSITUDES AND VICTORY, 1520–1521

The situation of this city is much like that of Venice, but only differs
in this that Venice is built upon the sea-water, and Mexico upon a lake,
which, seeming one, indeed is two.   THOMAS GAGE

ALTHOUGH they had been welcomed with peculiar honour by Montezuma: although they were
lodged in a palace where a troop of attendants ministered
to their needs and served their food, yet Cortes and his
few companions had an uneasy sense of imminent
danger: their progress over the causeways into the city
had revealed to them their perilous situation: for they
had crossed the surrounding water over several drawbridges, marching into a trap from which there was
no escape on foot or on horseback, so that their lives
seemed to depend on the caprice of Montezuma, whose
previous dealings had not been reassuring. After a week
of intense anxiety they came to an astonishing resolu-
tion—to seize, in the midst of his capital and of his
people, the person of Montezuma. They had professed
cordial amity to him, representing themselves as the
emissaries of a friendly monarch; and they had in the
end been treated by him with signal generosity. Yet this
outrage upon their host, an idolater and a partaker in
cannibal feasts, in their eyes needed no justification,
firmly believing, as they did, in the righteousness of
Castilian conquest and of Christian dominion over these
lands. In plain fact necessity was their justification.

Nevertheless a pretext was found: news came that a group of Spaniards had been waylaid and slain near Vera Cruz by an officer of Montezuma named Quahpopoca; and it was easy to throw the blame on the Emperor, who, if Quahpopoca's later confession was true, had indeed sanctioned the attack on the white men.

The whole night was spent in prayer as preparation for so daring and perilous a deed: and in the morning Cortes, accompanied by the two interpreters and by six armed companions, crossed the intervening space to Montezuma's palace. After interchange of greetings and of civil speeches, Cortes accused Montezuma of direct guilt or at least of complicity in Quahpopoca's 'treason', and invited the Emperor to accompany him to the Spaniards' quarters. The invitation was in fact a command: Montezuma, at first outraged and indignant, but finally cowed into submission by the menacing aspect of his armed visitors, entered his litter: the nobles of his court, barefooted and weeping, raised the litter on their shoulders and carried their sovereign to his father's palace where the strangers were lodged. A further humiliation followed: Quahpopoca was brought to Mexico by Montezuma's order and delivered to Cortes: he was burnt alive before the imperial palace, and the Emperor was placed in fetters until the execution was complete, while his shocked and weeping attendants held up the fetters lest they should hurt his limbs: when the burning was over, the fetters were removed by Cortes himself.

Cortes seldom struck without a politic aim. The Cempoalans and other coastal Indians, having found the Spaniards of Vera Cruz to be anything but divine, were in a state of uneasy sedition, but were terrified into submission by this shocking example.

From this time onwards Montezuma resigned himself to his fate, sometimes brooding in melancholy, sometimes cheerfully talking with the Spanish officers and challenging them to a game which was played with little golden balls. He always gave away his winnings and he often regaled his captors with gifts of gold, mantles and pretty women.

But in the nature of things, all was not peace. The 'King' of Tezcuco, nephew and colleague of Montezuma, attempted to rouse the princes of neighbouring cities and lead them to destroy the intruders. The attempt, which was a defiance of Montezuma's own authority, only served to strengthen Cortes' hold upon the country. The King of Tezcuco was imprisoned and his throne was given to his younger brother, a prince who could be trusted to be more amenable: three other nephews of Montezuma, lords of federated or dependent cities, were brought to the capital and placed in fetters.

But, for further security, other communication with the mainland was needed than the causeways with their treacherous drawbridges. Blacksmiths, rigging and metal were brought from Vera Cruz, and Montezuma himself sent out orders from his palace-prison that timber and labourers should be supplied for the building of three brigantines upon the lake, ostensibly for the recreation of the Spaniards and of their captive guest; who, when the work was completed, enjoyed the novel pleasure of sailing in a vessel with canvas spread to the wind and was thus conveyed to amuse himself with hunting upon an island which was a royal game preserve.

Montezuma now perforce declared himself a vassal of the remote, mysterious and powerful Spanish monarch, and sent officers throughout his dominions to

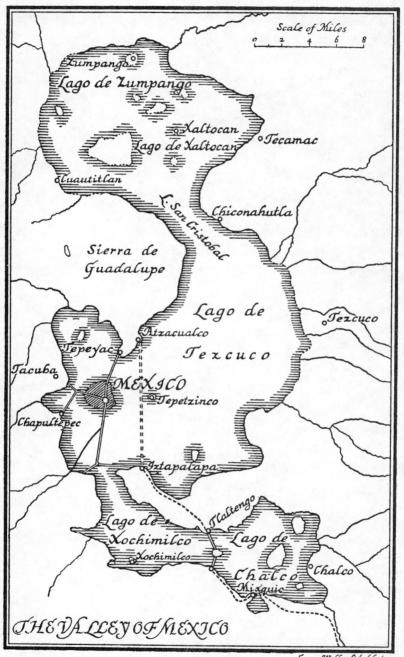

Scale of Miles

Zumpango

Lago de Zumpango

Xaltocan

Lago de Xaltocan

Tecamac

Huautitlan

L. San Cristobal

Chiconahutla

Sierra de Guadalupe

Lago de

Tezcuco

Tezcuco

Atzacualco

Tepeyac

Tacuba

MEXICO

Tepetzinco

Chapultepec

Iztapalapa

Tlaltengo

Lago de Xochimilco

Lago de Chalco

Xochimilco

Chalco

Mixquic

THE VALLEY OF MEXICO

Emery Walker Ltd. del. et sc.

gather gold and precious things for tribute to the Court of Spain:[1] he added part of the treasure accumulated by his father. 'One cannot believe', says Cortes, 'that any known prince in the world possesses such treasure.' Parties of Spaniards, conducted by Aztec officers to explore gold-mines, were everywhere peaceably received, even beyond Montezuma's dominions; and Cortes, with singular confidence, reduced his Spanish garrison in the capital to about 220 by sending 150 men to found a city on the coast near a suitable harbour. Yet it is not surprising that the people of the city, angered at the sight of these spoliations and at the calm assumption of authority by Cortes, became daily more restive under the burden of supporting these troublesome and not always well-conducted Spanish and Tlaxcalan guests. Montezuma warned Cortes of his precarious position in view of the increasing menace of popular discontent, urging him to depart while he could do so in safety: but the Spanish commander set aside the warnings and went on his way boldly taking possession of the country.

Possibly his confidence would have been justified but for a sudden check and interruption of his work. Some five months after his arrival in the capital, he was informed by Montezuma—whose swift runners brought him pictured records of all happenings—that eighteen ships had anchored at Ulloa carrying 800 infantry and 80 horsemen with many muskets, crossbows and artillery. Cortes, with politic dissimulation, declared himself delighted at the news: but he soon learnt that

[1] The treasure, shipped for Spain from Vera Cruz, was taken by a French corsair and passed into the possession of the French King, Francis I. When Charles V, not yet openly at war with France, remonstrated and claimed the treasure, the French King replied, 'Show me the testament of our father Adam, wherein all those lands are assigned to your Majesty'.

Panfilo Narvaez, the principal lieutenant of Velasquez in Cuba, an estimable person but always blundering and unlucky, had arrived with orders to occupy the land in the name of Velasquez, had denounced Cortes as a traitor and had claimed the allegiance of the perplexed Cempoalans and their neighbours. After discreetly sending messengers to open negotiations with the newcomers, which were at once rejected, but which, backed up by astute propaganda and by bribes, weakened Narvaez' hold upon his men, Cortes set out from Mexico with part of the Spaniards, leaving Pedro de Alvarado with the rest to hold the capital and guard Montezuma.[1]

Receiving reinforcements on his way to the coast, Cortes with 250 men fell upon Narvaez' quarters in the city of Cempoala on a stormy night. At the first onslaught Narvaez was a prisoner, having lost an eye in the scuffle. There were shouts 'victory for Cortes', and all Narvaez' men joined the ranks of the victor, who thus increased his army fourfold.

Narvaez brought another gruesome ally to Cortes, the smallpox, conveyed by a negro in his train. This plague, previously unknown on the continent, spread rapidly in a most fatal form: it is even said to have destroyed half the population of some provinces. Famine followed, for want of hands to till the ground: it was a weakened and diminished population which finally submitted to the conqueror.

Narvaez' men were needed, for Cortes had scarcely rested after his astonishing victory over his own countrymen, when news of disaster came; that the whole city of Mexico was in revolt, the brigantines on the lake

[1] Cortes says he took 70 Spaniards with him and left 150 with Alvarado. Since Cortes says that he attacked Narvaez with 250, this implies that 180 Spaniards joined him on the way. Diaz reverses the figures, saying that Cortes left 80 men with Alvarado and took the rest.

burnt and Alvarado besieged in his quarters. He had provoked the outbreak. When, by Alvarado's permission, the Aztec nobles, stripped of clothing but magnificently decked out with gold, jewels and gorgeous feathered plumes, were celebrating the festival of summer with a ceremonial dance, the Spaniards, at a given signal, had fallen upon them, unarmed, naked and helpless, and had massacred them all. Alvarado professed that he merely acted with due foresight, having knowledge of a conspiracy to destroy the Spaniards: Montezuma indignantly denied this, declaring that there was no reason or provocation for the slaughter.

Hastening back to the capital by forced marches and joined by some detachments on the way, Cortes led 1300 infantry and 96 horse, besides 4000 Tlaxcalan auxiliaries along the great southern causeway and thence into the city, not greeted now by great lords and curious crowds, but moving through the sullen silence of deserted streets. He reached his quarters, where Alvarado's men embraced the new-comers as their saviours. But none were safe: next day showers of missiles filled the courtyards of their dwelling, and part of the building was set on fire in ceaseless attacks. During the night the Spaniards repaired the damage: but at dawn the furious onslaught was renewed: the gaps made by every Spanish shot in the masses of assailants were filled up at once. In hopes of appeasing the people, Cortes led the captive King up to the roof to expostulate with his subjects. When 'the great Montezuma' appeared, clad in the imperial mantle of white and blue, crowned with the diadem of Aztec sovereignty and preceded by the bearer of the golden wand which heralded the approach of royalty, an awed silence fell upon the multitude: the fight stood still and many prostrated themselves in customary reverence at the sight of the priest-king. But when the monarch broke the silence with an address to his subjects, appealing for peace and declaring himself to be the friend of the strangers, there was an uneasy stir among the packed mass, followed by an outburst of furious rage: the storm of missiles was renewed: Montezuma was struck on the head by a stone hurled by his own people, refused all care and died in three days. The people saluted as his successor his kinsman Cuitlahuac, the prince who directed the attack on the Spaniards and finally some days later drove them from the city with the loss of more than half their number. For, although the Spaniards stormed the great temple-tower overlooking their quarters and hurled down the fighting men and the frantic bloodstained priests, they could not win the city. Veterans of the Italian wars 'swore that they had never seen such fierce fights . . . nor had they seen men close up their ranks with such courage'.

Many Spaniards were dead and all were wounded, the enemy daily reinforced: powder, food and water were failing: to remain in the city meant death by starvation or wounds or ceremonial sacrifice to the God of War. In this extremity Cortes decided to abandon for the time all that had been won and order a retreat by night over the western causeway leading to Tacuba, the shortest way to the mainland: the night of 30 June was fixed for the retreat: the men were told to take what treasure they chose; the rest was left behind: those who were wise and valued their lives took the jewels, of little bulk, and left the heavy gold. A movable bridge was made to span the gaps in the causeway: as soon as darkness fell it was dragged into position across the first gap and the whole army, cavalry, guns, infantry and

Tlaxcalan auxiliaries, passed over it, not without casualties, for such a move could not be made in silence and secrecy. When all had passed, it was found impossible to move the bridge, jammed tight by the weight which had passed over it. Thus the second gap lay open before the retreating men, a gulf of deep water. A scene of dreadful confusion followed: the lake was crowded with canoes, their occupants thrusting with lances at the horses and dragging down the men to be drowned or carried off for sacrifice. To most of the men who had come with Narvaez the weight of gold which they carried brought death: artillery and powder were all lost: only twenty-three horses came through alive; the children of Montezuma, the captive 'kings' and other Aztec prisoners, all perished on this 'Sorrowful Night'. The survivors, Spaniards and Tlaxcalans, who had contrived to cross the water by swimming or treading on the bodies of men and horses, reached the city of Tacuba; but, pursued and attacked, retreated to a fortress-like temple on a hill, where they found food and rested for the night. In the following six days the exhausted and diminishing troop marched nine leagues, continually losing stragglers who were carried off for sacrifice.

Before reaching friendly Tlaxcala, they had to fight once more. Famished, weary and wounded, they were attacked by a great host of mocking and confident Mexicans, the captains resplendent with their brilliant plumes. 'They were so many', says Cortes, 'that they hindered one another and could neither fight nor fly.' Yet the Spaniards seemed to be overwhelmed by mere force of numbers, when Cortes with a few companions fought his way on horseback to 'the place where the Mexican Captain-General was with his banner dis-

played, with rich golden armour and silvery plumes . . .
with many other chieftains wearing great plumes'. The
royal standard was struck down, its bearer pierced by a
Spanish lance; thereupon the attack slackened; the
horsemen pressed the enemy, and 'we followed up our
victory killing and wounding. Then our friends the
Tlascalans were very lions and with the arms which they
seized they behaved stoutly', says Diaz.

Otumba, where this battle was fought, is a name
which sounds in the ear of Spaniards as Plassey or
Quebec to an Englishman. 'The Battle of Otumba',
says Prescott, 'one of the decisive battles of all history,
demonstrated conclusively that it was the Spaniards
themselves, not their superior equipment, that conquered the Aztec Empire. Only men of extraordinary
physical strength and courage could have escaped an-
nihilation through sheer weight of numbers'. It should
be added that the Spaniards had no artillery at Otumba
and no powder for the few muskets which they had
saved from the confused struggle of the 'Sorrowful
Night'.

The exhausted victors struggled on to Tlaxcala,
where the news of their astonishing success won for
them a hospitable reception, much-needed food, rest
and care for their wounds.

Here news came of fresh disasters. Two parties of
Spaniards, travelling from Vera Cruz to join Cortes in
Mexico, supposing him to be in peaceful possession,
were killed on the road or captured for sacrifice. The
survivors of Narvaez' men, who were with Cortes at
Tlaxcala, were disillusioned, dispirited and bent on
escaping to the coast: but Cortes, supported by his old
companions, refused further retreat, declaring that his
present force was equal to that which had marched out

to conquest from Cempoala a year earlier. He resolutely set himself, aided by a great Tlaxcalan army, to gain or regain the neighbouring cities subject to the Aztecs. Those which submitted were 'pardoned' and subjected to Spanish allegiance. In places where, after due reading of the 'requisition', resistance was offered, all the inhabitants were branded on the face as slaves. Cortes himself was averse from needless destruction, but was unable to restrain his triumphant Tlaxcalan auxiliaries from sack, slaughter and feeding on the bodies of the slain. A Spanish city, named Segura de la Frontera, was founded to secure the new conquests and guard the road to Vera Cruz.

Meantime Spanish reinforcements were arriving from Vera Cruz, whose population had increased. Francisco de Garay, Governor of Jamaica, had sent four expeditions to make a settlement at Pánuco. Great part of his men, horses and artillery found their way to the camp of Cortes. Recruits and stores came from Cuba destined for Narvaez: they were decoyed into the service of his conqueror. Munitions, horses and men came from Santo Domingo. But Cortes knew that horse, foot and artillery were powerless against the water-girt city of Mexico. Accordingly he conceived the apparently fantastic design of building a fleet of thirteen vessels to be transported in sections across the mountains and launched upon the lake. Rigging, tow and iron were brought from Vera Cruz to Tlaxcala: pitch was procured from the neighbouring wooded mountains: Tlaxcalan workmen, directed by Martín López, a dexterous ship's carpenter, cut and shaped the timber. After prudently allowing all malcontents to return to Cuba, Cortes, on 26 December 1520, just six months after the tragedy of the *Noche Triste*, reviewed his troops at Tlaxcala—550 foot, forty horse and eight small guns. Two days later they marched out, followed by a vast host of Tlaxcalans, who had received some drilling from Spanish officers. Having traversed the mountain pass, they looked down once more upon the plain of Mexico with its lakes and cities; 'and although we had much pleasure in seeing them', says Cortes, 'yet thinking of the hurt we had suffered there, some sorrow visited us, and we all promised never to come out thence without victory, or to leave our lives there. And with this determination we all went on as gay as if we were going to a festival.'

A determined and exasperated enemy, fully prepared, was awaiting the attack. Montezuma's successor, victor over the Spaniards on the 'Sorrowful Night', had died of smallpox after a reign of eighty days. The throne had passed to Guatemoc (or Quauhtemoc), a young prince of resolute spirit and energy, who had gathered his warriors in his capital and accumulated provisions and arms within the city.

On the last day of the year 1520 the invading army entered Tezcuco, the second royal city of the Aztecs, whence the inhabitants fled at the approach of the Spaniards. But Cortes had brought with him from Tlaxcala a young Aztec prince who had accepted baptism and a Spanish name, who dined daily at the commander's table and spent the evening in friendly talk with him. By recognising this youth, a prince of royal Aztec blood, as King of Tezcuco Cortes acquired a certain authoritative status both in the city of Tezcuco, whither the people gradually returned, and also in the surrounding country. In Tezcuco and in the neighbourhood 'we found', says Cortes, 'the blood of our brothers and companions spilt and sacrificed in all the towers and mosques, a thing so pitiful that it renewed all our past tribulations', and in a house near Tezcuco 'they found these words written with charcoal on a white wall "here was kept prisoner the unhappy Juan Yuste" . . . a thing to break the hearts of those who saw it'.

With Tezcuco as headquarters, three months were devoted to a preliminary campaign round the lake, strengthening the alliance of friendly cities and chastising the recalcitrant—with general success, but not without reverses; at Iztapalapa, in whose gardens and palaces the Spaniards had been welcomed fourteen months earlier, the enemy turned a rush of water upon the invaders by opening a dyke and the Spaniards narrowly escaped drowning. But great part of the city of Iztapalapa was burnt and thousands of the inhabitants were slain, 'for our allies the Tlascalans', says Diaz, 'when they saw the victory which God gave us, thought of nothing but killing right and left'. In an attack on Xochimilco the Spaniards were driven back; many suffered the dreadful fate of being taken alive; and Cortes, unhorsed and grasped by eager enemy hands, was only saved from capture and sacrifice by the devotion of a Tlaxcalan Indian—whom he afterwards sought in vain—and of a Spanish soldier named Olea, who was badly wounded in protecting his commander. But during those months Cortes with steady tenacity strengthened his hold upon the country: he also secured his hold upon his own men: he discovered that some malcontents were plotting to murder the captains and escape to Cuba: Cortes acted promptly: the army first learnt the existence of the plot by seeing the body of the ringleader hanging at the door of his quarters. Cortes had snatched from the culprit's hand a list of the conspirators, but with prudent generosity concealed his knowledge and gave out that the guilty man had swallowed the incriminating paper.

Meantime a long string of Indian porters, guarded by 300 Spaniards and a host of Tlaxcalans, carried on their backs the materials for thirteen vessels a distance of eighteen leagues over the mountains from Tlaxcala to Tezcuco. For six hours Cortes stood watching the triumphant procession defile past him. The timbers were put together and the vessels were completed, while thousands of Indians laboured for fifty days digging a canal half a league long from Tezcuco to the lake. A reservoir was constructed at the head of the canal. On 28 April all was ready. Father Olmedo said mass and blessed the boats: all the Spaniards received the Sacrament: the reservoir was opened and the rush of water floated the thirteen vessels into the lake amid martial music and salvos of artillery. Cortes then reviewed his troops: in spite of considerable losses, they had increased to 900 men through fresh arrivals from the islands or from Spain, attracted by the fame of the commander and the hope of booty. There were 86 horsemen and above 100 crossbowmen and musketeers.

By the end of May 1521 all was ready for the siege. The aqueduct bringing fresh water to the city had been cut. A great army of Tlaxcalans hastened to Tezcuco at Cortes' summons, all eager to destroy their ancient enemy.

The land attack by the three causeways was assigned to three parties under Alvarado, Olid and Sandoval. Cortes himself at first commanded the twelve brigantines (one of the thirteen having been rejected as unserviceable): 'the key of the whole war', he says. He soon proved their value. 'The wind being good, we broke into the midst' of a fleet of canoes, 'and smashed many canoes and killed or drowned many enemies—the greatest thing in the world to see'. The brigantines never entirely succeeded in stopping canoes from bringing supplies to the city: 'yet there was never a day', says Diaz, 'when the brigantines did not bring in canoes and many Indians hanging from the yards'. Moreover it was only through the defence and support supplied by these vessels that advance against the city along the causeways was possible.

In the first assault on the city the Spaniards fought their way to the great temple-pyramid, stormed the stairway and reached the summit, but failed to hold it. In two other assaults, supported and protected by the brigantines, they advanced along the causeways, penetrated the streets, set fire to houses and killed many men, the Tlaxcalans holding up before the defenders their countrymen's limbs and crying out 'we will sup off these to-night'.

As the Aztecs lost ground, the dependent cities threw off their allegiance and gave valuable aid to Cortes. Yet twice at least the Spaniards were driven back in rout. An attack on the great market-place in the north of the city failed disastrously, and Cortes, entangled in the disorderly crush of the retreat along the causeway, was saved a second time from capture by the same Olea, who died in defending him. On that day, says Diaz, over seventy Spaniards were captured, and Alvarado's detachment, which was nearest to the city saw their captive comrades driven with blows up the stairs of the pyramid and forced to dance before the idol before being stretched upon the sacrificial stone, while the great serpent-skin drum, audible two leagues around, throbbed in triumph. Ten days in succession the drum sounded for this ghastly festival: the last to suffer was Cortes' page, who had been captured while aiding his master to mount his horse and escape. After these disasters many of the Indian auxiliaries abandoned the siege and dispersed to their homes in discouragement, although they did not renew their allegiance to the Aztecs.

At last Cortes, who wished to preserve his conquests and not to destroy them, reluctantly reached the dreadful conclusion that the city must be levelled piece-meal. 'I knew not', he says, 'how to free ourselves without destroying their city—the most beautiful city in the world . . . we found them more undaunted then ever . . . the plan was to demolish every house as we penetrated into the city and not to advance a step until all was level with the ground'. The Tlaxcalans exulted in this work of ruin, which grieved Cortes: repeatedly during the siege he offered to Guatemoc an honourable capitulation, promising to recognise him as King; but the Aztec prince stubbornly refused all terms, even when most of the city, including the great pyramid, was lost and when his people were perishing of pestilence from the heaped-up corpses and also of hunger—for they spared the bodies of their own people.

But starvation, pestilence and destruction, besides wounds and death in ceaseless combat, gradually and inevitably did their work. After nearly three months of incessant fighting, about one-fourth part of the city remained standing, defended by emaciated and exhausted survivors. On 13 August, while the brigantines were engaged in destroying the houses, a number of Indian canoes put out into the lake attempting to escape: the Spanish vessels pursued them with sails and oars: one García Holguín, captain of a swift brigantine, singled out a conspicuous canoe, overtook it and made as if to shoot. One of those in the canoe stood up and said, 'Do not shoot; I am the King of this city . . . take me to Malinche'. When Cortes was told of this capture, he prepared a guest-chamber with food; and when the Aztec prince was led into his presence, he received the prisoner with an embrace. Then Guatemoc said to Cortes, 'Malinche, I have done my duty in defence of my city . . . take that dagger in your belt and kill me with it'. Cortes answered that 'he esteemed him all the more for his bravery in defending the city'.

'That night', says Diaz, 'there was rain, thunder and lightning . . . and when Guatemoc was taken prisoner, all of us soldiers found ourselves as deaf as if one had been standing on the top of a belfry with many bells ringing and as if at the height of the ringing they had suddenly ceased to ring. And I say this purposely; for during all the ninety-three days that we were besieging this city, the Mexican squadrons both night and day were raising such shouts and cries and whistlings, preparing the troops and warriors who were to fight on the causeways; others summoning the canoes which were to fight with the brigantines and to attack us on the bridges; others marshalling those who were to drive down stakes and make breaches in the causeways and deepen the water and make breastworks; others preparing stones, javelins and arrows, and the women providing round stones for the slings; and from the temples the drums and horns and the great drum and other wailing trumpets never ceased to sound; so that night and day we had great noise such that we could not hear one another: and when Guatemoc was taken, the shouts and noise ceased: and thus I say it was as if till then we had been standing on a belfry.' The old soldier, careless of grammatical forms and using an unstudied vocabulary, could not better the vivid picture. He goes on to tell us that 'Guatemoc showed gentle breeding in form and features, a long and cheerful countenance, eyes which looked at one gravely and pleasantly'.

The Spanish conqueror permitted or commanded the evacuation of the ruined city. For three days and nights a slow procession of homeless fugitives streamed along the causeways to an unknown fate, 'so thin and foul and yellow and stinking that it was pity to see them', and the place where the Aztec monarchs had reigned was left empty.

Cortes stained his victory and belied his first gener-ous impulse by yielding to the clamour of the soldiers and of the royal treasurer that his vanquished guest the Aztec king should be tortured into revealing a supposed hidden treasure. Nothing was revealed, and the pest-ilential ruins of the capital yielded little booty to the angry and disappointed soldiery. It was surmised that the treasure of Montezuma, cast away and lost that it might not become the spoil of the conqueror, lay buried in the mud beneath the waters of the lake.

Yet the wealth of the country was no fable: that wealth existed and still exists in its rich mines, its pas-tures and the varied products of its soil.

CHAPTER VIII

CORTES

When that Lord was made prisoner, the war immediately ceased.

CORTES

It was no good to say to Cortes, 'Señor, let me rest, for I am most weary of service'.

BERNAL DIAZ

HERNAN CORTES, at the age of thirty-five, had accomplished an astonishing and singular achievement. With a few adventurous followers he had conquered a warrior people and a magnificent empire; for upon the fall of the Aztec capital the whole dominion of the Aztecs fell into the grasp of the conqueror: the rulers of surrounding regions sent envoys or came themselves to acknowledge his authority, not only those who had been tributary to Montezuma, but also more distant chieftains who had rejected Aztec sovereignty but now accepted that of Spain, astounded as they were by the amazing victory achieved by the Spaniards. Among others the independent King of Mechoacan, an extensive province touching the Pacific Ocean, sent his brother to view the ruins of the imperial capital and to ask the protection of its conqueror.

In order to complete the work of imperial subjugation Cortes sent out his captains in all directions in command of small detachments to accept or compel the allegiance of the surrounding tribes and cities: he himself led an expedition to the unruly region of Panuco and there set up, with due formality, a Spanish city. But Garay, Governor of Jamaica, the jealous rival of Cortes, also sent thither a body of Spanish settlers, who ravaged the country in vagabond groups and by outrageous robbery of women and of goods provoked a general rising in which many Spaniards perished. Terrible retribution followed: Cortes sent Sandoval to pacify Panuco: he did so by burning 400 chiefs in the presence of their people: he then nominated or acknowledged the successors of these victims as native chiefs of the people and left the country beaten down into uneasy submission.

For three years the tireless energy of the chief was fully occupied. Upon the site of the ruined capital there quickly rose under his eye, in the characteristic rectangular form, the first edifices of a spacious and stately Spanish city, a work which cost the lives of many Indian labourers: as a means of security and defence a fortified harbour was constructed on the lake to shelter the flotilla of brigantines, which was kept ready in case of need. Having failed to get artillery and powder from Spain, Cortes manufactured both on the spot: iron was unknown in New Spain: soft copper was plentiful, but useless for the forging of guns without tin to harden it: after anxious search some tin was found, and Cortes soon had bronze guns. Nitre was abundant, and sulphur for making powder was obtained by a hazardous descent into a volcanic crater. Ships were built on the Pacific coast to explore strange shores and to search for the non-existent strait. All the materials for shipbuilding, except timber, were brought from Spain and conveyed across 200 leagues of mountainous country to the west coast. An accidental fire destroyed these stores, but a ship from Castile brought fresh supplies, which were conveyed across the continent, and the ships were completed. 'I cannot express', wrote Cortes to the Emperor in October 1524, 'how much I value these ships. For I hold it certain that with them, if God will, I shall bring it about that your Caesarian Majesty shall be lord of more kingdoms and lordships than are known in Spain up till now and . . . that your Highness need do no more in order to be monarch of the world'.

The tribes and provinces, shaken, weakened and in some cases halved in population by the smallpox epidemic and by the scarcity which always follows pestilence and war, looked to the Spanish conqueror for guidance: he provided for their government by recognising or nominating chieftains to rule them as before, for Cortes, alone among the Spanish conquerors, seems to have desired the preservation of native institutions as the basis of Spanish sovereignty: but circumstances were too strong for him: his men, who had followed him as volunteers without pay and with little booty, now looked for the reward of conquest; and Cortes, contrary to royal command and to his own judgement, was obliged to satisfy them by assigning a *repartimiento* or group of Indians to be vassals and serfs to every Spaniard who settled down as a *vecino* or householder. This system, already adopted elsewhere and developed into the formal *encomienda* or feudal fief,[1] was obviously damaging to the traditional institutions of tribe and village.

The astonishing success achieved by Cortes and the dominion which he had added to the Crown of Spain finally won royal sanction for all his floutings of authority.

---

[1] It is worth quoting an apt remark of Las Casas: 'The *repartimientos* ('assignments' or 'allotments') which, in order to give them a coat of varnish, were called *encomiendas* ('feudal fiefs' or 'charges').'

In October 1522, fourteen months after the fall of Mexico, the Emperor Charles V, after due enquiry, appointed Cortes to be Governor and Captain-General of New Spain. The appointment was justified by his zeal and sagacity in promulgating Ordinances of Government and by his ceaseless efforts to extend and enrich the dominions of the Crown. Two expeditions were despatched to distant regions: Pedro de Alvarado led a well-equipped expedition 200 leagues to the southeast, there to open out a fresh phase of conquest, to be narrated later: Cristobal de Olid was sent by sea to make a settlement on the north coast of Honduras in order to open out a country where, according to travellers' tales, the fishermen weighted their nets with a mixture of gold and copper, and to discover the legendary strait. Having reached Honduras, Olid disavowed the authority of Cortes and set up as a Conquistador on his own account; but the conqueror of Mexico was determined that no one else should treat him as he had treated Velasquez. An expedition which he sent by sea to reduce Olid to order met with disaster: thereupon Cortes himself, in order to chastise his mutinous captain, marched eastwards across the base of the Yucatan peninsula, a distance which he estimated at 500 leagues: he set out surrounded by great state, served upon gold and silver plate, attended by a troop of servants, entertained by musicians, jugglers and acrobats, and carrying in his train two captive kings, Guatemoc and his cousin the King of Tacuba. This daring march through unknown country, although it was the one great blunder of Cortes' career and contributed little to the conquest, was an extraordinary achievement, in which it was only the resourcefulness and determination of the leader which repeatedly saved his men from perishing in dark, pathless, tropical forests, in climbing craggy mountains where many horses perished and in the passage of deep rivers and of wide swamps, one of which was traversed by constructing a floating bridge with 1000 tree-trunks, each over fifty feet in length.

During a halt at an Indian town Guatemoc and the King of Tacuba were accused of conspiracy and were hanged by Cortes' order, upon the evidence of informers. Diaz, who was with the expedition, declares that the sentence was unjust and was disapproved by the whole army. The act has found few defenders.

When finally, emerging from the wilds, they reached a Spanish settlement on the north coast of Honduras, Cortes was so emaciated and broken in health—and for a time, even in spirit—as to be hardly recognisable. The mutiny which he had come to quell had already collapsed; for Olid had suffered death at the hands of Cortes' friends. But the Spanish settlements were feeble and uneasy, weakened by contentions between the men of Mexico sent thither by Cortes, and the men from Darien. The persuasive or authoritative presence of Cortes did much to assuage these disputes and to strengthen the Spanish occupation of Honduras.

He was recalled from further exploration to the south in search of a strait by the urgent summons of his friends in Mexico, where during his two years' absence (1524–26) all was in confusion, the royal officials quarrelling for supremacy and only unanimous in persecuting the friends of Cortes, who with the other expeditionaries had long been given up for dead. Cortes left many of his men, among them Bernal Diaz, under one Luis Marín with orders to march southward. To their great delight they met Pedro de Alvarado, who was hastening northwards to join Cortes but was relieved to find his services were not needed, for he had enough to do in the pacification of his own province and in fixing frontiers with Pedrarias' men from Darien who had reached the limits of Alvarado's Guatemalan conquests. After some months Alvarado accompanied and guided Marin and his men back to Mexico by a more southerly and more practicable route, although, as usual, they had their fill of fighting on the way with Indians who resented the passage of these arrogant and hungry foragers.

Meantime Cortes embarked at Trujillo on the north coast of Honduras and, after repeated delays from tempest and from accident, reached Vera Cruz by sea, whence he travelled to Mexico, welcomed everywhere on the road with enthusiasm by Spaniards and by Indians alike. The jealousies and disputes which pursued him in the capital hardly belong to the present subject. Meantime his efforts to extend the dominions of the Castilian Crown were unceasing, both through expeditions by land and through maritime exploration of both coasts, Atlantic and Pacific, of the realm which he had conquered and of the provinces which lay beyond it. He even despatched an expedition in 1527 across the Pacific to the Spice Islands, as will be related in another chapter (Chapter XI).

In 1529, exasperated by intrigues and accusations, Cortes sailed for Spain and landed at Palos with a retinue of forty Indian nobles, many attendants wearing their tribal costumes, much treasure, a collection of strange animals, plants and fruits and also beautiful specimens of Mexican handicraft in gold, feathers and dyed cotton. The dwarfs, jugglers and tumblers whom he brought so delighted the Emperor that they were sent to Rome to entertain the Pope. Charles received Cortes with signal marks of honour, confirmed his rank as Captain-General with the right to explore, gave him the title of Marqués del Valle de Oaxaca and an *encomienda* consisting of that city and twenty-eight dependent villages—a princely fief. The Emperor granted his requests that the Tlaxcalans should be for ever exempt from tribute, that two colleges should be endowed for the sons and for the daughters of Mexican nobles, that provision should be made for building churches and schools and that generous dowries should be provided for Montezuma's daughters. But, notwithstanding these marks of favour, Cortes, upon returning to New Spain with the rank of Captain-General, found himself in an ambiguous and subordinate position, deprived of all effective authority; for the Government of New Spain was now in the hands of an Audiencia, a Court or Council consisting of Spanish magistrates, until the arrival of the first Viceroy, Antonio de Mendoza, in 1535 initiated the regular system of viceregal government which continued for three centuries. The sanguinary excesses and scandalous misgovernment of the gold-hunting and slave-driving Nuño de Guzmán, first as Governor of Panuco and then as President of the Audiencia, cannot here be narrated in detail. Nor do the disheartening disputes of Cortes with the Audiencia and the Viceroy fall within the history of the conquest.

But Cortes followed up that conquest by equipping four expeditions which sailed upon the Pacific—one of them commanded by Cortes himself—exploring the coasts and searching for a strait. Thus Cortes was the first discoverer of the coasts of California, a country which fitly drew its name from one of the romances of chivalry, just as in the pages of Don Quixote the conqueror of Mexico is reckoned among the chevaleresque heroes, Amadis of Gaul and the rest: this comparison with the heroes of medieval fable is all the more apt from the fact that one of the little fleets set out upon the Pacific by the Marquis sailed northwards to seek and win the fabulous 'Seven cities of Cíbola' in rivalry with the Viceroy Mendoza who was aiming at the same opulent discovery by land. More useful if more prosaic was the energy which Cortes devoted to cultivating his estates and introducing European seeds and plants. But, mortified by contentions concerning his privileges and vassals, after nine years he carried his claims and his litigation to Spain, not welcomed as before but coldly received at Court and not admitted to play a part on the great European stage. He did not return to New Spain, and died in his native country in 1547 at the age of sixty-three. To some, whose view is not focused upon European courts and camps, he stands out as the greatest Spaniard of a great age.

The empire which had been conquered or founded by Cortes expanded northwards during three centuries until it extended beyond San Francisco and embraced great part of the lands now forming the southern part of the United States, so that, as Humboldt remarks, the Spanish language was spoken over a distance equal to the length of Africa. A preliminary phase of that expansion, one which falls within the lifetime of Cortes himself, has been narrated in another volume of this series, *The Explorers of North America*, in a chapter well entitled 'Empires of Dream', and need not be retold here: but since four of those men who were drawn by the lure of the 'Seven Cities' or of some undiscovered realm of treasure appear as Conquistadores in other parts of the present volume, their names at least should

be mentioned here: in 1528 Panfilo de Narvaez, the unlucky rival of Cortes, led 400 men to Florida: after
nearly eight years of strange adventures four survivors
reached New Spain, extricated from the wilderness by
the resourceful prudence of Alvar Núñez Cabeza de
Vaca, who appears in Chapter XXVI as Governor of
Paraguay. Fray Marcos de Niza, who saw one of the
Seven Cities, had seen some years earlier the treasures
of Peru and Quito: Hernando de Soto, one of the foremost conquerors of Peru, who has won a reputation for
chivalry by not consenting to the death of Atahualpa,
but who according to Oviedo was much addicted to the
'infernal sport' (*montería infernal*) of hunting Indians
with dogs, led a brilliant company of 600 into the wilds
of North America and was buried there under the
waters of the Mississippi. But this brief mention of ven-
tures fruitless or not immediately fruitful must conclude
by emphasising once more the solid and lasting results
of the work done by Hernan Cortes.

It should be added that within five and twenty years
of Cortes' death the Philippine Islands were added to
the Spanish Empire and were thenceforth administered
as a dependency of New Spain: a remote dependency,
for it took more than a year to receive a reply to a despatch sent from Mexico to Manila: but the conquest of
the Philippines meant in some small degree the fulfilment of Columbus' ambition or dream of reaching the
Asiatic world by a westward route.

CHAPTER IX

GUATEMALA, 1523–1542

ALTHOUGH, after the story of Cortes and Mexico, the conquests which follow in adjacent regions may seem something of an anticlimax, yet the expedition of Alvarado mentioned in the previous chapter calls for brief narrative apart, since that expedition brought an extensive country under Spanish dominion and also won for the leader an independent command, signal favour at Court and a fame only second, although second by a long interval, to that of Cortes himself as empire-builder in the Caribbean region. Moreover, in the portrait-gallery of the Conquistadores, Alvarado, the chief of Cortes' captains, arrests the attention as a notable figure, handsome, valiant, richly attired, of polished aspect and gracious manners, but headstrong and violent in his rapacious ambition and, if not actually delighting in the wanton torture of helpless and innocent victims, completely callous in inflicting it. The varied and rapid adventures of his impulsive career and its tragic ending outdo all romance. The telling of it is facilitated by the recent publication in America of a biography of Alvarado by Mr. J. E. Kelly.

In December 1523 Pedro de Alvarado set out from Mexico with a brilliant company to penetrate the great mountainous country which lies south-eastwards beyond the Isthmus of Tehuantepec, having been enjoined by Cortes to win the land by peaceful means and to treat the people with loving-kindness. The scourge of smallpox swept the country before him and prepared the way; but his march was not an easy one, for the people about Tehuantepec, nominally subject to Spain, were rising in revolt and were only pacified by hard fighting. Thence the way led through dense uninhabited forest to the cultivated land of Guatemala which he sought.

The inhabitants of Guatemala were a vigorous and intelligent people, mostly of the Maya stock, who possessed a culture generally resembling that of the Mexican region and in some ways superior to it. They were trained in wielding the same weapons of war, but were more astute in stratagem and more skilful in the defence of their cities, which were built in strong natural positions and in most cases were only accessible by narrow approaches easily destroyed or defended. The subjugation of such people in battles and in successive sieges called for signal military qualities: Alvarado possessed these qualities; but the friendly and gentle methods enjoined by Cortes did not suit his unscrupulous greed and restless wayward ambition.

As previously in Darien and in New Spain, the country was won by means of the inhabitants; for the normal condition of the Guatemalan tribes was war, the two principal tribes, Calchiquels and Quiches, being perpetually in conflict: the former welcomed the effective aid of the Spaniards against the enemy tribe and then found too late that these powerful allies had become their masters. The decisive event of the campaign was the fall of Utitlan, the capital of the Quiches. 'This city', says Alvarado in his report to Cortes, 'is very strong, and there are only two ways of entering it, one by more than thirty steep stone steps and the other by a causeway made by hand, much of which was already cut away . . . it is more like a robbers' stronghold than a city.' Here the chiefs welcomed the Spaniards with a show of friendliness 'thinking that they would lodge me there . . . and would set fire to the town some night and burn us all in it'. Alvarado perceived the danger, seized the two approaches, retired to the open country, skirmishing on the way, got possession of the chiefs 'by the cunning with which I approached them and through presents which I gave them'. He burnt these chiefs and, calling Indian allies to his aid from the city of Guatemala ten leagues away, he burnt the city of Utitlan, crushed all resistance, set up as chiefs two sons of the men whom he had executed and branded as slaves all the prisoners.

Fixing his headquarters near the friendly city of Guatemala, he next attacked and subdued the town of Atitlan, situated on the margin of a lake and approached by a raised causeway. Next came a successful incursion into the country now forming the Republic of Salvador. The foundation of the Spanish city of Guatemala in July 1524, seven months after his entry into the country, marks the end of the first stage of conquest. But two more years were spent in 'pacification' and in the suppression of revolts, provoked, as Cortes himself declared to the Emperor, by ill-treatment. For Alvarado and his men, particularly his brothers who served as his captains, were accomplished plunderers, slave-hunters, and extortioners by terror and torture. Pascual de Andagoya, a contemporary historian generally moderate in tone, summarises the conquest in a few expressive words: 'Don Pedro de Alvarado went to the provinces of Guatemala with all the troops he could collect in Mexico, and those provinces were among the richest and most populous in all this land. There was much resistance made to him and the Indians often fortified themselves in rocky places. Alvarado committed great cruelties and pacified the land at great cost to the inhabitants. He took away many people for the expedition which he made to Peru and made slaves ... so that there has been a great diminution in the numbers of inhabitants in that land.'

Like most of the Conquistadores he had to deal with discontent among some of his own men, and also with the rival claims of other conquerors; for a troop despatched from Darien by Pedrarias clashed with a fresh advance of Alvarado into Salvador. Alvarado handled this difficulty with diplomatic skill and vigour and succeeded in holding the ground which he had won.

His services as conqueror received recognition when he visited Spain in 1527. He returned to Guatemala as a Knight of the Order of Santiago, Adelantado of Guatemala with large powers of government, and the husband of a noble bride who, however, died at Vera Cruz before reaching her destination. Fresh trouble followed, of a familiar kind, when the Audiencia of Mexico sent a commission to enquire into the administration of Guatemala; and a second territorial dispute arose with the men who came from Darien and Nicaragua. Both these difficulties were overcome and in 1530 Alvarado ruled an extensive and expanding dominion with unquestioned authority.

Here the story must suffer a digression. For the limits of Guatemala did not bound the expansive ambition of Alvarado, and although 500 Indian slaves washed the river sand to find gold dust for the Governor, the harvest of treasure was disappointing; and at the beginning of 1534 he abandoned his government, plunging into a wild enterprise in search of fresh conquest and richer fortune. Materials for the shipwrights had been conveyed on the backs of Indians 300 miles over rough mountains from the Atlantic to the Pacific: vessels were built, and Alvarado was about to embark for the west, 'for the discovery and conquest of the Indies and the mainland in the South Sea', when sensational news came, that Pizarro and Almagro had conquered a great empire far to the south and had gathered treasures far surpassing all the wealth of New Spain. Alvarado changed his plan. Interpreting royal commands with convenient laxity, and disregarding local protests concerning his duties as Governor, he named his brother Jorge as Deputy-Governor of Guatemala and set sail not westward but south-eastward and then southward, with the most imposing force which had yet sailed the Pacific Ocean, 500 Spaniards, 227 horses and 2000 Guatemalan slaves. He reported afterwards to the Emperor that he had been driven by storms to the coast of Quito from his westward voyage and that his attempted conquest was an after-thought, the result of accident: but in fact his deliberate object was to win a golden kingdom before the conquerors of Peru should carry their arms northwards. After a voyage of 1500 miles his army disembarked on the coast of Quito at the place afterwards known as Puerto Viejo. At first these wooded tropical shores, lying on the outskirts of the great dominion of the Incas, seemed to promise, in the Indian villages where they foraged and looted, the fulfilment of their ambition. 'Alvarado's men', we are told, 'found many vases full of gold, silver and gems, besides many emeralds.' Some of these they smashed by testing them with hammers, thinking that the genuine emerald would resist a blow like a diamond. The promise of wealth proved a delusion; for before the end of their journey all the treasure was abandoned for want of strength to carry it, as they travelled 'through the most difficult country of mountainous rivers, swamps and thick unhealthy jungles . . . opening roads by the sword . . . many of my people fell ill and the sickness was so severe that the day after they were stricken they died . . . in this way more than eighty men (Spaniards) died'. They suffered all the varied trials of hunger, exposure, exhaustion, terrifying showers of volcanic ash as they journeyed through swampy tropical jungle, through a parched stony desert and over towering mountains across slopes of snow where many Indian slaves and some Spaniards were struck down by the icy blasts to lie where they fell. At last, half a year after they had disembarked at Puerto Viejo, they descended, much diminished in number, from the rampart of the western Cordillera to the lofty plateau beyond—only to find that they had not won the race. As they passed along the great Inca highway which traversed the country from north to south, Alvarado was astonished and dismayed at seeing tracks of horses; and soon afterwards they saw approaching a troop of armed Spaniards, horse and foot. The conquerors of Peru, as was to be expected, had reached the lofty table-land of Quito before him: Belalcázar, conspicuous among Pizarro's captains, had entered the country some ten months earlier, had made alliance with some of the native tribes, and with their help had overcome the main body of resistance: he had already occupied the capital and had established a Spanish municipality at Riobamba. Moreover, when the news of Alvarado's designs reached Peru, Almagro himself, Pizarro's partner in Peruvian conquest, hastened

northwards to thwart the intruder and joined forces
with Belalcazar. Yet the Guatemalan troops outnum-
bered the combined forces of these two captains and a
conflict seemed imminent, all the more so when Antonio
Picado, Alvarado's secretary, an astute person who
guessed what would pay him best, deserted to Almagro,
who refused to give him up. But meantime Almagro's
men, mingling with the travel-worn and hungry new-
comers, talked temptingly of the magnificent treasures
of Peru. Cries of 'Peace! Peace!' were heard among the
wearied men. Alvarado was aware of the legal and moral
weakness of his claim, particularly when the Alcalde of
the infant city of Riobamba, accompanied by a notary,
entered his camp and required him to cause no scandal
and to leave the country in peace. Negotiations were
opened; and finally a contract was drawn up—a document which is still in existence, dated 26 August 1534
—whereby Alvarado sold his ships and armament to
Almagro for 100,000 pesos de oro. Leaving Belalcazar
to conquer and govern Quito as a lieutenant of Pizarro,
the two other captains rode away southwards together
in amicable company at the head of their troops on the
long journey to visit Pizarro at Pachacamac,[1] where the
conqueror of Peru was choosing a site for his future
capital. The conqueror of Guatemala was received with
courteous ceremony, and some time was spent in feasting and in *juegos de cañas*, tourneys of canes, held in his
honour: bull-fights were impossible, for as yet there
were no horned cattle in Peru. The stipulated sum was
duly weighed out in gold bars, 1000 pounds full
weight, to Alvarado: the current report that during the

---

[1] Alvarado in his letter to the King says that he met Pizarro at Jauja; this
may be a confusion of names; but it is more probable that they met at Jauja
and rode thence to the coast at Pachacamac together.

festivities Almagro won back half of the sum at play is too good to be altogether true. Almost all the men of Guatemala joined the forces of Almagro, and in the course of their later service they shocked Pedro Pizarro, the historian of the conquest of Peru—by no means a squeamish person—by their proficiency in plundering. On the other hand, by one of those contrasts which diversify Spanish history, among the men of Guatemala who remained in Peru were several hidalgos whose character and later services were worthy of their lineage: Alonso de Alvarado (apparently no relative of Pedro), noted for faithful and loyal service; Pedro Alvarez Holguín, who afterwards commanded a royal army; Garcilaso de la Vega, a gallant young cavalier, whose son afterwards wrote a history of these events; Lorenzo de Aldana, who was repeatedly employed in matters requiring discretion and fidelity; Diego de Rojas, later a pioneer in the conquest of the river Plate. Antonio Picado, a man of very different stamp, became secretary to Pizarro and later met a tragic end.

During the following years there was much buying and selling of Guatemalan slaves in Peru.

On his return to Guatemala after eighteen months' absence the Governor was received with festive rejoicings. Nor did the disaster of Quito seriously damage his reputation; for upon visiting Spain three years later he was confirmed in his government of Guatemala, and was also empowered to make an expedition to the 'islands and provinces of the South Sea towards the West', that is to say to cross the Pacific in order to win whatever lands he might find. He brought back from Spain another noble bride, the sister of his deceased wife. He wrote from the coast to the Cabildo of Guatemala that she was accompanied by twenty maidens of good family and unmarried, though he did not think they would long remain so. The sequel is too characteristic to be omitted: when these high-born damsels arrived at the capital and saw their prospective bridegrooms, grizzled, weather-beaten and war-battered veterans, they did not conceal their scornful disappointment: 'one was maimed, another lame, another had lost an eye'. One of these despised warriors simply remarked, 'I will take the daughter of a cacique'.

Pedro Alvarado seemed to be at the height of his achievements: but his career was near its end. Again he equipped an imposing armament to sail westward across the Pacific, and again was diverted from that quest by a more alluring chimera, the rumour of a region more abounding in treasure than anything yet discovered, a country pictured by imagination under the fantastic name of the 'Seven Cities of Cibola'. Vasquez de Coronado, despatched by the Viceroy Mendoza with 300 men to win that land, had lately returned 'poor and naked' with 100 men. Yet Mendoza was determined to pursue the search; and hearing that Alvarado's powerful fleet had arrived on the west coast of New Spain in the first stage of their intended voyage across the Pacific, he proposed to the Adelantado a joint enterprise to win that opulent land. The two chiefs met and arranged conditions. But Alvarado, before sailing northwards, was asked to aid in suppressing a serious Indian revolt which had spread over the north of New Spain. Alvarado consented, led his men, horse and foot, to the central point of danger, and with his wonted impetuosity, disregarding the advice of those who knew the ground, he rushed to the attack of a strongly fortified height held by the insurgents, who, by rolling boulders down the steep hill, drove back the assailants. The Spaniards retired, fighting as they went and saved from destruction by the valour of Alvarado, who commanded the rearguard. The fight was over, the Indians had retired to their fastness, and Alvarado, having dismounted, was leading his horse along a steep hill-side, when a horse urged by a nervous and agitated rider slipped upon sloping stones, fell against Alvarado and crushed him, impeded as he was by his heavy armour. He died after a few days on 29 June 1541. A year later his widow, who succeeded him in his government, perished in an earthquake which destroyed the city of Guatemala. The city was rebuilt on a new site, and the country which Alvarado had conquered remained as one of the kingdoms of the Crown of Spain.

CHAPTER X

MAGELLAN, 1519–1522

All States, that are liberall of naturalization towards Strangers, are fit for Empire. . . . I have marveiled sometimes at Spaine, how they claspe and containe so large Dominions with so few Naturall Spaniards: But sure, the whole Compasse of Spaine is a very Great Body of a Tree. . . . And besides, though they have not that usage to Naturalize liberally; yet they have that which is next to it; That is, To employ, almost indifferently, all Nations in the Militia of ordinary Soldiers: yea, and sometimes in their Highest Commands.   FRANCIS BACON

SIGNAL proof of the wise generosity of Spain in her great age is to be found in the names of four famous navigators who became Spaniards by adoption and held 'Highest Commands': Columbus the Genoese; Amerigo Vespucci of Florentine birth; the Anglo-Venetian Sebastian Cabot, and the Portuguese Fernão de Magalhães, who assumed Spanish nationality and a Spanish name as Fernando de Magallanes.

The magnificent story of maritime exploration about and beyond the coasts of the New World cannot here find place. It is only possible to trace briefly those known voyages directly concerned with the work of the Conquistadores. Chief among these are the first voyage of Columbus and, twenty-seven years later, the voyage of Magellan, which has been generally regarded as the greatest achievement in the history of oceanic discovery. Magellan accomplished that which Columbus had attempted, the discovery of the westward route to the Far East and to the Spice Islands; and, although the farther voyage was no part of his original design and although he did not live to accomplish it himself, he was in command of the first voyage round the world. That voyage added to the map of the world the widest of the Oceans, revolutionised the geographical conceptions of mankind and in some sort revealed the world to its inhabitants. Again, he did more than any other man to teach the Spaniards the form and the extent of the lands which they had found and the dominions which were falling into their hands. Moreover, his voyage extended those dominions by leading the way to the acquisition of the Philippine Islands, lying far beyond the utmost limits of the New World. The islands were, in a sense, a second and more remote New World, since their very existence was unknown to Europe. But they were in fact part of that Asiatic region, that 'India' of which Columbus had talked and dreamed.

Magellan's voyage was no isolated effort. The southern voyages of Vicente Yañez Pinzon and of Lepe, mentioned on page 33, and the famous voyage of the Portuguese Cabral in 1500 were followed up by other explorers both Spanish and Portuguese who sailed far into the Southern Hemisphere. Two Portuguese expeditions are recorded, under Jaques and under Coelho in 1501 and 1503. One of these is said to have reached latitude 52° south, that is to say almost as far as the strait afterwards traversed by Magellan. But the most notable forerunner of Magellan was Juan de Solis, 'the most excellent man of his time in his art', who finding his native place Lebrija 'too small for his thoughts', went to sea as a youth, entered the royal service as a salaried piloto or navigating officer in 1508 and in the same year sailed westward in company with Vicente Yañez Pinzon

and coasted round the Caribbean Sea. On the death of
Vespucci in 1511 Solis was appointed Piloto Mayor.
A year later he received an extraordinary commission,
to round the Cape of Good Hope, and, after touching
at Ceylon, to take possession of the 'Island of Maluque
which lies within our demarcation'; continuing his
voyage to Sumatra, Pegu, the land of the Chinese and
that of the 'Jungos', he was to take possession of all
these for the Crown of Castile. After long preparation
this grandiose design, which throws much light on
Magellan's later voyage, was abandoned. However, in
1514 Solis was commissioned to sail southwards along
the Atlantic coast of South America, to enter the South
Sea and sail northward to the Pacific coast of the
Isthmus. In October 1515 he set sail with three little
ships provisioned for thirty months and carrying a com-
plement of sixty men. After touching at several points
on the Brazilian coast, he entered in February 1516
(the height of summer) the vast estuary named by him
El Mar Dulce, 'the Freshwater Sea', which seemed
possibly to offer the desired westward passage. The
three ships sailed along the northern shore (now the
Republic of Uruguay), a country of grassy undulating
plain, sparsely inhabited by savage tribes of hunters
and fishers. When some of these beckoned the strangers
ashore with friendly signs, Solis rowed to land in the
ship's boat: he and his few companions were at once
killed and their bodies devoured in sight of the horrified ships' crews, who hastily set sail for home.

Thus ended the enterprise which, if it had succeeded,
would have anticipated by ten years the Pacific explorations of Pizarro carried out from the opposite direction. Little was known of those southern lands, and no
navigator had found a passage to the other Ocean.

Ferdinand Magellan—to use the anglicised form of the name—belonged to an ancient family of the lesser Portuguese nobility. Educated as a page at the Court of Lisbon, he saw fleet after fleet sail out from the Tagus to round the Cape of Good Hope and to win for Portugal empire in the Indian Ocean and wealth from the Spice Trade. In 1504, being then about twenty-five, he sailed for India, spent seven years of strenuous service on sea and land and of hard fighting against Indians, Malays, Arabs and Egyptians on the coasts of Mozambique, of India and of Malaya, was wounded more than once, and distinguished himself by courage and resource in fight and in shipwreck. He was a man of short stature but of great strength and endurance and of a determined, commanding countenance. It is probable that he never saw the Spice Islands: but their situation and character were revealed to him through the Portuguese expedition of three ships which sailed at the end of 1511 from Malacca to Amboyna and Banda and achieved the first direct contact of Europe with the opulent region of the Spiceries, the object of so many dreams and so many efforts. Two of the three ships returned to Malacca laden with spices. The third, commanded by Magellan's friend Serrão, was wrecked. Serrao, after most sensational adventures, made friends with the Rajah of the island of Ternate, the home of cloves, became commander of the Rajah's forces, which he led to victory over the rival Prince of the island of Tidore, married a Javanese wife and spent the last eight years of his life in the Moluccas, whence he wrote to Magellan that 'he had discovered another new world, larger and richer than that found by Vasco da Gama'.

In June 1512 Magellan was back in Lisbon. War service in Morocco followed, and a wound which lamed him for life; but Magellan, an experienced captain eager for service, fell into disfavour with King Manoel and found himself unemployed. To his friend Serrao in the Moluccas he wrote, 'I will be with you soon, if not by Portugal, then by way of Spain'. Finally in 1517, availing himself of a traditional legal right of the Peninsular nobility, which had been often exercised by Castilian nobles departing to take temporary service under some Moorish prince, he formally 'denaturalised' himself, had a farewell interview with King Manoel and passed to Seville, hoping to procure in Spain the means of accomplishing his great design of penetrating the long-sought strait and sailing westward to the Far East and to the Spice Islands. Magellan has hardly received due credit for a cogent reason why in seeking a route to the Moluccas he should enter the service of the Spanish Crown. He believed, or succeeded in persuading himself, that the Moluccas lay within the Spanish demarcation and that the Portuguese had no claim to them: this was the basis of his proposal to the Crown of Spain.

At Seville, in company with one Faleiro, a Portuguese geographer who had joined his enterprise, he obtained the favour of a high official of the Casa de Contratacion, who brought the two Portuguese to the Court at Valladolid. Here Fonseca, President of the Council of the Indies, supported their design and commended it to the young King Charles I, afterwards Emperor. Financial aid was promised by a wealthy Spanish merchant, Cristóbal de Haro, partner in an Antwerp trading firm. Finally in March 1518 Charles signed a 'capitulation', undertaking to equip five ships provisioned for two years in order to 'discover, in the dominions which belong to us in the Ocean Sea within the limits of our demarcation, islands and mainlands and rich spiceries'. This document stipulated that they 'should not explore nor do anything within the demarcation of the Portuguese King'.

More than a year was spent at Seville in the task of manning and equipping ships. The delays and jealousies, partly due to Portuguese efforts to thwart the expedition, drove Faleiro, an irritable and rancorous person, out of his mind. But Magellan's determination and the orders of the King overcame all obstacles, and at last in August 1519 five ships, old and not very well-conditioned, dropped down the Great River. Magellan sent a brief farewell message to the King reiterating his belief that the Moluccas lay within the Spanish demarcation and that Portugal had no claim to them; and on 30 September 1519 the little Castilian fleet put to sea on the voyage which was to circle the globe, carrying about 270 men of whom less than two-thirds were Spaniards. There were thirty-seven Portuguese, about thirty Italians and nineteen Frenchmen, besides Germans, Flemings, Greeks, Negroes, Malays and one Englishman. The best contemporary narrative is that of Pigafetta, an Italian cavalier who sailed with Magellan (translated for the Hakluyt Society, 1874). The story is well told in F. H. H. Guillemard's book *Ferdinand Magellan* (London 1890). During a tedious voyage through equatorial waters, Juan de Cartagena, captain of the ship *Trinidad*, who had been mentioned in official documents as *conjunta persona* with Magellan, showed signs of insubordination. Magellan seized the Spaniard with his own hands, placed him under arrest and deprived him of his command. Having reached the Brazilian coast near the present city of Pernambuco they followed the coast southward, examining every inlet: they looked into the Río de Solís (the estuary of the river Plate), and finding only fresh water continued their southward course. In March 1520, six months after their departure from Spain, they were compelled by boisterous weather to anchor in the sheltered bay of San Julián in latitude 49° 20′ south; and here Magellan determined to spend the winter.

The necessary reduction of rations, the bitter cold and the dubious issue of so prolonged a voyage, caused discontent among the heterogeneous company: on 1 April, Palm Sunday, a group of Spanish officers mutinied and mastered three of the five ships: thereupon Magellan struck hard. The leading mutineer was struck down dead on the deck of the ship which he had seized and which was now boarded and overpowered by loyal men. Magellan, thus becoming master of three ships, beat down all resistance. A second guilty captain was beheaded, and there were no more signs of mutiny.

The refitting of the ships, the loss of one ship driven ashore on an exploring expedition, the southward move in August to the anchorage of Santa Cruz—these were episodes of the seven wintry months of waiting. To the stalwart barbarians of the coast—magnified by later imaginative memory into giants—they gave the name of Patagones, 'big-feet', from their clumsy moccasins; hence the name Patagonia, later given to the whole country.

In mid-October, upon the approach of the summer season, the voyage was resumed; and after three days—thirteen months since the departure from Spain—'we saw an opening like a bay', says the pilot. They had reached the Strait.

And here a question occurs, whether Magellan had any previous knowledge of the existence of a strait in the far south. There was a wide but by no means universal belief that such a strait existed; but it cannot be said with certainty whether this belief was based on knowledge gathered in previous voyages or whether it was a matter of conjecture and probability. In any case Magellan was the first to penetrate the Strait and to reveal its extent and position.

Five weeks were spent in tracing a way through 300 miles of tortuous and labyrinthine passages, beset by many rocks and reefs and swept by gales from the west, passages which in parts wind, like a Norwegian fiord, between mountains seamed by glaciers—waters which have since been the scene of many wrecks; so that sailing ships prefer the tempests round Cape Horn to the treacherous perils of the Strait. One ship deserted and returned to Spain. Magellan, after vain search for the missing vessel, continued the voyage, declaring that 'if they had to eat the leather on the yards, he would still go on'. On 28 November the three remaining ships sighted the longed-for Cape, Cabo Deseado, and sailed out upon the waters of a strange ocean, which on account of the fair weather prevailing at the moment—a rare occurrence in that latitude—they named the Peaceful Sea, El Mar Pacífico.

For ninety-eight days they sailed over a sea 'so vast that the human mind can scarcely grasp it', sighting no land except two uninhabited islets which yielded neither water nor sustenance. Magellan's rhetorical figure became a hard fact: they ate the leather with which the main-yard was covered: 'we ate biscuit, but in truth it was biscuit no longer but a powder full of worms . . . we used sawdust for food and rats were such a delicacy that we paid half a ducat apiece for them'. Scurvy broke out; some died and few were sound.

On 6 March 1520 land was sighted and a number of *praus*—light native boats—shot out to meet them. They had reached a group of unknown islands which they called Ladrones from the expert thievery of the islanders. Refreshed by fruit and vegetables, the explorers sailed on; and after a week came to the great archipelago which they named the 'Islands of Saint Lazarus', later known as the Philippine Islands. These islands, although unknown to Europe, were much visited by Chinese and other Asiatic traders: a Malay slave whom Magellan had brought with him from his Oriental service was able to act as interpreter; and Magellan thus learnt that he had accomplished his great design; he had found the way to the longitude of the Spice Islands, lying due south of the Philippines. He had traced a way across the unknown portion of the world and by sailing to the west had reached the meridian which the Portuguese had attained by sailing to the east.

But the triumph was marred by tragedy. Having made an alliance with the 'Moorish' King of the island of Sebu, who accepted Christianity with many of his people, Magellan offered to help his new friend and proselyte against a rival prince in an adjoining island. Over-confident in the weapons and the valour of Europeans, he led sixty men to what he expected to be an easy victory. He was overpowered by numbers and fell in an obscure skirmish. 'They killed our mirror, our light, our comfort and our true guide. When they wounded him, he turned back many times to see whether we were all in the boats.'

Upon the death of Magellan the King of Sebu, disillusioned about the power of his Christian allies, invited twenty-nine Spanish officers to a banquet and massacred all but two, who contrived to escape. To the survivors of the expedition, who numbered 115, seventeen months of trial remained before a handful of them reached European shores. One of the three ships was burnt as unserviceable; the remaining two ships, the *Victoria* and the *Trinidad*, after various strange adventures and some piratical proceedings in the course of a foraging cruise through the Malayan Archipelago, finally reached the lofty volcanic islands where cloves and nutmegs grew. 'On Wednesday the 6th of November (1521) we sighted four lofty islands. . . . The pilot told us that those four islands were Maluco. Therefore we thanked God and for joy we discharged all our artillery. It was no wonder that we were so glad, for we had passed twenty-seven months less two days in our search for Maluco.'

They had come to a group of island principalities enriched by their fragrant harvests of spice—cloves, nutmegs, ginger, mace, cinnamon—and enjoying, under the vertical sun of the Equator, the simple and leisurely civilisation of the Malay countries. Two days later the Spanish ships anchored opposite the capital of the island of Tidore, and saluted the place with a salvo of artillery. Next day the Mohammedan sultan of the island, Almanzor by name, a person of stately presence and royal dignity, astrologer and prophet as well as king, came on board attended by his suite and, with the courtesy of an Oriental prince, offered to the Spaniards a generous welcome and refreshment from the long tossings and perils of the sea. The Spaniards, eager for trade, loaded him and his attendants with gifts; and a few days later Almanzor promised a supply of cloves partly from his own island, partly from the friendly island of Gilolo. Almanzor kept his word: a storehouse was opened for the use of the Spaniards, who were soon engaged in barter with the islanders, getting cloves in exchange for red and yellow cloth, hatchets, bronze, glass goblets, quicksilver, linen, knives, scissors, caps, and gongs from Brunei in Borneo.

The Spaniards appeared to have a clear field for trade and possibly for dominion. Although the Portuguese from their settlement at Malacca had been trading for some years with the Moluccas—chiefly with Ternate, whose king had welcomed them—they had not yet established any posts in the islands nor asserted dominion over them. This was evident from the fact that the Sultan of Ternate sent some of his brothers to Tidore to make a treaty with the Spaniards, and a crowd of *praus* laden with cloves hurried from Ternate to Tidore to get European goods by barter. Treaties were signed with other island kings, who thus appeared to recognise the sovereignty of the Emperor.

The two ships were laden with cloves: five Spaniards were chosen to remain in charge of the storehouse and of Spanish interests in the islands. The sails were set and farewells taken of the friendly king and people, when the *Trinidad* was found to have sprung a leak. It was decided that she should remain for repairs and sail later for Panama. The *Victoria*, commanded by Sebastián del Cano, an experienced navigator from the Basque coast, started homewards alone on 21 December 1521. A voyage round the world had been no part of Magellan's design: on the contrary, he had hoped to trace a westward route by which Spanish ships might sail to the Moluccas and return to Spain laden with spices. That westward route had been found and followed to the end, but winds and waves and the breadth of the sea forbade return by the same way. The *Victoria*, after sufferings and vicissitudes which cannot here be told, reached Europe in a voyage of nine months by the Portuguese route round the Cape of Good Hope. In September 1522, three years after the fleet of five ships had started from Spain, this one ship sailed into the Guadalquivir with eighteen exhausted survivors of the first circumnavigation of the earth. The sale of her cargo of cloves paid all the expenses of the five ships and the whole expedition.

To the commander Juan Sebastian del Cano a crest was granted, a terrestrial globe encircled with the legend *Primus circumdedisti me*. The addition to his coat of arms, twelve cloves, three nutmegs, two bars of cinnamon—supporters the Kings of Tidore and Gilolo—indicates that the Emperor and the Council of the Indies believed the objects of the voyage to have been accomplished and the Spice Trade to have been secured for Spain, together with dominion over the Moluccas.

The tragic story of the *Trinidad* may be briefly told. Having been unloaded, repaired and reloaded at Tidore, she sailed with a crew of fifty-four for Panama, in order that a long-cherished hope might be accomplished by conveying the spices of the East across the Isthmus to the North Sea and so to Spain. She failed to cross the Pacific Ocean: after seven months at sea she was driven back to the Moluccas, having lost three-fifths of her company from starvation and disease. The survivors fell into the hands of the Portuguese, who were now establishing themselves in the islands. After years of captivity the commander and three others found their way back to Spain round the Cape of Good Hope in Portuguese ships.

CHAPTER XI

THE PACIFIC

Wherever the sun shines, there is Spain.

THE homecoming of the *Victoria* and the lucrative sale of her cargo roused excited hopes in Spain and indignant apprehension in Portugal: from Lisbon came urgent remonstrances against Spanish encroachment on the Portuguese delimitation: the Spaniards denied any encroachment. Finally in 1524 there met at Badajoz in Spain and at Elvas in Portugal on alternate days a Commission of geographers and navigators, Portuguese and Spanish. After wrangling for nearly two months over maps, globes and longitudes, the Commission dispersed with nothing settled; and Charles V resolved to secure the Spice Trade for Spain. A *Casa de Contratación de Especería*—a 'Board of Trade for Spicery'—was set up at Corunna, as being the most convenient port for the merchants of Flanders, Germany and England who were the chief purchasers of spices. In order that Corunna might outdo Lisbon an imposing expedition sailed from Corunna at the end of July 1525, six ships and a *patache* commanded by a veteran soldier, the Comendador Loaisa, who was appointed Commander of the fleet and Governor of the Moluccas: for the Emperor still firmly held that the Moluccas lay within the Spanish delimitation, and commanded Loaisa not to touch land or explore within the delimitation of the King of Portugal.

Loaisa with his seven vessels followed the track of Magellan. Twice they entered the strait and twice were driven back. One ship was wrecked: two others failed to traverse the strait and returned to the Atlantic in dismay at ceaseless hardship and peril. At last, in May 1526, ten months out from Spain, the squadron, reduced to three ships and the *patache*, doubled Cabo Deseado and entered the Pacific. Six days later the four vessels were scattered by tempest and never met again.

The strange adventure of the *patache* demands an anticipatory digression. The officers of the little vessel, short of food and water—for her stores were on board Loaisa's flagship—despaired of crossing the Pacific and determined to steer northward in hopes of reaching New Spain, the nearest known land where food and succour could be found. After two months of voyaging northward through unknown seas, they found themselves off an inhabited coast. They had no skiff, but the chaplain at the risk of his life attempted to get to land in a large wooden chest: he was saved from drowning by five Indians who swam out and helped him ashore. For a time he lay exhausted on the beach. When he recovered, he was conducted by his rescuers to a large Indian town, whose chief and people showed not only cordial generosity but also profound respect for the priest and for the rest of the ship's company, whom the Indians hastened to convey ashore. They had reached the southern coast of Tehuantepec. After four days the Spanish Governor of the district arrived, borne in a hammock by Indian servants; and it was decided that the chaplain—for the commander was prostrated by illness—should travel to the capital and tell the whole strange story to Cortes. They received a cordial welcome in the city of Mexico from the Captain-General, who was bent on finding a way to the Spice Islands and hoped that the trade in the spices of the East might pass to Spain through the realms which he had conquered, either by the long-sought shadowy strait or by carriage overland from sea to sea. By an odd coincidence Cortes received, a few days after the arrival of the new-comers, a letter from the Emperor commanding him to send ships to the Moluccas in order to get news of Loaisa's squadron and ascertain the fate of the *Trinidad*; for after the lapse of five years, no news of Magellan's flagship had reached Spain. Cortes at once pushed forward the despatch of three ships under Alvaro de Saavedra, a kinsman of his own. One of these ships, as will presently appear, succeeded in reaching the Moluccas but never returned to New Spain.

But the main narrative must resume the story of Loaisa. His flagship, after passing Cabo Deseado in May 1526, sailed on alone, the men half starved and toiling daily at the pumps. After two months with no land in sight, Loaisa died: royal orders had named del Cano as his successor: four days later del Cano also died 'and they both received a sailor's obsequies, a *Pater noster* and an *Ave Maria* and burial in the sea'. A commander was chosen in place of del Cano; and, as other officers died, their places were filled by general vote. In September 1526, ninety-eight days from Cabo Deseado and thirteen months from Corunna, they reached the Ladrones and a month later the Moluccas, where they found that the Portuguese had established a fort on the island of Ternate and had burnt the capital of Tidore as a punishment for trading with the Spaniards in 1521. Some of the island kings welcomed the new-comers as allies against the Portuguese; and for over three years this handful of Spaniards, under officers elected by vote, unable to communicate with Spain yet hoping vainly for instructions or succour from the Emperor, waged a desultory and inconclusive war against the Portuguese, who were constantly reinforced from Malacca, while the number of the Spaniards

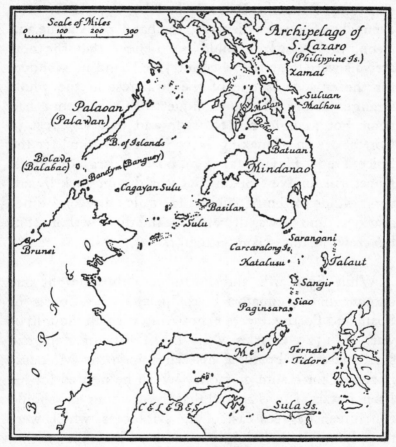

Scale of Miles
0   100   200   300

Archipelago of
S. Lazaro
(Philippine Is.)
Zamal
Suluan
Malhou
Palaoan
(Palawan)
B. of Islands
Matan
Bohol
Batuan
Bolava
(Balabac)
Bandym (Banguey)
Mindanao
Cagayan Sulu
Basilan
Sulu
Brunei
Sarangani
Carcaralong Is.
Katalusu
Talaut
Sangir
Siao
Paginsara
Menado
Ternate
Tidore
CELEBES
Sula Is.

THE SPICE ISLANDS

was constantly reduced by death and by desertion to the Portuguese; for, notwithstanding this bitter conflict between kindred and neighbouring peoples, the Spaniards and Portuguese hardly regarded one another as foreigners. When the single Spanish ship sank, they built another, which also met with disaster: and the conflict went on in sea-fights between fleets of *praus*, manned by the native allies or subjects of either side. After fifteen months unexpected aid came when Saavedra in March 1528 arrived from New Spain with one ship out of the three despatched by Cortes. At first, even when Saavedra displayed the banner of Castile and Leon, the Spaniards could not believe that the new arrivals were their fellow-countrymen: and no wonder; for the episode is one of the strangest in the whole strange history of the Conquest. But Saavedra had come not to fight but to trade and to give effect to Cortes' dream of making New Spain a channel for the Spice Trade. Having taken on board a cargo of cloves, he set sail for New Spain, but was driven back by adverse winds to the Moluccas. He sailed a second time: a second time he was driven back and died, with most of his crew, in this second attempt.

While Spaniards and Portuguese thus fought one another in an equatorial archipelago, the Courts of Spain and Portugal were negotiating with no thought of war. In 1529 Charles V by the Treaty of Zaragoza surrendered to Portugal his claim upon the Moluccas in return for a sum of money which he needed for his French wars. It was agreed that the dividing line should run fifteen degrees east of the Moluccas, which were thus definitely and rightly recognised as falling within the Portuguese delimitation. No news of this agreement reached the Spice Islands, where the conflict continued —inevitably in favour of the Portuguese. In 1530 there were only forty Spaniards left, who came to an accommodation with the Portuguese, in fact an admission of defeat. Four years later the seventeen still surviving

Spaniards were amicably conveyed by the Portuguese to India, whence two years afterwards they made their way to Spain in Portuguese ships.

Spain had failed to win the Moluccas and the Spice Trade. Nevertheless, Magellan and those who followed him did not fail as Conquistadores. For the 'Islands of Saint Lazarus', first discovered by him, although lying far within the delimitation of Portugal, finally fell under the dominion of Spain. An expedition, sent thither from New Spain in 1542, changed their name, calling them the Philippine Islands in honour of Prince Philip. Twenty-two years later Philip, now king, sent an expedition from New Spain under Legaspi to win the islands; and the Philippines became a far-distant dependency of the Vice-royalty of New Spain. Indeed by a strange destiny these islands remained in Spanish hands long after all her Continental possessions in the New World had broken away and become independent: moreover Spanish occupation has left a notable monument in the fact that the inhabitants of the Philippines, almost alone among Oriental peoples, profess Christianity.[1] Every year for more than two centuries a Spanish galleon laden with Chinese silks and in part also with spices sailed from Manila in the Philippines to Acapulco in New Spain. Perhaps it is not too great an exaggeration to say that Magellan gave some effect to the proud prophecy of Balboa, who had claimed for the Crown of Castile 'all that sea with the provinces and kingdoms adjacent thereto'; for the greater part of the Pacific Ocean, first sighted by a Castilian warrior, first navigated by Castilian ships and first traversed by a Castilian fleet, was during nearly two centuries, but for occasional incursions by corsairs or enemies, a Spanish lake.

[1] So also do the people of Goa, Portuguese India.

CHAPTER XII

THE DISCOVERY OF PERU, 1524–1530

Francisco Pizarro spent more than three years in this discovery, passing through great labours, hunger, perils, fears and mockery.

GOMARA

THERE is a temptation to write the history of the Spanish conquest in superlatives: but superlatives fall short in narrating the fall of the Inca empire: and indeed the plainest and simplest language is best for matters which need no rhetorical exposition to proclaim their marvels.

There are several contemporary narratives of these events, mostly written with much simplicity. Two call for mention: Pedro Pizarro, who at the age of fifteen joined his cousin Francisco as page and served throughout the conquest, afterwards settled down as a *vecino* and *encomendero* in the city of Arequipa. In 1572 he published a brief straightforward narrative of the events which he had witnessed, a narrative of the highest value, notwithstanding his natural bias concerning the disputes between Pizarro and Almagro: Oviedo, although he never visited Peru, yet knew all the actors in this history and, as official chronicler of the Indies, had all documents and all information placed at his disposal: he was himself intimately concerned; for his only son was among the conquerors of Peru and, after surviving all the perils of Almagro's expedition to Chile, perished on the return march in a flooded river near Arequipa. During the early part of the enterprise, Oviedo held office in Panama, witnessed all the preparations and saw the ships sail out of the harbour. Later he was Governor of the Castle of Santo Domingo, a place which was still in some sort the metropolis of the Spanish Indies and a port of call for ships sailing to and from Europe. There he was in touch with all that passed: he saw the settlers in Española deserting their estates to seek fortune in Peru and leaving the island exposed to the attacks of French corsairs.

The story has a strange and fantastic native background which can only be briefly indicated here, but may be studied in the pages of Mr. T. A. Joyce (*South American Archæology*) and of Mr. P. A. Means (*Ancient Civilisations of the Andes*), who have described the vast and elaborately organised empire of the Incas, abounding in countless stores of gold and silver, extending more than 2000 miles from north to south and comprising approximately the more habitable parts of the present republics of Ecuador, Peru, Bolivia and northern Chile; for the Inca polity had made little impression on the tropical forests east of the Andes. 'At the time when Pizarro entered the Peruvian Empire', says Mr. Joyce, 'the Inca had evolved, if not a civilisation, at least a very magnificent barbarism: their empire was well organised and governed according to a traditional code of laws: the various provinces were administered by a hierarchy of officials who collected tribute and administered justice, and large armies could be quickly raised and maintained on lengthy campaigns in any part of the dominions. . . . The Inca's court was brilliant in the extreme; all the utensils of the royal household were of gold or silver, and magnificent gardens were attached to the palace in which every kind of plant was imitated in the precious metals. Not even his own relations could enter the presence of the ruler without removing their shoes and carrying burdens on their backs.' Describing the temple of the Sun or 'House of Gold' at Cuzco, he says, 'The walls, built of accurately fitting rectangular blocks of stone, were covered with sheets of the precious metal and studded with jewels. One end formed an apse which contained the image of the sun, a huge circular plate of gold which has never been discovered.'

During four centuries a line of Inca monarchs, revered and almost worshipped as the semi-divine Children of the Sun, had extended the territories of their empire, 'combining guile and diplomacy with military aggression', says Mr. Means, an enthusiastic eulogist of the Incas. The empire was held together by a system of roads, astonishing to the Spaniards, which traversed ravines and rivers by hanging bridges of interwoven ozier cables, and surmounted the heights by steps cut in the rock. The Inca system was extended and secured by the transplantation of populations, groups of loyal colonists being settled in the newly conquered lands to spread the official language (*Quichua* or *Quechua*), to exhibit the benefits of Inca rule and to inculcate a submissive loyalty. 'The people', says Means, 'were conquered by arms but reconciled by kindness.' The Inca polity recognised no private property but assigned to every family a plot of land sufficient for its support, claiming on the other hand that every man should be an obedient servant of the State, or rather of the Inca sovereign. The accounts of tribute, of administration and of armies were kept by an elaborate system of knotted cords, for there was no kind of writing. Although still living mainly in the Stone Age, the Peruvians made more use of copper implements than did the Mexicans: their temples, fortresses and public buildings were of magnificent solidity, and roofed with thick layers of thatch. The wheel was unknown, but upon the Andine plateau and in the mountain region, although not upon the coast, the Peruvians possessed a beast of burden of limited capacity in the llama, the curious 'camel-sheep' of the Andes.

Although not such hard fighters as the people of New Spain, to whom war was the normal state of things, the Peruvians were better armed: in addition to slings, arrows, javelins and lances, sometimes merely of hard wood, but sometimes tipped with copper, they had battle-axes of copper hard enough to cleave a skull, and spiked maces of the same metal or sometimes of silver, made for the hands of the nobles; they also wielded the lasso and the *boleadora*, the characteristic weapon of the Pampa Indian and the Argentine gaucho: for defensive armour they used shields and thick quilted jackets.

The home of the aristocratic Inca clan and the region of their imperial expansion in its earlier stages was strangely remote and difficult of access: they dwelt upon the great Andine plateau stretching generally from north to south at a height above sea-level varying from 9000 to 13,000 feet, hedged in by the two gigantic ramparts of the Eastern and the Western Cordillera and traversed by a third irregular chain approximately parallel to these. In order to penetrate the essential part of the Inca dominion, it was necessary to surmount the Western Cordillera, which runs parallel to the Pacific Ocean and separates the coastal plain from the Andine plateau. The ways which lead up from the coast between the towering mountain heights to the plateau rise through passes which themselves reach the altitude of Alpine peaks. The invaders of such a country had to contend with extraordinary physical difficulties which may here be emphasised once for all in order to avoid reiteration at every stage of advance: but these difficulties were in great part smoothed away by the existence of the great imperial roads, the store-houses, granaries and resting-places which the Incas had provided in order to facilitate the passage of their own armies and messengers.

It should be added that the Inca polity emerged from an earlier civilisation (in the comprehensive sense of the word) of great antiquity, which has left massive architectural remains about Lake Titicaca, overlooked by snowy peaks more than 22,000 feet in height; also that the Incas, descending with their armies from their home on the table-land, had subjugated or moulded into their own pattern several centres of culture on the coast, among them the remarkable monarchy of Chimu, which had been conquered about a century before the coming of the Spaniards. It is obvious that these coastal annexations and also the recent conquest of Quito in the north and part of Chile in the south, while they increased the extent, wealth and apparent power of the Inca empire, by no means strengthened it for self-defence: the Spanish conquerors met little determined resistance either in the coastal region or in the northern part of the empire. The diversity and the deliberately artificial character of Inca political expansion are illustrated by the fact that migration to the low-lying coastal region was often fatal to dwellers in the rarefied air of the table-land.

Nevertheless the Spaniards here found not a loose

congeries of tribes often warring among themselves, as in New Spain, but an industrious and law-abiding people normally living under a well-ordered and apparently stable political system. Yet that seeming-solid structure, shaken by the recent outbreak of strife within itself, collapsed almost at a touch before a rude adventurer leading a few volunteers. In tracing the story of that tragedy and that triumph the reader does not know whether most to admire the persevering valour and startling audacity of the conquerors or to be appalled at their crimes of violence, cruelty, lust, avarice and ambition, or to be thrilled and horrified by the successive shocks of internecine strife, the nemesis which finally consumed them all. That welter of discord and destruction did not undo the remarkable work of civic organisation which those same men had accomplished, and the outcome was the conquest of half a continent, the establishment of a *Pax Hispanica* which endured, with occasional interruptions, for nearly three centuries and the hispanisation of lands now comprising nine extensive republics.

Francisco Pizarro, the Conqueror of Peru, a man of robust frame, high courage and strong determination, was the illegitimate son of a poor gentleman of Estremadura: he had the upbringing of a peasant, was unable to read—an accomplishment not necessary to a conqueror, as Mr. Cunninghame Graham remarks; and even as Marquis and Governor of Peru, Pizarro never learnt to sign his own name. The story that as a youth he was put to herd his father's swine is probable enough: whether it is true that he ran away from home because he had lost some pigs stampeded by flies is a question of no great consequence. At all events, he passed to the Indies 'with a cloak and sword', proved his quality as a stout soldier and was left in command of the diminishing remnant of Ojeda's men on the Spanish Main when that commander departed to seek succour.[1] He accompanied Balboa in his discovery of the South Sea and afterwards served under Pedrarias, by whose orders he arrested and led to trial and execution his former chief Balboa. He then became a *vecino* or householder of the city of Panama, living as a stock-farmer and *encomendero* or lord of Indian serfs. Here he entered into a business partnership with an intimate friend, Diego de Almagro, an illiterate and obscure adventurer like himself, son of nameless peasant farmers in the Castilian village of Almagro: hating the dullness of rural labour, he went to Court and became servant to one of the four *alcaldes de la corte*, magistrates attached to the precincts of the Court. Here having stabbed an antagonist in some youthful quarrel, he thought it prudent, 'even though his master was a judge', not to await arrest: after various wanderings he found his way to the Indies and passed to Darien. Serving under various captains as 'a poor soldier and a good companion', he acquired by careful prudence property, slaves and Indians. He was a man of small stature and a countenance far from handsome, but of extraordinary vigour and endurance: he could outmarch the Indians themselves, says Oviedo, even in the most difficult country, and never showed signs of fatigue. Almagro was much beloved for his generosity, freehanded kindness and sociable gaiety; so much so that Oviedo, no admirer of violence and oppression, speaks of him reminiscently with warm affection. The two comrades were joined by a third partner, the priest Fernando de Luque, schoolmaster of the Cathedral Church, a friend of the Governor Pedrarias, and

[1] See p. 49.

accordingly lord of better Indians than those allotted to Pizarro and Almagro. The triple partnership flourished through mining, farming and the labour of slaves and Indians, largely owing to the energy and business capacity of Almagro.

For nine years past, ever since the discovery of the South Sea by Balboa in 1513, there had been much talk of rich lands awaiting conquest in the south: and in 1522 Pascual de Andagoya, an experienced captain, sailed from Panama eastward and southward in search of these lands. He penetrated a province called Birú, a name which afterwards received a wide application: there he heard fuller details concerning the magnificent sovereigns ruling over lands of marvellous wealth far to the south. Having been injured by an accidental fall —an involuntary plunge into a river as he said himself, according to others a fall from his horse—Andagoya returned to Panama. He had sailed hardly beyond the Isthmian region: but his voyage and the stories which he brought back were the prologue to a history more sensational than any romance.

The captain whom Pedrarias appointed to follow up Andagoya's discoveries died. Thereupon the three partners determined to discover and win those opulent lands, although Pizarro and Almagro—who were to lead the enterprise as captains, while Luque took charge of their interests in Panama—were both of them over fifty years of age, elderly men according to the standard of those days, men who had fought much, endured much and might seem to have earned comfortable ease. But that was not the spirit of the Conquistadores. The three partners obtained permission from Pedrarias, who, although contributing nothing, claimed a share in the profits. Luque provided the funds, acting probably as agent for the judge Espinosa, who had condemned Balboa. The sum was to be 20,000 *castellanos* or *pesos de oro* (the terms are identical) at the rate of 100 *castellanos* to the pound weight of gold, for no coin was current, and all payments were made by weight in gold. Two hundred pounds' weight in gold bars was duly delivered; and a formal contract was drawn up by a notary which stipulated that the proceeds of the enterprise should be divided equally between the three partners. The townspeople derided the talk of profits and Luque was nicknamed *Fernando el Loco*, 'the mad priest', for associating himself with such a hare-brained enterprise.

Nevertheless, undeterred by great expense and long delays, the three partners pushed forward the equipment of a ship and the recruiting of men; at last in December 1524 Pizarro set out with one vessel and about 100 men, besides Indian servants, leaving Almagro to follow with a second ship. This was the beginning of four years spent in preliminary efforts and in expeditions which seemingly led to nothing but exhaustion, sickness, starvation, mortality and the wasting of all resources with no return. But the indomitable perseverance, patient endurance and dogged courage of Pizarro admitted no failure. Three times in as many years the enterprise was at a standstill, and it seemed impossible that the survivors, exhausted, impoverished, starving and half naked, could advance another step. In this first voyage the names *Pueblo Quemado*, 'Burnt Village', and *Puerto de la Hambre*, 'Port Famine', where twenty-seven men died, record incidents in the trouble which they endured, as they fought the winds unable to advance more than 100 leagues along the coast, or tramped through swamps and rain-soaked forests in search of food; Pizarro himself received seven wounds and was stretched upon the ground in combat with savage Indians, but escaped by his own strength and agility. He and his companions looked in vain for the sail which should bring Almagro with food and men. Compelled at last by exhaustion, hunger and loss of men to return northwards, Pizarro sent the ship to Panama, but landed himself at a village some leagues short of the city, refusing to acknowledge retreat by treading the streets of Panama until the conquest of Peru should be in sight. Here he was found by Almagro, who had sailed from Panama three months later than Pizarro with one ship and about seventy men recruited among the vagabonds of the city, had followed his partner along the coast, had lost an eye in fight with Indians—an accident which further disfigured his uncomely countenance—had found traces of the landing of the Spaniards, but, never coming in sight of them, had returned to Panama, and now came thence to confer with Pizarro.

They had spent all they had: but so far from despairing, the partners borrowed funds from Gaspar de Espinosa, the alcalde who had sat in judgement on Balboa. So confident were they of success that they bought out Pedrarias, who relinquished all share in the prospective profits of the enterprise; and early in 1526, having with difficulty got together about 160 men and a few horses, both captains with two vessels again sailed down the coast of the present republic of Colombia. Falling upon an Indian town they found food and some gold: and here Pizarro remained, sending one ship forward to the south under the pilot, Bartolomé Ruiz —henceforth famous in the annals of discovery—while

Almagro returned in the other ship to Panama to seek reinforcements. Ruiz did his work well: he visited several places on the coast of the present republic of Ecuador and crossed the equatorial line, the first European to pass the line in the Pacific. As he advanced, he found increasing evidences of civilisation, frequent villages, lands carefully cultivated, ornaments of the precious metals and people clothed in garments of fine wool, delicately embroidered and dyed with brilliant colours. His return brought encouragement to the exhausted survivors of Pizarro's men, of whom many had perished of hardship and hunger or by the attacks of Indians and wild beasts. The arrival of Almagro from Panama bringing men and food brought further relief; and the united expedition sailed southwards to follow up the discoveries of Ruiz. His reports of a rich and settled country were found to be true: but landing near a considerable town close to the Equator, they found themselves not strong enough to face a crowd of hostile natives, although there was a momentary respite through the dismay of the Indians at seeing a monstrous animal apparently break into two parts when Pizarro was accidentally thrown from his horse.

They were too few for advance and conquest: some were for abandoning the enterprise: but Almagro proposed that he should return to Panama to recruit volunteers, and that Pizarro should await his return in some suitable spot. Pizarro protested that hunger and suffering were his share, while Almagro sailed backwards and forwards at his ease. A violent quarrel, presage of future trouble, was appeased by their companions. Pizarro agreed to remain with part of the company on the island of Gallo, about two degrees north of the line, beyond reach of native attacks, but a dreadful abode owing to ceaseless tropical rain, intolerable plagues of mosquitoes and scarcity of food. Pizarro despatched the second vessel to Panama, thus cutting off all retreat; but by constructing a boat and passing to the larger island of Gorgona, twenty-five leagues to the north, they found slightly better conditions. Here, after long waiting, they were visited by ships bearing, not Almagro and reinforcements, but an emissary charged by the Governor of Panama to carry home the survivors of these foolhardy men.

The reappearance of Almagro at Panama for the third time had caused indignant dismay, and the Governor, Pedro de los Ríos, recently appointed as successor to Pedrarias, resolved to cut short an enterprise so far only fruitful in the miserable death of many men. But the same ships which brought this command to Pizarro brought also messages from Almagro and Luque imploring him not to abandon the enterprise. Pizarro needed no prompting: tracing a line upon the sand he declared that all might return to Panama, but that those who wished to pursue the conquest should cross the line: thirteen men stepped across the line and stood beside their captain: the names of these men, who gave half of South America to Spain, have been preserved. The rhetorical appeal put into the mouth of Pizarro by later writers is unknown to witnesses on the spot: Pizarro's eloquence lay in the force of his character and his stubborn refusal to go back; and in any case the action is sufficiently dramatic in its bare simplicity. It was an instant of utmost anxiety and extreme moment in the destinies of the New World: seldom has a single gesture been so decisive in determining the course of history.

Pizarro and his thirteen companions endured seven

months of starvation and torrential rain before a sail appeared from the north: it was Almagro, bringing food and munitions but no recruits beyond the crew of the vessel.

With the one small ship and handful of men the enterprise was renewed. Guided by the pilot Ruiz, they sailed straight for the Gulf of Guayaquil and anchored off the town of Túmbez, whose inhabitants crowded on the beach to view the strange floating castle. A Greek sailor, Pedro de Candia, the ship's gunner, a man of imposing strength and stature, landed as emissary clad in shining armour and bearing a cross. One story relates that the people let loose upon the intruder a caged 'lion and tiger' (puma and jaguar), which, so far from tearing him in pieces, fawned upon him and enjoyed his caresses, thus convincing the people that there was something preternatural about these visitors. Pedro de Candia returned on board confirming all reports concerning the solidity of the buildings, the arts of the people, the abundance of gold and silver and the greatness of the sovereign ruling over a vast, wealthy and organised empire. Pizarro himself went ashore and was hospitably received by the chief of the place and by an Inca noble who happened to be there. After a brief stay, he sailed on along the coast, visiting several places, carefully avoiding any show of acquisitive ambition and cultivating friendly intercourse: everywhere he found his most brilliant hopes confirmed. After sailing farther than any previous voyager and reaching the ninth degree south of the Equator, his companions insisted on return and he turned his prow northwards, amicably revisiting several places on the way. After a cruise of eighteen months the vessel anchored off Panama.

Yet Pizarro's magnificent reports won no favour

from the Governor: the money was all gone: nothing was to be done in Panama. Luque, who was the brain of the undertaking, declared that they must apply to the Emperor himself: although the cautious Luque distrusted the egotistic ambition of Pizarro, the genial Almagro insisted that Pizarro himself must be their emissary. A sum of money was somehow raised to pay his expenses; and in the late summer of 1528 Pizarro appeared at Court at Toledo. In proof of his story he brought some llamas, some fine woven fabrics of vicuña wool and—more eloquent still—various vessels and ornaments of gold and silver: the time was propitious, for Hernan Cortes also appeared at Court at the height of his fame and achievements, fresh from the conquest of New Spain. The Emperor listened to Pizarro's story; and at last in July 1529, more than a year after Pizarro's arrival in Spain, a 'capitulation' was signed by the Queen Regent, on behalf of the Emperor, absent in Italy. By this instrument Pizarro was appointed Governor, Captain-General, Adelantado and Alguacil Mayor of Peru for life, with a sufficient salary, to be drawn from the revenues of the land which he should win: Almagro was appointed Governor of Tumbez with a salary less than half of that assigned to Pizarro: the thirteen who had remained with their captain at Gorgona were raised to the rank of hidalgos, and various privileges were granted to those who should accompany Pizarro to conquest and settlement. 'In return for these grants and titles', says Gomara, 'Pizarro promised great wealth and kingdoms: in order to attract men, he announced more riches than he knew of, but less than the reality.'

Fortified by his new dignities, Pizarro visited his native place Trujillo in Estremadura and there added to his company his four brothers or half-brothers, 'as proud as they were poor', of whom only one, Hernando Pizarro, was legitimate:[1] a young cousin, Pedro Pizarro, joined him as page. Accompanied by these and other volunteers, he re-embarked for the New World and entered Panama with much state. But Almagro, on hearing the result of the mission, complained bitterly of the inferior treatment granted to him and would not listen to Pizarro's explanation that the Emperor, knowing by experience the evils of a dual command, had refused his urgent request for equality between himself and Almagro. Pizarro promised future honours and rewards by way of redress: but the haughty Hernando Pizarro resented the complaints of the low-born Almagro, and the quarrel was with difficulty patched up.

Royal favour, the new dignities of Pizarro and his magnificent promises did not make men forget the sufferings and mortality of the three previous voyages, and volunteers were slow to come forward. At last, at the end of 1530, six years from his first setting out, Pizarro and his brothers, after the customary solemn Mass and Communion of all the expeditionaries, sailed from Panama with about 180 men and twenty-seven horses to the conquest of a great empire. Almagro, as before, remained in Panama to recruit men and follow with reinforcements.

[1] His half-brother Martín de Alcántara may also have been legitimate, being the son of Pizarro's mother—probably married to Alcantara's father.

CHAPTER XIII

THE CONQUEST OF PERU, 1530–1535

In those early days any Spaniard, even the poorest soldier, thought the whole of Peru was little for himself alone.

GOMARA

SIX years had passed since Pizarro's first setting-out from Panama. Before a decisive move could be made, nearly two more years were to be spent in pre-liminary efforts, in establishing bases on the coast and in attracting by means of booty fresh recruits from Panama in order to repair casualties and strengthen the scanty force. But there was no more going back: in thirteen days from Panama the little expedition arrived at the Bay of San Mateo, one degree north of the Equator, a point which they had previously taken more than two years to reach. Landing here, marching along the coast and living on the country as they went, they came to a town called Coaque, whence the in-habitants fled, leaving large booty in gold, silver and emeralds. The soldiers, believing that the true emerald would resist a blow like the diamond, tested their genuineness with a hammer and smashed many gems; but the booty sent back to Panama brought welcome recruits. After half a year of rest at Coaque, a plague of large ulcers, fatal to some and horrible to all, hastened their departure southwards. They marched under a torrid sun beating down on coats of mail and quilted jackets to the Gulf of Guayaquil. An attempt to occupy the island of Puná as a base of operations was abandoned; but the islanders, who had proved recalcitrant, were chastised; and the rich city of Tumbez on the adjoining mainland, after pacific persuasion had failed, was beaten into subjection and much booty was taken. Here two ships arrived from Nicaragua, bringing welcome reinforcements under Hernando de Soto, a spirited cavalier and notable commander, one of the foremost Conquistadores of Peru and afterwards celebrated in the exploration of North America. Pizarro was thus able to leave a garrison at Tumbez, while he marched some five-and-twenty leagues farther south and found at the mouth of the river Chira a suitable harbour to serve as a base for a march into the interior and for communication with Panama.

Here Pizarro founded the city of San Miguel in regular Spanish fashion, tracing out the central plaza and the streets, appointing magistrates and councillors and assigning the Indians of the neighbourhood as vassals (*encomendados*) to the householders, not without the use of swords and crossbows and the burning of some 'rebellious' chiefs.

And now, after eight years of tedious and costly preliminaries, the Governor found himself on the threshold of his great enterprise. The delays had in a sense been fortunate for the conqueror and fatal to the Inca empire; for that empire was torn by sanguinary and destructive civil war between brothers, so that every passing month destroyed its fighting men and lessened its power of resistance. About seven years before Pizarro's arrival at San Miguel, the Inca sovereign Huayna Capac died, a ruthless and cruel conqueror but also a determined and able ruler who was obeyed and reverenced as well as feared. The rightful heir to the whole empire was Huascar, son of his lawful wife; but his favourite among the numerous offspring of his harem was a spirited and active youth named Atahualpa, born of another woman. Huayna Capac broke the Inca tradition and policy by dividing his dominions: the northern province of Quito, recently subdued by the Inca arms, was to be ruled by the warlike, ambitious and (as it proved) unscrupulous Atahualpa. Huascar, a prince of generous and easy character, was to inherit the rest of the empire. Policy as well as paternal affection may have been a motive for the division. The Carangues, a tribe dwelling to the south of Quito, had rebelled: Huayna Capac, after suppressing the revolt, beheaded all the fighting men, throwing their bodies into a lake and contemptuously exclaiming, 'Now you are all boys'. He may have thought it wise to place a strong ruler over this recently subjugated region, remote from the seat of government at Cuzco.

For some time Atahualpa reigned in Quito and Huascar in Cuzco, the imperial capital, in apparent concord. But concord between the half-brothers was unreal; and while Pizarro was preparing his final expedition from Panama, civil war flamed out. Its early incidents are uncertain: but finally Atahualpa's generals won a crushing victory in the northern part of the Peruvian plateau, followed by a massacre of prisoners and by a campaign of extermination against the neighbouring tribes which had supported Huascar. Advancing southward towards Cuzco, the rebel commanders were again victorious in the battle of Ambato, where heaps of bones years afterwards testified to the slaughter. They swept away all further resistance, entered Cuzco, made Huascar prisoner, and established Atahualpa's authority by force, bloodshed and terror, killing almost the whole imperial lineage, that there might be no rival to the power of the conqueror, who now assumed the scarlet fringe or fillet, the symbol of supreme and divine authority over wide dominions: he chose as his residence the town of Cajamarca, surrounded by a fertile and beautiful region in northern Peru. The natural character of the Peruvian people or peoples and their long experience of discipline—sometimes a stern discipline—under an absolute paternal autocracy disposed them to submission and acquiescence: accordingly the usurper was generally revered and almost worshipped as a true child of the sun and lord of the Inca dominions. He was surrounded by all the traditional state of Inca sovereignty: the greatest nobles only approached him barefoot, with downcast eyes and bearing on their shoulders a symbolical burden.

Having heard of these recent civil wars, Pizarro, after 'pacifying' the neighbourhood of San Miguel, determined to cross the desert of Sechura and the coastal plain, to surmount the huge barrier of the Western Cordillera and to visit Atahualpa at Cajamarca. Leaving about eighty men at San Miguel to hold the country, he set out with the rest. After the first stage of his march he wisely dismissed all who chose to return to San Miguel and advanced into the heart of the empire with 62 horsemen and 106 infantry, of whom twenty were crossbowmen and three were musketeers: there were also a few small cannon which shot stone balls. The Spaniards were hospitably lodged and fed in the villages which they passed: but the contemporary narratives, usually almost bald in their simplicity, are here tinged by the intense anxiety and watchful caution with which the little army, losing many horses by the way, ascended the freezing heights of the Andine pass, sometimes passing through narrow defiles and even under the walls of a fortress where a small force could have overwhelmed them all. But they were allowed to pass unmolested and to descend into the plateau which lies between the great parallel ranges, meeting by the way messengers with gifts from Atahualpa, who, surrounded as he was by a great host of warriors in his camp near Cajamarca, believed that this handful of intruders was delivering itself into his power. As the Spaniards entered the valley of Cajamarca and approached the city, the Inca camp lay before them, containing, so they were assured, at least 30,000 fighting men. The watch-fires at night looked like the countless stars in a clear sky.

On 15 November 1532, forty-five days after setting out from San Miguel, Pizarro led his men in battle array into the city of Cajamarca, which appeared to be deserted. Riding through silent and empty streets, he came to a wide open space or square surrounded by a clay wall: low buildings containing large chambers opened upon the square, and in these the commander quartered his men. Without delay he sent fifteen horse under one of his most gallant captains, Hernando de Soto, followed by twenty more under Hernando Pizarro with a message inviting the Inca to visit 'his brother' in Cajamarca. The two Spanish cavaliers approached the Indian monarch, who was seated amidst a ceremonious group of nobles and officials in the courtyard of a pleasure-house erected over a hot spring which here welled from the earth. Hernando Pizarro approached on horseback and, without dismounting, delivered his message, which was translated into Quichua by an Indian youth named Filipillo who had been taken into the service of the Spaniards that he might learn Castilian and act as interpreter. The Emperor answered nothing and sat motionless. But when Hernando respectfully begged for a reply, Atahualpa answered that he was keeping a fast until the next day, when with some of his nobles he would visit the Spanish commander and order what should be done.

De Soto now, exhibiting the paces of his charger and his own horsemanship, pulled up his horse at full gallop at the very feet of the Emperor, who maintained his impassive dignity; but some of his attendants who shrank back in fear from the career of this strange animal were afterwards beheaded, according to the Spanish historians, for showing timidity before the strangers. After being regaled with *chicha* or maize beer in large golden vases, the cavaliers returned to announce to their commander the promised visit of the Emperor.

Pizarro prepared to receive the royal visit after his own fashion. The night was spent in prayer and in polishing the arms. Next day the men, both horse and foot, were all concealed, except one sentinel posted on a watch-tower. Orders were given for complete silence until the shout of *Santiago* and a musket-shot should give the signal to artillery, muskets and crossbows: then all were to fall-to with sword and lance, trusting in God who would give the victory to His servants. Twenty men, under Pizarro himself, were told off to seize the Emperor's person.

All day successive bodies of armed men, numbering in all many thousands, were seen to issue from the native camp and advance towards the city. About noon the Emperor, seated on a golden throne in a litter borne by great nobles, which rose 'like a gleaming castle of gold' above the throng of attendants, was carried slowly over the plain. Before him a body of men swept the road, removing every straw: others followed dancing and singing: a body-guard in splendid array surrounded the litter. Having approached the city of Cajamarca, Atahualpa halted, intending to sleep outside the place: but as sunset drew near and suspense among the Spaniards increased, Pizarro sent a message inviting the Emperor to supper. Atahualpa then was borne into the city and advanced into the silent and empty square, attended—according to the Spanish estimate—by about 5000 men, apparently unarmed but suspected of concealing slings, stones and darts under their cloaks. If this was true, it availed them nothing.

Atahualpa halted in the centre of the square and looked about, seeing no one. 'Where are the strangers?' he asked, and was assured by his attendants that the Spaniards were hiding from fear. 'And the truth is', says Pedro Pizarro, 'that some of us were shivering from fright.' Then Valverde, the Spanish chaplain, advanced alone and, approaching the monarch, pronounced a discourse based on the famous 'requisition' concerning the Christian religion, the authority of the Pope and the supremacy of the Spanish king. Upon hearing this lecture, ludicrously mistranslated into Quichua by the Indian youth Filipillo but intelligible with respect to the claim of supremacy, Atahualpa answered with indignant scorn; and when a breviary was handed to him as evidence of the truth, he threw it upon the ground. Thereupon the signal was given by a musket-shot: the battle-cry of *Santiago* was raised: cannon, muskets and crossbows shot their missiles:

horsemen and infantry rushed into the square striking down the defenceless people: some, under the impulse of terror, broke down the containing wall with the pressure of their bodies and fled over the plain, pursued by the lances of the horsemen. The Spaniards suffered one casualty: Pizarro was wounded in the hand by one of his own men in protecting the life of Atahualpa, who was dragged from his litter with his vesture torn from his body and was carried to Pizarro's quarters. 'As the Indians were unarmed', says Hernando Pizarro, 'they were defeated without danger to any Christian.'

The lowest Spanish estimate of the slain was 2000: they were probably twice that number. But night was coming on and the slaughter only lasted half an hour. The empire of the Incas, which had stood and grown for centuries, fell in that half-hour.

Pizarro, after exhorting his men to join him in thanksgiving for the great miracle, went to supper, placing Atahualpa beside him at the same table. Next day the Indian camp was pillaged and great booty taken; for all the vessels of the royal household were of silver and gold. The captive Indians were then gathered in the square: every Spaniard took all the men whom he needed for his service and the rest were released. The Spanish soldiers, for the sake of future security, wished to kill all the fighting men or at least to cut off their hands; but Pizarro refused, declaring that they should trust in God for future victory.

Atahualpa in captivity was treated as a reigning prince, served by the women of his harem and attended by Inca nobles, who waited in an outer chamber and only entered at the Emperor's call, always with the customary marks of humility. He learnt to play chess and conversed freely with his captors, narrating his war with his half-brother and adding, after a few days, that Huascar was now dead. Pizarro refused to believe such unwelcome news, but it was true: the men guarding Huascar had killed him; and no one doubted that Atahualpa had sent orders for the deed, lest the rightful monarch should seize the opportunity to recover his throne.

Before long the captive saw a chance of winning his freedom. Observing the strange eagerness of the Spaniards to acquire gold, he made them a promise which sounds like a fantastic fairy-tale: raising his arm above his head, he offered, by way of ransom for his release, to fill the room in which he stood, measuring seventeen feet by twelve, with plates and vessels of gold up to the highest stretch of his uplifted hand—all this to be done within two months. Pizarro accepted the contract: an extraordinary blunder if he had any intention of fulfilling it. A line was traced round the walls of the room at the agreed height, over seven feet: Atahualpa sent out his autocratic orders: day by day his vassals came, marching in single file like trains of mules and carrying on their backs burdens of gold which were thrown upon the floor. The pile rose steadily, but the two months had almost passed before it reached the line traced upon the wall. By Atahualpa's wish, three Spaniards were sent to Cuzco to hasten the collection: they were carried in litters by Indian porters along the great road, a distance of nearly 200 leagues, to the capital: here, although much gold had been hidden, they were astounded at the store which remained and also at the size and solidity of the buildings: 700 sheets of gold which covered the walls of the great temple were torn down and sent to Cajamarca to be added to the heap. Meantime, Hernando Pizarro was despatched on a difficult journey of 100 leagues over the western mountains to the famous sanctuary of Pachacamac on the coast. He returned empty-handed: the priests had concealed the treasure. But his journey was not fruitless; for, hearing that Atahualpa's chief general, Chalcuchima, was encamped with a large army in the valley of Jauja, Hernando returned by that more devious and troublesome route and succeeded in persuading the menacing warrior to abandon any hostile design and to accompany him peaceably to Cajamarca. The Indian chief was, in fact, delivering himself up to captivity and to a death which was not long delayed.

Here, in order to explain later events, a digression is necessary. Three generals had served Atahualpa in his campaigns of usurpation and slaughter, Chalcuchima, Quizquiz (whose fate will be told later) and Rumiñavi. The last-named, as soon as Atahualpa had fallen into the hands of the Spaniards, threw off his allegiance to his unfortunate sovereign and determined to make himself independent master of Quito, the extensive northern kingdom which had been Atahualpa's first dominion. Rumiñavi led thither from Cajamarca an army, probably about 5000 men: some represent him as a noble patriot defending his country, others as a sanguinary and rapacious tyrant. There is probably some truth in both views, as in the case of military usurpers elsewhere. At all events, trained in the cruel and despotic school of Atahualpa, he evidently turned his schooling to account, for when the Spaniards invaded Quito a year later their chief opponent was Rumiñavi; and, on the other hand, many of the inhabitants hating the domination of Rumiñavi made common cause with the Spaniards.

To resume the story of Atahualpa and Pizarro: the Spanish emissaries, both those sent to Cuzco and those sent to Pachacamac, were everywhere received and served with friendly and even cordial hospitality. The people seemed to have accepted quietly the change of masters, perhaps by command of Atahualpa himself: a few scores of intruders appeared to have the Inca empire in their hands.

Atahualpa had spent three months in captivity when in February 1533 Almagro marched into Cajamarca with the long-looked-for reinforcements—150 foot and 50 horse: the many vicissitudes and trials which had delayed their coming cannot here find place. After this increase in the numbers of the invaders only two obstacles stood in the way of advance, the distribution of Atahualpa's huge ransom and the disposal of his person. To solve the first of these problems a business was carefully organised and accomplished which has no parallel in the history of the world. For more than a month a squad of Indian goldsmiths were compelled to labour at melting down and casting into gold and silver bars of equal weight a vast quantity of plates, vessels, and artistic objects, the handiwork of their own craft. When this lamentable destruction was complete, Pizarro arranged the distribution. 'He was most Christian', says his page, 'in depriving no man of that which he deserved'. The treasure was found to weigh 1,326,539 'pesos of good gold', ($13265\frac{2}{5}$ pounds weight) and 26,000 pounds of silver. But since the weighing had been a rapid business with a liberal over-allowance at every balancing of the steel-yard, the amount was, in fact, much more. The royal fifth was duly set aside, together with some artistic objects to please the Emperor's eye and bear witness to the greatness of his newly-won dominions. Almagro's men, who claimed that they should share equally with the rest, were finally bought off with a moderate sum. Every one of Pizarro's men received a weight of uncoined gold and silver apportioned to the rank and services of each. Pizarro's own share was enormous; that of his chief captains meant a large fortune. Every cavalryman received nearly 90 pounds weight of gold and above 180 pounds of silver. Some of the infantry men received half that amount: others had to be satisfied with less. But, if the treasure afterwards distributed at Cuzco be added, most of the Spaniards received a portion which, had it been in Spain, might have enriched a thrifty man for life. On the other hand, the value in Peru was problematic: the men had food and servants for nothing, it is true, but the horses were shod with silver for want of iron; a Spanish cloak cost at least a pound weight of gold, a sword about half that amount, and a horse was worth a huge sum in gold. A few of the men carried home their gains to Spain; others dissipated them in gambling and idle expenditure. Of those who remained in Peru not many survived to enjoy their wealth.

Hernando Pizarro, a man of education and of a bearing fit for courts, was chosen to carry to Spain the fifth part due to the King. The bearer of this truly royal treasure was rewarded with the Cross of Santiago; and some two years later he returned to Peru bringing the King's signature to titles, dignities and territorial grants conferred upon the two captains—matters to be related in the next chapter. The choice of Hernando as emissary to Spain was a politic one, for his haughty temper caused discord between the chiefs and later was the cause of great evils. His absence was also convenient in another way: he had shown a certain chivalrous and friendly sympathy with the unfortunate Atahualpa, and would not have consented to the crime which followed.

There still remained the question what was to be done with the captive Atahualpa, who had paid the agreed ransom and earned his release. The question was discussed among the Spaniards as one of expediency, not of justice, although the pretence of justice was observed: it was decided to put the captive Emperor out of the way in the quickest and readiest fashion. Atahualpa was accused of 'treason', of ordering the assembly of armies to attack the Spaniards, partly on the evidence of the rascally young interpreter Filipillo, who had been denounced by Atahualpa for violating the sanctity of the royal harem and now avenged his private grudge by false evidence. De Soto, who, like Hernando Pizarro, was a friend and probable champion of Atahualpa, was despatched with five horsemen to investigate the rumoured gathering of enemy forces: he returned declaring that there was not an armed man to be found anywhere, and that the whole country was at peace. He was too late; in his absence, notwithstanding protests from some of the Spaniards, Atahualpa had been condemned in a mock trial to be burnt as a traitor. That same evening all the Spaniards gathered to witness the execution. Atahualpa, having been assured that, by accepting baptism, he would suffer the lesser penalty of strangling instead of fire, submitted to the exhortations of Valverde, was baptized at the stake, and after commending his children to the care of Pizarro, submitted with Indian stoicism to his fate. Christian burial followed; but it is believed that his people disinterred the bones to give them due obsequies in the city of Quito after the ancestral custom of the Inca lords.

Such is the story usually told—sentence of death by fire, commuted to the *garrote* (strangling) upon submission to baptism: but Pedro Pizarro, who witnessed all these scenes, gives a more probable account: according to him the sentence was that Atahualpa should be strangled and that his dead body should be burnt, because he had taken his sisters as wives. But Atahualpa had told his people that after death his father, the sun, would resuscitate him and send him back to his subjects on earth. Accordingly, on being assured that if he accepted baptism his body would not be burnt, he agreed, lest his people should think the prophecy frustrated on seeing his body consumed by fire. It seems improbable that Pedro should have invented so curious and characteristic a story. It may be added that some indignity to the corpse was a common part of a capital sentence in Spain: thus a sentence of quartering, passed upon traitors, often meant quartering after execution. The same witness adds that, as Atahualpa was led to execution, the crowds of natives who were present lay upon the ground 'like drunken men', that some of the Inca's women hanged themselves in order to go and serve him in the other world: two of his women, beating drums, chanted the deeds of their master, and then passed through the chambers where he had lodged, calling him by name in every corner.

The historian Oviedo, who bore office among the Conquistadores, who firmly believed in the righteousness of the conquest and records with evident approval and in a tone of religious triumph the massacre of Cajamarca and the capture of Atahualpa, writes thus of this later crime: 'Experience has shown how ill-advised and worse done was the taking of Atabalipa's life: wherewith, besides the sin against God, they took from our lord the Emperor and from the Spaniards themselves ... innumerable treasures which that prince would have given them; and none of his vassals would have moved or risen, as they rose and rebelled when he was gone. It is well known that the Governor guaranteed to him his life. . . . All this was contrived by evil men or by the error or ill counsel of the Governor; and they brought against him an accusation ill composed and worse written, one of the leaders being an uneasy, turbulent and dishonest priest, with a notary of no conscience and poor capacity. . . .'

The doers of the crime soon repented of their blunder: Pizarro the Governor, Valverde the priest, and Riquelme the Royal Treasurer bandied reproaches, accusing one another of the deed. They had, in fact, destroyed the basis of their own authority and the means of securing the conquest. Pizarro attempted to repair the injury to his own authority by setting up a puppet Inca, one of the surviving sons of Huayna Capac named Toparca. Pizarro invested Toparca with the imperial fringe, professed to recognise the sovereign authority of his own creature, and carried this titular monarch in his train upon his southward march. For the Governor, now reinforced by many volunteers from Panama or from Spain, led out 590 Spaniards, besides Indian attendants, on the road to Cuzco after he had detached 150 men to strengthen the garrison of San Miguel under Belalcazar, a brave and able captain, famous later as the conqueror of Quito.

Belalcazar, like Almagro, was the son of a peasant

farmer, and knew no name but that of his native village in Estremadura. As a youth he ran away from home, because, in trying to extricate an ass which had become bogged, he gave the poor beast in a fit of exasperation such a severe blow on the neck as to kill it: rather than face parental anger he disappeared—so says the historian Castellanos. The story is curiously like that of Pizarro and his stampeded pigs: but it is significant that the early biographies of Pizarro, Almagro and Belalcazar, all resemble the opening of a picaresque novel; and the autobiography of another Conquistador, Alonso Enríquez de Guzmán, to be cited later, reads throughout like a picaresque romance. The young Belalcazar, leaving the dead ass in its hole, made his way to Seville, the goal of vagabonds and adventurers, and there joined Pedrarias' expedition to Darien. He did good service in Panama and Nicaragua, on one occasion saving the Governor's life in a tight place: he was well known to Pizarro and Almagro, and was invited by them to join the Peruvian enterprise. His appointment as commander at San Miguel started him upon a successful but finally tragic career of adventurous ambition. Having secured the necessary base on the coast, Pizarro and his men moved southwards from Cajamarca, traversing the great central table-land of Peru by the Inca road and meeting no resistance until, after peaceably travelling two-thirds of the total distance, they came to the valley of Jauja, where a host of hostile Indians gathered on the farther bank of a river was swept away by the Spanish horsemen. The Governor here made a halt, having resolved to found a Spanish city in this rich and beautiful valley, whose name *Jauja* has been adopted into the Spanish language to signify a rich fairyland.

While the ordering of the city of Jauja was in progress, de Soto was sent ahead with sixty horsemen to prepare the way to Cuzco: he was hard pressed by ambushed Indians in mountainous ways and was in utmost danger, when the trumpets of Almagro, advancing to his support, were heard: de Soto's trumpets replied; and the Indians, dismayed by this apparently magical multiplication of the Christians at the critical instant, scattered and disappeared.

The Spaniards, angered by this unexpected and, in their view, criminal resistance, vented their chagrin upon Chalcuchima, Atahualpa's general, who accompanied their march perforce: he was accused of having instigated the rising; and when some days later the puppet Inca Toparca died, fresh suspicion or pretended suspicion fell upon the unhappy prisoner. He was burnt alive as a traitor, protesting his innocence, and when exhorted to accept baptism, simply replying that he 'did not understand the religion of the white men'.

After some skirmishing in the last stages of the march, Pizarro led 480 Spaniards in battle array into the imperial city of Cuzco on 15 November 1533, just a year after his entry into Cajamarca. He rode through streets, packed with a throng of gazers, to the central square, where his men were lodged in great public halls. They were soon at work plundering the city: they ransacked palaces, temples and sepulchres; they stripped the royal mummies of their jewels; and in defiance of Pizarro's orders to respect the persons and property of the inhabitants, they broke into houses and sometimes tortured the people to extort supposed hidden treasure. Pedro Pizarro declares that none of Pizarro's men dared take so much as an ear of maize without the Governor's leave: this was probably true on the march, but in Cuzco no such strict discipline was observed. The quantity of treasure found in the city itself was disappointing; but, added to the booty taken on the road from Cajamarca, it made a magnificent pile. In one place they had found ten planks of solid silver, described as being each of them twenty feet long, a foot broad and three inches thick. The Indian goldsmiths were again commanded to destroy the artistic handiwork of their ancestors; and after the royal fifth had been set aside, every Spaniard received a bountiful portion. 'It was a thing worthy to be seen,' says Pizarro's secretary, 'this house where the melting took place, full of so much gold in plates of eight and ten pounds each and in vessels and vases and pieces of various forms.' A circle of gold representing the sun was left intact and assigned to a soldier named Leguizana: he lost it in a night's gambling, whence came a proverbial saying, 'To play away the sun before sunrise'. It is probable that other objects were not melted down, but were weighed and distributed intact to the soldiers. This was certainly done later; for goldsmiths and furnaces could not always be at hand when booty was gathered; moreover, when a town was pillaged, a man kept what he had got. Thus Alonso Enriquez de Guzman, a gay and unscrupulous gentleman-adventurer who came to Peru in 1535 and has left an entertaining autobiography, tells us that he possessed 20,000 *castellanos* of good weight and size in the form of water-pots and other objects.

The Governor, having taken possession of the city, proceeded to secure the European occupation of the place, after the regular constitutional Spanish fashion, by setting up in due form and with solemn public ceremonial a Spanish municipality for the city of

Cuzco. A town council (*cabildo*) was constituted by the nomination of eight councillors (*regidores*), among them Juan and Gonzalo, brothers of the Governor; and in March 1534, four months after the entry into the capital, the two alcaldes took the oath of office in the great square in presence of all the Spaniards and a crowd of natives. To every Spaniard who settled in Cuzco as a householder (*vecino*) were assigned a house or building site in the city, a grant of land for cultivation outside and an *encomienda* or fief of Indian vassals. The municipality thus formed soon undertook, as in all similar cases, the administration of a wide district.

While Spanish authority was thus regularly established on a constitutional basis, an attempt was made to give some constitutional colour to that authority in the eyes of the natives by reviving the semblance or pretence of Inca sovereignty. After the death of Toparca and before the entry into Cuzco, an Inca noble named Manco visited the Governor's camp attended by a showy retinue and claiming to be the rightful heir to the throne, as the eldest legitimate son of Huayna Capac. Pizarro readily accepted the part of king-maker, avowed that he had come to the country as the champion of legitimate monarchy, and at a solemn public function he himself, as representing the all-embracing supremacy of the Spanish sovereign, bound the imperial fringe upon Manco's brow, declaring him, amid the acclamations of his gratified subjects, to be the true successor to the great Huayna Capac and to Huascar. Manco repaid his debt to Pizarro by leading out a force of Indian warriors to aid the Spaniards in suppressing a revolt raised by Quizquiz, the only surviving general of Atahualpa and therefore an enemy to the house of Huascar: ostensibly both the Spaniards and their Indian auxiliaries were fighting for rightful authority against the faction of Quito and the adherents of the usurper. After a short campaign Quizquiz was killed by his own men, sick of hopeless resistance to the combined forces of the Spaniards and the Inca Manco; and the trouble disappeared for the time.

Another anxiety supervened when news came that Pedro de Alvarado was leading a strong force from Guatemala to the conquest of Quito. Almagro hurried northwards from Cuzco to avert or anticipate the danger: visiting San Miguel on the way to pick up reinforcements, he was alarmed to find that the ambitious and active Belalcazar, Governor of that place, finding himself much strengthened in his command by the arrival of men from Panama and Nicaragua, had set out for Quito some months earlier; he had been invited by some emissaries of the Cañari tribe to come and deliver them from the hated dominion of the usurper Rumiñavi: a surprising incident, since the Spaniards found themselves accepted in the character of deliverers from oppression, not through any diplomatic wiles of their own, as in the case of Cortes and the tributary subjects of Montezuma, but upon the unsolicited invitation of some of the inhabitants. Almagro hastened after Belalcazar from San Miguel, and joined him in the early part of 1534 on the heights of Quito, near Riobamba, where Belalcazar had established a Spanish municipal settlement after defeating Rumiñavi. It has been already related on page 116 how the united[1] forces of Almagro and Belalcazar frustrated Alvarado's designs of conquest. Belalcazar

[1] Their union was possibly facilitated by the fact that they were *compadres*, Belalcazar having stood god-father in Panama to Almagro's son Diego.

was left in Quito as lieutenant-governor of that kingdom, to pursue a fresh phase of ambitious conquest and push his arms far to the north; Almagro, after accompanying Alvarado to his meeting with Pizarro at Pachacamac, marched back to Cuzco at the head of an army trebled in number by the addition of most of Alvarado's men to his own troops, with a reputation enhanced by the notable power of leadership and of diplomacy which he had shown.

The conquest seemed to be complete and secure, and the Governor proceeded to signalise its apogee by setting up a new seat of government, which should be wholly Spanish in character, for the whole realm. The division of the Empire by Huayna Capac and the civil war which followed had shown that Cuzco, far to the south and seated upon its lofty plateau, was too remote to serve as the seat of government. The recently founded Spanish city of San Miguel was too far north. The Governor, leaving his brothers Juan and Gonzalo in command at Cuzco, travelled to the coast and finally chose a site two leagues from the sea and near the convenient harbour of Callao in the valley of Rimac. Here in January 1535 he inaugurated the City of the Kings (*Ciudad de los Reyes*), so named in honour of the Feast of the Epiphany. Indian labourers were collected from a wide district to give solid and stately form to the purely Spanish city which under the more convenient name of Lima (corrupted from *Rimac*) was to be for two centuries the capital of half a continent, although for some ten years longer Cuzco continued to be the official capital. In the new city the Governor built for himself a palace with its garden of fruits and flowers and its court for the game of bowls, of which Pizarro was an enthusiastic player. A coat-of-arms, three crowns and a star, was afterwards granted by the Crown to the City of the Kings.

With the foundation of Lima in 1535 the story of the conquest of Peru by rights should end. If the victors had acted with reasonable discretion, if a Cortes or a Balboa had been in command, the historian would merely have to round off his narrative by indicating the process of consolidating and extending the work already accomplished. But this apparently assured success was but the beginning of great disasters: a native revolt which threatened to undo all that had been done was provoked by the violent excesses of the conquerors and was facilitated by their dissensions; and hardly had this danger passed when those dissensions flamed out into a series of sanguinary and fatal conflicts among the Spaniards themselves, which darkened the history of the conquest and left a shadow on the later history of Peru.

CHAPTER XIV

CUZCO

Fighting at the same time with enemies, with the elements and with hunger.
HERRERA

IN dealing with Pedro de Alvarado the two chiefs had worked heartily together: the long-standing jealousy between them seemed to have died down when suddenly it flamed out dangerously. Just when Almagro, at the height of success, was leading back to Cuzco the most imposing force to be found in Peru, he heard through his friends arriving from Spain that the Emperor had conferred upon him, with the title of Adelantado, an independent government to the south of that already granted to Pizarro. The news was unofficial, without documents or details, but Almagro at once asserted that Cuzco, the historic capital, which was regarded as the chief prize of victory, lay within his limits and belonged to him. The two Pizarro brothers had been ordered by the Governor to yield the command in Cuzco to Almagro as their superior officer on his return from Quito; but they were now told to reject his claim of independent authority and to retain the command. Almagro, having entered Cuzco with his army, protested vehemently against this treatment, and the two parties were on the point of coming to blows, when the Governor hastened from Lima to avert such a calamity. However, upon his arrival at Cuzco he stood stiffly upon his rights, and a break seemed imminent until some peacemaker persuaded the two captains to renew their ancient compact: they attended Mass together; and, joining hands over the consecrated Host, they swore not to calumniate one another, not to send separate reports to the Emperor and to share equally all future profits, a scene which recalls the famous story of the oath exacted from King Alfonso VI by the Cid. The need of so solemn an engagement is evidence of the profound distrust bred between old comrades by success and victory, a distrust not to be healed even by the most binding oaths.

A month after this singular ceremony, Almagro set out on his southward march to occupy his new vaguely-defined Government and also to provide employment and booty for new-comers from Spain and for the impoverished men of Guatemala, many of them hidalgos, who had failed in their attempt upon Quito and had won nothing in Peru. To some of these Almagro freely lent gold and silver to provide equipment; and when the expedition returned profitless he publicly tore up the bonds and forgave the debts with cheerful talk. To other recruits he gave with careless profusion: a man who asked for a ring was told to fill his two hands with gold: another, who presented to the Adelantado (as he was henceforth called) the first European cat to be found in Peru, received a gift of a pound weight of gold.

Relieved of his rival's presence, Pizarro returned to Lima. Hither came his brother Hernando bringing news from Spain of the gracious reception granted at Court to the Peruvian treasure and to its bearer; he brought also the royal decrees which conferred a Marquisate on Francisco (henceforth known as 'the Marquis'), extended his Government seventy leagues to the south beyond its former limits and granted to Almagro a territory to the south of this. Pizarro's Government, to be entitled New Castile, was to extend 270 leagues southwards from Santiago, a place situated a little north of the Equator: Almagro's territory, to be called New Toledo, was to extend 200 leagues from the southern limit of New Castile: the Bishop of Panama was appointed as judge or rather surveyor to define the limits on the spot after consulting the most skilful pilots: the Bishop in due course visited Peru, but returned to his diocese without deciding anything. Thus there was no authoritative ruling about the dividing line or about the possession of Cuzco: the geographical notions of the authorities in Spain were extremely hazy;[1] and the conquerors of Peru were by no means agreed about distances or methods of measurement. It may be added that the name New Toledo never came into general use and that of New Castile was soon disused.

Hernando, having delivered at Lima his message from Spain, was despatched to join his two brothers at Cuzco and assume the command there while the Marquis continued his constructive work of planning, building and colonising at Lima, at Trujillo, so named after his native place in Estremadura, and at other places on the coast.

THE EXPEDITION TO CHILE, 1535–1537

Almagro was absent nearly two years (July 1535 to March 1537). The expedition, which sought another

---

[1] A curious proof of this vagueness appears in the grant to Pedro de Mendoza, the first founder of Buenos Aires, of 200 leagues of the Pacific coast to the south of Almagro's territory, a grant made in this same year 1535.

golden Peru, was an epic of hardship, endurance, mortality and disappointment, but of splendid leadership by the Adelantado. He chose as his lieutenant one Rodrigo Orgoñez, a veteran of the Italian wars, a stout and skilful soldier, devoted to his commander; to provide food, a flock of llamas was driven with the troops and a supply of maize was carried which was renewed at various halts: the herds of swine, which accompanied all later expeditions, were not yet to be found in Peru, the pig being an imported European beast. Altogether 570 Spaniards and some thousands of Indian attendants marched out from Cuzco in several detachments at intervals of time; 'for if they had gone together, most of them would have perished of hunger and the natives of the land would have been destroyed'. The Adelantado himself led the second detachment, numbering 200 Spaniards, accompanied by Manco's younger brother the Inca Paulu, who attached himself permanently to the white men and rendered valuable service during this expedition by inculcating peace on the inhabitants where they passed and by raising supplies of food. Almagro's company took the Inca military road which led southwards skirting the western shore of Lake Titicaca and traversing the highest and bleakest part of the plateau (now part of the republic of Bolivia) through the province of Charcas. Had they known that this apparently poor land was soon to become a proverb for its amazing wealth in silver, the fatal conflict over Cuzco might never have arisen. Before the expedition reached the southern limit of the tableland at Tupiza some 230 leagues from Cuzco, many of the Indians died of cold and exhaustion—for it was the depth of winter—on the icy wind-swept heights. From Tupiza they went down by the long steep descent to the valley of Salta (now in the north-west of the Argentine Republic). Here there was a halt of two months until the approach of summer should make possible the most difficult stage of the journey, the passage westward through a broken mountainous region, thence by the pass of San Francisco over the freezing height of the Cordillera and down towards the Pacific to Copiapo in the coastal plain of northern Chile. According to Oviedo, 1500 Indians, two Spaniards, 150 negroes and 112 horses perished in this passage of the mountains and many of the survivors were frostbitten: other accounts give a much greater mortality among the Spaniards. The next detachment, which followed some time later, found the frozen carcasses of the horses and fed on their still untainted flesh, for the torment of hunger pursued all these expeditions. Having descended from the mountains westward towards the Pacific coast and having reached the northern part of the land which they sought, Almagro and his men journeyed southwards from Copiapo by easy ways through a productive country where food was abundant, accepting or compelling the submission of the tribes as they went, denouncing idolatry everywhere and proclaiming the supreme dominion of the Catholic Church and of the Spanish king, but gathering little booty. Three Spaniards having been killed by Indians, thirty Indian chiefs were burnt alive: 'This chastisement was necessary', says the contemporary chronicler Oviedo, 'and was so effective that the land was secured and a Spaniard's Indian servant could pass everywhere without hurt.' Oviedo's successor, the historian Herrera, writing sixty years later, says that the sentence was unjust and seemed great cruelty to all.

Having thus travelled some 2400 miles by a cir-

cuitous route of indescribable difficulty, having reached
the central part of Chile and having found nothing to
please him, Almagro sent forward an exploring party
which probably reached the river Maule in latitude
36° south, the farthest limit of Inca influence, for the
country of the unconquerable Araucanian Indians lay
beyond. This party returned reporting that all the land
was sterile and forbidding—a strange report and a
strange judgement on the part of Almagro concerning
a country of singular beauty and fertility, blessed with
a benign climate, a country which has been called the
'Californian slope of South America': in part the men
were disheartened by the trials which they had under-
gone: but their chief complaint was the paucity of gold.
Moreover the return of Almagro was hastened by the
news that all Peru was in revolt and that Cuzco was
besieged by the Indians: on his way northwards he also
met an officer, Juan de Herrada by name, bearing the
royal decree which named him Adelantado and defined the limits of his government: he at once resolved
once more to claim Cuzco as standing within those
limits. For the return northwards to Peru he chose
the coastal route, much shorter than the mountain
way but hardly less terrible in its own kind; for it
led through long stretches of waterless desert, one of
them, the desert of Atacama, measuring more than
100 leagues in length. Almagro proved his qualities
as a commander by leading his army safely back to
Peru: he ascended from the coast by way of Arequipa,
a city distant about sixty leagues from Cuzco by a
mountain road. The last trial of the journey was the
torment of snow-blindness which afflicted his army for
two days.

His apparently profitless expedition, with all its

sufferings, was the prologue to the conquest of Chile undertaken three years later by Valdivia.

During Almagro's absence strange things had happened in Peru; and the main narrative must be resumed at the date of his departure for Chile.

At that time the Spaniards appeared to hold safely the lands which they had conquered. In seeming security they divided and scattered their forces. Great part of their fighting men marched far away under Almagro: expeditions set out under various captains to suppress sporadic resistance and to complete 'pacification' spreading the dominion of Castile and the religion of the Cross: many Spaniards settled down as *encomenderos* on isolated estates to live by the labour of submissive Indian vassals: Belalcazar, detached in the far north, was establishing the power of Spain throughout the kingdom of Quito and even carrying his arms northwards into lands now forming part of the republic of Colombia. Pizarro, now ruler and administrator rather than soldier, was engaged in peaceful administration, establishing centres of European civilisation by planting groups of Spaniards in newly founded cities on the coast. Cuzco, the centre of Inca tradition and still the seat of a shadowy Inca Court, was actually left with a garrison of about 200 Spaniards and a few Indian auxiliaries under Hernando Pizarro as Governor of the city.

This seeming quietude was broken by a violent rebellion headed by the Inca Manco.

THE SIEGE OF CUZCO, 1536

That prince, although in theory or rather in pretence recognised by the Spaniards as sovereign of the whole Inca empire, was in fact held captive in Cuzco by Hernando Pizarro, not indeed actually imprisoned, but always guarded and confined to the city. Feeling bitterly the mockery of his position, he attempted escape, which was frustrated through information laid against him by some Cañari warriors stationed in Cuzco. Manco was then placed under stronger guard; and any bully among the rude soldiers was allowed to inflict on him the most outrageous affronts. Finally Manco obtained his release by playing upon the Spaniard's cupidity for gold: he promised Hernando to bring back to the city from a secret cavern in the mountains a life-size golden statue of his father the great Inca Huayna Capac: once outside the city, he took to the mountains and called his subjects to arms to destroy the Spaniards.

Oviedo puts into the mouth of an Inca noble the provocations which moved that aristocratic ruling clan to revolt. After describing the ease, leisure and tranquillity of their life before the coming of the invaders, the Indian noble continues, 'Now, since you Christians have come, from freemen you have made us slaves and from lords have made us your servants. The Inca lost his reputation and freedom and we our liberty and refreshment. In place of being served, we served you . . . we lived in your houses, abandoning our own. You have been so ungrateful that instead of treating us well and justly, you took our wives and daughters for concubines: you robbed our property, burning us and tearing us with dogs in order to take it from us, insulting our persons with evil words; and that which we feel with most dismay is that a natural lord whom God gave us, who was esteemed, served, loved and obeyed, should be treated as the least among us.' Alonso Enriquez de

Guzman, who was Camp-Master in the garrison of Cuzco at the time and afterwards joined the party of Almagro, gives independently in his autobiography the substance of the same speech; which was therefore presumably uttered in fact and not merely composed by Oviedo in the character of historical chorus. Such were the feelings of the ruling class: but the submissive and docile peasantry, accustomed to obey commands and to acquiesce in conquest, who commonly received their new masters not only peaceably but cordially, also suffered grievous wrong. Wherever the invaders chose to settle, the population of a wide district became serfs, compelled to build the cities where their new masters should dwell and to till the lands which should feed the strangers. The chief trouble of the Spaniards in these early days was their food-supply, and their chief tribulation was hunger: accordingly whenever a troop of a few score Spaniards, accompanied by some hundreds of Indian servants, rested in some friendly village of small farmers, they left hunger and destitution behind them. One sentence of Oviedo is instructive. After briefly mentioning the occupation of a place from which the Indian garrison had fled, he adds, 'The Spaniards, pursuing them, took many women and sheep (llamas) and other spoils'.

No wonder then that the Inca Manco was able to assemble a great army and lay siege to Cuzco, so that countless watch-fires glimmered round the city at night: the besiegers occupied the great fortress which still overlooks the city: with burning missiles hurled from thence they set fire to the thatched roofs of the houses: the fire raged for days and consumed half the city: parties of the enemy entered through the clouds of smoke and erected barricades across the streets to impede the movements of the horses. The Spaniards, who were never dislodged from their quarters in the great square, determined that the fortress must be taken: accordingly a night attack was planned. Juan Pizarro, a cavalier twenty-five years of age, much beloved for his high spirit and pleasant ways, led the assault bareheaded, for a wound on the jaw prevented the wearing of his helmet. A stone slung from the ramparts struck him on the head and inflicted a mortal wound, of which he died a fortnight later: yet, though prostrated, he urged on his men until they captured the first terrace. At dawn Hernando himself renewed the assault: an Inca noble standing on the highest parapet struck down with his battle-axe every assailant who mounted the scaling-ladders, until, seeing the fortress lost, he wrapped his mantle about his head and threw himself from the topmost height. Notwithstanding this success, the little garrison of Cuzco—200 or perhaps 240 Spaniards, 'half of them lame or maimed', says Alonso Enriquez the Camp-Master—never had rest. Hernando Pizarro, leading a sortie and driving back the enemy, found in his path the heads of five Spaniards together with 1000 letters despatched from Lima. As time passed without succour and as famine was felt, there was talk of abandoning the place and making a dash for the coast. The enemy vauntingly shouted to them that Lima and Trujillo were besieged or taken, that every Spaniard in the country was slain.

There was some truth in the boast. Most of the Christians who were living on their estates throughout the country were killed. Manco actually sent an army to besiege Lima: but that city, near the sea and surrounded by a plain suitable for cavalry, was never seriously in danger, for the horse was still a terror to the natives. Moreover those Indians who had been forced to serve the Spaniards in Lima as *yanaconas*, that is to say personal servants or retainers and attendants, went out from the city at night and brought back food for their Spanish masters—an incident which reminds us that the Spanish household has always had a patriarchal character, that of all European peoples the Spaniards were the most humane slave-owners, and that the Spanish master commonly regarded all his servants, whether slaves or free, as members of his family.

But although Lima itself was safe, the mountain ways leading thence to Cuzco were beset by Manco's troops: four times the Marquis sent armed bodies to succour his brothers in Cuzco: they were waylaid and slain—more than 300 in all—in the mountain passes, except a few kept in captivity by Manco to serve as armourers; for the weapons taken from the Spaniards were turned against their countrymen in Cuzco and a few audacious Inca chiefs even mounted some of the horses. Thus, all communication being intercepted, the fate of Cuzco was unknown in Lima and the ruler of Cuzco, knowing nothing of Lima, feared the worst. The Marquis in this emergency publicly admitted the set-back to the conquest by exceptional action: he sent out from Lima urgent messages to the governors of Panama, Nicaragua, Guatemala and New Spain, and even to the distant Audiencia of Santo Domingo, imploring aid to avert the loss of these rich conquests. Hernan Cortes in response sent from New Spain a ship laden with victuals and munitions, together with a personal gift of rich clothing for Pizarro: Gaspar de Espinosa, who was a principal shareholder in the enterprise of Peru, brought 250 men from Panama: other ships came bringing aid. But when these succours arrived after inevitable months of delay, they were not needed; for although the fighting was not over, the imminent danger was past and Cuzco, with the survivors of its little garrison, was safe. Before long, the arms of these Spanish reinforcements were to be turned against their own countrymen. Indeed this was the fate of the last and strongest expedition of relief despatched from Lima by Pizarro towards the end of 1536 under Alonzo de Alvarado, one of the men of Guatemala, who marched only as far as Jauja and there lingered unaccountably for five months instead of joining hands with the defenders of Cuzco against Manco.

After surrounding the city of Cuzco for more than half a year (February to August 1536), the Inca Manco found himself unable to feed so great an army; moreover seed-time was approaching and the farmer-soldiers were called home by necessity. In September he disbanded most of his forces; but he still maintained a formidable army in the field, making his headquarters in the fortress of Tambo. Although the Spaniards were now able to sweep in llamas and maize from the surrounding country, every sally meant a skirmish: a war of raids and of combats between small parties continued, and for another six months the scanty defenders, to whom the loss of a single man was a grave disaster, were never safe.

Hernando determined upon a bold stroke; to assault the fortress of Tambo and seize the person of the Inca. He led eighty horsemen, a few infantry and a body of Indian auxiliaries by a night march and attacked the place at dawn. But the Indians were on the watch and received the assailants with such a shower of missiles as forced them to retire, while the Inca Manco was seen on horseback within the enclosure animating the defenders. The Spaniards attacked a second time and again they were repulsed. The Indians, breaking an embankment, flooded the ground behind the assailants: and Hernando Pizarro led his defeated men in a difficult retreat back to Cuzco, his brother Gonzalo twice turning to drive back with a cavalry charge the Indian troops which harassed their rear; 'for the Indians after victory', says Pedro Pizarro, 'are devils in pursuing their enemy, although they are like a lot of wet chickens when they fly'. It was the last triumph of the Inca, as Prescott remarks.

In April 1537, more than a year after the siege had begun, Almagro, marching over the mountains from Arequipa on his return from the expedition to Chile, approached Cuzco. He opened negotiations with his former friend Manco, who was still harassing the defenders of the city with a considerable army. Manco replied recalling the insults and wrongs suffered at the hands of the Spaniards, but without definitely rejecting Almagro's overtures. However, suspecting the Adelantado's good faith and probably unwilling to make terms with any Spaniard, Manco attempted a surprise attack on Almagro's camp; but the veterans of Chile were not to be caught unaware, and the natives were driven back in rout. The great revolt of the Indians had in fact spent its force and almost died down.

Almagro now sent a summons to the Spanish municipality of Cuzco demanding to be admitted as master of the place. Hernando brushed aside the civic authorities, took the matter into his own hands and opened negotiations with Almagro. But negotiation meant little: the latter, in command of his veteran troops returning from Chile, was the stronger of the two. Alleging afterwards in justification that Hernando had broken a truce, Almagro burst into the city one stormy night: a party, told off to arrest Hernando, attacked the house where he and his brother Gonzalo slept, guarded by a watch of twenty men. Hernando, roused from sleep, armed himself in haste and vigorously faced his assailants. But they set fire to the thatched roof, and the inmates, forced to come out, were overpowered by numbers. Next day the town council unanimously accepted the Adelantado's authority: he was received in the church with a *Te Deum*: Hernando and Gonzalo, the brothers of the Marquis, were imprisoned: Almagro was master of Cuzco.

CHAPTER XV

THE WAR OF LAS SALINAS, 1537-1538

In this land the dispositions of the people are so variable and change-
able that what they promise to-day they disown to-morrow, only thinking of their own interests. So it is that no one can trust in the word
of another, for on the first occasion it will be broken.

CIEZA DE LEON

ALMAGRO considered that he had merely used
unavoidable force in claiming his right as Governor
of New Toledo, entering his own capital and arresting
criminal intruders. But force could not halt at a given
point: Alonso de Alvarado, after delaying five months
near Jauja, as is told in the previous chapter, advanced
to the bridge of Abancay, which spanned a tributary
of the Apurimac about seven leagues from Cuzco:
Almagro sent envoys to him demanding recognition as
master of the city. After a first courteous reception by
Alvarado and amicable conversation over the dinner-
table, the envoys were put in fetters, threatened and
roughly handled—an experience which is described in
lively fashion by one of the victims, Alonso Enriquez,
in his autobiography. Orgoñez, Almagro's lieutenant,
thereupon urged his chief to behead the two Pizarro
brothers who were held captive within the city. The
Adelantado declined such extreme advice both now
and when it was reiterated later: but he led out his
men and encamped at the bridge of Abancay facing
Alvarado's camp which was pitched on the opposite

side of the river; that same night after dark Orgoñez, with part of the men of Chile, forded the river higher up and, although bleeding profusely from a wound in the mouth, fell upon the enemy camp. Alvarado's lieutenant Pedro de Lerma, angered at having been passed over for the chief command, joined the assailants by previous agreement. Alvarado's men, taken by surprise and unable to distinguish friend from foe, as Lerma and his men turned against them, were huddled into confusion; and when daylight came Almagro led back to Cuzco a body of prisoners and deserters or new adherents equal in number to his own troops (12 July 1537).

Before following up this victory over his own countrymen, it was necessary to dispose of the Inca Manco, who still kept the field with a diminished and disheartened army. Almagro, now old and infirm, sent the veteran Orgoñez against the Inca, who, seeing his army melt away at the approach of the Spaniards, fled, almost alone, to the remote fastnesses of the mountains, all his wives but one, according to current report, having committed suicide, a sacrifice usually reserved for the obsequies of an Inca. Almagro then enthroned as nominal sovereign his own satellite, the young Inca Paulu, who was adorned with the scarlet fringe, the symbol of empire, and exhibited for the homage of his subjects. It was a provocative encroachment on Pizarro's authority; for even if Cuzco lay within Almagro's limits, this did not constitute him king-maker for the whole realm of the Incas.

The native revolt had been suppressed; or rather perhaps it had gradually dissolved in face of the superior valour and arms of the conquerors. Had the attack on Cuzco been vigorously pushed by Manco's

army, the tiny garrison of white men could hardly have
escaped; but the natives never overcame their dread
of horses and of fire-arms, and they never came to close
quarters with the Spanish steel: the empire of the Incas
was not to be won back from the conquerors by en-
circling cities and laying ambushes in Andine defiles.
It is said also that Manco exercised among his own
people a cruel and capricious tyranny unsuited to his
precarious position.

An anticipatory paragraph may here be dedicated
to the later destiny of the house of Huayna Capac.
Manco survived his defeat eight years and reigned, a
dispossessed and fugitive monarch, among the Indian
tribes of the mountains. During the disordered times
which followed the War of Las Salinas he and his
irregular native troops infested the country between
Cuzco and the sea and gave much trouble by raids and
ambushes, cutting off detached parties and burning
homesteads. In 1545 he was killed in a quarrel over
a game of bowls by some runaway Spaniards whom he
had befriended and received at his court. At Manco's
death the scarlet fringe, the symbol of former grandeur,
passed to his son, who accepted amicable offers of peace
from the Spaniards, visited Cuzco and finally abdicated
in 1559 in favour of King Philip II of Spain, thereby completely recognising Spanish dominion for the
sake of peace. Yet his two brothers in succession
claimed the remnant of imperial authority and were
obeyed as sovereigns by their vassals in a remote
region difficult of access. The second of these, Tupac
Amaru, the last Inca to assume the symbols of sovereignty, declined a proffered accommodation with the
Spaniards, fell into the hands of Francisco de Toledo,

Viceroy of Peru, and was put to death by him at Cuzco in 1571.

The narrative must turn back from the tragic story of the Inca dynasty to the not less tragic story of the Spanish conquerors. With the defeat and flight of Manco in August 1537 the conquest of Peru—a conquest which ought never to have been endangered—appeared to be accomplished a second time and only to need completion by extending authority to outlying regions and by establishing order in parts already subjugated. The epilogue in fact was far different: a long section of Prescott's book bears the title 'Civil Wars of the Conquerors'. These wars have been fully and admirably related by a careful historian, Cieza de Léon, who went to the Indies as a young boy and spent his life there. He travelled over the whole of Peru and wrote an exact geographical account of its countries, provinces and cities. He came to Popayan, the province adjoining Quito, in 1538, and passed later into Peru: thus he did not himself take part in these earlier wars, but he visited the scenes not long afterwards, examined the battlefields, witnessed the desolation caused by the passage of armies, questioned those who had been actors in these passages of history and listened to their reminiscences.

For nine months after the battle of Abancay (July 1537 to April 1538) war between Pizarro and Almagro was imminent but was kept off by attempts at peaceful settlement. The first intermediary was the old friend and partner of the two captains, Gaspar de Espinosa, who had brought men from Panama to Lima to save the enterprise of Peru during the insurrection of Manco. Espinosa now travelled from Lima to Cuzco in hopes of reconciling his old associates: finding Almagro obdurate, he quoted the Spanish proverb *El vencido vencido y el vencedor perdido*—'The vanquished vanquished and the vanquisher undone'. Before he was able to effect anything or to enter upon the government of a province which was to be the reward for his share in the enterprise, Espinosa died—one of the many, the great majority indeed, who did not live to grasp the prizes of victory.

Almagro, arrogantly misled by his recent victories over Spaniards and over Indians, now declared that Lima itself, the capital founded by Pizarro, lay within his own limits; accordingly, two months after the fight of Abancay he marched down to the coast, leaving Gonzalo Pizarro and Alonso de Alvarado under strong guard in Cuzco and taking Hernando with him as a prisoner, in spite of the repeated advice of Orgoñez that all three should be put to death, since 'a dead dog neither bites nor barks'.

Moving northwards along the coast to Chincha (about thirty leagues from Lima), he set up with the accustomed elaborate formalities a city—destined to be short-lived—called by his own name, thus challenging the Marquis on his own ground. While Almagro was thus establishing his authority, news reached him that Gonzalo and Alvarado, having tampered with their guards in Cuzco, had escaped from prison and made their way to join the Marquis at Lima: Hernando was still a prisoner in the Adelantado's camp.

For weeks envoys and messages passed and repassed between Lima and Chincha. Meantime Pizarro was vigorously arming. In point of strength the advantage was all on his side: through the port of Callao stores, arms and men constantly arrived at Lima: Pizarro's urgent messages had brought strong reinforcements, among them men from Flanders armed with the latest type of musket, so that two companies of musketeers were formed—a novelty in Peru, where hitherto musketeers had not formed a separate arm owing to the paucity of fire-arms. Moreover many adventurers, attracted by stories of Peruvian wealth, came to Lima from Spain and from the Antilles. Meantime in Cuzco, which was Almagro's base, secluded on the remote Andine heights and now almost cut off from the outside world by imminent civil war, the men of Chile were forging pikes of copper and silver for want of iron. But as long as Hernando was kept prisoner, Pizarro's hands were tied; he was determined first to obtain the release of his brother by peaceful means and then to get possession of Cuzco.

After long negotiation, it was agreed to submit the matter to the arbitration of a priest named Bobadilla, trusted by all for his known probity. The two captains met at a point midway between Lima and Chincha in a *tambo*, one of the rest-houses maintained on the Inca highways. Almagro advanced, saluting his old companion with easy cordiality: Pizarro responded stiffly and broke into resentful reproaches; an altercation followed, until one of Pizarro's men, moved by an impulse of chivalry, sang outside the window the opening lines of a popular ballad:

> Tiempo es ya, caballero,
> Tiempo es de andar de aquí.
>
> (It is time, oh cavalier,
>   It is time to go from here.)

Almagro took the hint, left the room, mounted his horse and galloped away: Gonzalo Pizarro had been posted in the neighbourhood with thirty horse: whether an ambush was intended cannot be known; but suspicion and resentment grew.

Bobadilla's decision (15 November 1537) was unfavourable to Almagro, who at once repudiated it with scorn. Thereupon Pizarro, in order to obtain his brother's release, agreed that Almagro should hold Cuzco until the matter should be settled by royal authority, that Hernando should be released on condition of undertaking to depart for Spain and that peace should be observed. Hernando was at once released by the too trustful Almagro, who speeded his parting prisoner and guest with banqueting and courteous escort towards Lima, where Hernando was received with great rejoicing. Orgoñez, drawing his hand across his throat with a significant gesture, prophesied what the issue would be.

On the day following Hernando's release an emissary who had been despatched to Spain, Pedro Anzures (Peranzures) by name, disembarked at Callao, the port of Lima, bearing a royal order that, pending the King's decision, each of the two captains should hold what he had conquered and occupied. The Marquis at once declared that this order gave Cuzco to him and that the royal decree annulled the agreement which he had solemnly concluded with Almagro: accordingly he commanded his brother Hernando to recover Cuzco by force. This meant war: Almagro, far from his base, from armouries and stores, retreated over the mountains carried in a litter by Indians and leaving the command of the troops to Orgoñez: Hernando followed from Lima with a larger and better equipped force, including the two companies of musketeers. Had Orgoñez turned and attacked while the pursuers, unaccustomed to the heights, were prostrated with mountain sickness, he would probably have destroyed them; but the decision was to make for Cuzco. Ten days were spent there in preparation before the armies met on 6 April 1538, about a league outside the city on a plain known as Las Salinas, from the pits where salt was gathered from a salt spring. The men of Chile numbered about 600, of whom about fifteen had muskets. Hernando had about 800 men, including a body of crossbowmen and about 80 musketeers. 'These were the arms which beat us', says Alonso Enriquez. Hernando chose as his Camp-Master Pedro de Valdivia, a veteran of the Italian wars, one of the finest soldiers and captains in the history of the conquest, afterwards to win fame as conqueror of Chile and there to meet a tragic end.

As they joined battle both sides shouted their invocation to Santiago, the warrior patron saint of Spain; 'The King and Pizarro'—'The King and Almagro' were the cries with which the armies clashed. Crowds of Indians, come from afar, thronged the surrounding heights to see their conquerors destroy one another. Almagro, prostrated by the dreadful ailment which afflicted many of the Spaniards throughout the conquest, was carried in a litter to view the combat from a distance. He saw his troops beaten and driven in flight: Orgoñez, wounded by a musket-shot and his horse killed under him, still strove to rally the fugitives, but was surrounded by six soldiers. 'Is there among you', he asked, 'some caballero to whom I may yield myself?' One Fuentes, a servant of Hernando Pizarro, replied 'Yes, yield yourself to me'. So they took him prisoner, and 'Fuentes, with great cruelty, cut off his head', says Cieza de Leon. The battle lasted a little more than two hours. Pedro Pizarro, who fought in the battle, says that the losses, including both sides, were 200. When the fight was over the crowd of Indians, including those who had been auxiliaries on either side, swept over the battlefield to plunder the dead. Meantime, the victorious soldiers scattered through the city, pillaging, quarrelling over the spoil, fighting one another and pursuing the Indian women, who ran from place to place.

Almagro was taken from the battlefield to the city, mounted behind a soldier on a mule. A trial was instituted against him, and for over two months accusations poured in until the 'process'—all in writing after the Spanish custom—covered 2000 folio sheets and reached, as Alonso Enriquez remarks with humorous hyperbole, up to the waist of a medium-sized man. It is needless to summarise the charges, for they had little to do with the decision. Cieza gives fairly Hernando's arguments to justify his action on the ground of political necessity: the certainty of attempted rescue on the way if the prisoner were sent to Lima for embarkation to Spain; the danger of an Almagrist rising in Cuzco itself to break open the prison; and lastly (the decisive reason according to Hernando) the discovery of a plot in the camp of Pedro de Candia to march on Cuzco, kill Hernando and liberate Almagro. At this time Pedro de Candia and his men were probably struggling through the wilds far from Cuzco;[1] and although Hernando may possibly have got wind of a plot through the strange rapidity of rumour among the Indians, Oviedo's account of the matter is more convincing: 'One night suddenly', he says, 'when all the neighbours and people in the city of Cuzco were in silence and repose, the alarm was sounded and it was given out

[1] See the next chapter.

that Candia's people were coming and with them Mesa, a mulato (Candia's Camp-Master), and that they were within two leagues of Cuzco and were coming to release Almagro; but all this was mockery and lies, and when morning came, Monday 8th of July . . . after two hours it was known that Hernando Pizarro had sentenced Don Diego de Almagro to death.' The old man pleaded for his life on his knees to Hernando: 'I was the first ladder', he said, 'by which you and your brother mounted up. When I held you as you now hold me and all counselled your death, I alone gave you life.' Claiming the right of an independent governor, he appealed to the Emperor: Hernando denied the right. The prisoner then appealed to the Marquis, whose lieutenant, no more, Hernando was. But Hernando was inexorable and reproached his aged and infirm prisoner for timidity unworthy of a cavalier. 'I am human and may fear death, since Christ Himself feared it', he replied; 'and I fear not only for myself but for all my friends who are in danger.' Hernando sternly told him to prepare for death. Almagro then made his will, naming as his heirs the Emperor and the young Diego Almagro, a youth of eighteen years, son of the Adelantado by an Indian woman of Panama. After making his confession and receiving the last rites of the Church, he was strangled in the prison.

Almagro's friend, Alonso Enriquez, who narrowly escaped the same fate, has left a moving account of the old warrior's end: and when soon afterwards Enriquez returned to Spain, he caused a ballad to be made, in the traditional octosyllabic Spanish metre, about the fate of 'the great Don Diego de Almagro, strong, noble and most loyal, who in the South Sea did notable deeds; such that for any of them he deserves to be crowned'—

a ballad to be sung in Spanish streets to the familiar tune of '*El buen Conde Hernán González*' in order to move compassion for the victim and stir up odium against Hernando Pizarro, who was then awaiting his trial in a Spanish prison.

CHAPTER XVI

THE PATH OF WAR

Now that the Inca Kings have lost their power, all these palaces and buildings, with other grand works of theirs, have fallen into ruin, so that the vestiges of some of their buildings alone remain. As they are built of beautiful stone and the masonry is excellent, they will endure for ages as memorials.   CIEZA DE LEON

Of those who went into Peru, eighty out of a hundred died.

          BENZONI

IN order not to confuse the narrative, little has been said about the effect of those marches, encampments and combats on the peaceful inhabitants who tilled the land. In describing Pizarro's forced marches upon the news of the siege of Cuzco, Cieza writes: 'The natives of the fruitful villages, seeing the powerful force led by the Governor, came out to serve him and bring him provisions; and although the Governor had excellent intentions about pacifying and tranquillising the provinces, I will not omit to say that great wickednesses and violences were committed against the natives by the Spaniards, who took from them their women and from some their property also: and—what is most lamentable—in order to make them carry baggage and superfluous things which need not have been brought at all, the Spaniards put them in chains; and as they walked through the deserts of deep sand and the burdens were big and the sun was powerful and there was no tree to give them shade nor stream to provide them with water, the poor Indians became weary; and instead of letting them rest, the Spaniards gave them hard beatings, saying that they did it from rascality. They were so ill-treated that many of them fell on the ground; and some of the Spaniards, in order not to spend time in removing the fallen men from the chain, cut off their heads with little fear of God. In this way many of the Indians perished; for there used to be a great number of them in these valleys; and through the evil treatment which they suffered from former Governors and Captains, they have come to the present diminution; and many of these valleys are depopulated and are so deserted that there is nothing to be seen but the ruined buildings and the sepulchres of the dead and the rivers which run through the valleys.' Again speaking of Almagro's arrival in the coastal region on his march from Cuzco, Cieza writes: 'They ill-treated the unhappy Indians who for their own sins and those of their ancestors deserved the chastisement or great plague which by the hand of the Spaniards—our Lord God permitting it—has come upon them. . . . Hardly had one army of the Christians passed when the other army came; and if the first had little fear of God and had no charity to prevent the deaths of so many thousands, the others feared God less . . . moreover Almagro and his men paid attention to nothing except to attain their desire and possess the government, and thus there disappeared from these valleys between Lima and Nasca the greater part of the inhabitants, dying from hunger and from being carried captive in chains and from many other harms which they suffered; and having come to the valley of Nasca, the Adelantado set up his camp in the place which seemed most suitable: and the Spaniards provided themselves at their pleasure and at the cost of the poor Indians. . . . And of the Indians who came from the mountains carrying the King's gold and other baggage some were left dead on the road and others were so injured in their feet that they had not the use of their feet as long as they lived.'

Yet Cieza, although throughout his history he is stern in judging the Pizarro brothers, declares that the Marquis had excellent intentions. It is true that Pizarro held it to be right that native chieftains should be burnt as rebels if they resisted after hearing the 'requisition': but depopulation and destruction were not at all the things at which he aimed; he not only desired to win wealth, fame and power for himself, but also to win vassals for the Crown of Castile and neophytes for the Catholic Church; moreover the wealth and power which he desired for himself depended on the preservation of a subject population. Thus after his first success he turned at once to the peaceful tasks of government and construction. But when he was called away from this work by the outbreak of fresh strife, then the need of victory overrode all else, and the lives of his subjects counted for nothing against military necessity. The war of Las Salinas undid the work of conquest and set the clock back. The natives were shaken in allegiance, arguing, 'These Christian captains lie in calling themselves servants of a great lord beyond the sea, for in our country the servants of a great lord do not make war on one another'. Victory brought not peace but disorder due to the undisciplined brutality bred by civil wars. When defenceless Spanish prisoners were robbed, murdered and tortured, it is not surprising to read: 'Many faults have been committed by the Spaniards in this kingdom and assuredly I should wish not to write these things since they were done by my own countrymen. They did not regard the benefits granted by God, who was pleased that they and no other nation should win the great kingdoms and provinces of these Indies. After the victory of Las Salinas many of those who had fought for the Pizarros dispersed through the provinces of the west and north, robbing all they could from the Indians: they forced the Indians by torture to give up the flocks that were hidden for fear of thieves; and they drove away great flocks for sale in Lima and sold them for almost nothing . . . and the poor Indians went from hill to hill complaining of their ill-treatment.' It should be noted that Cieza was not an eye-witness; at this time he was himself among the explorers and conquerors of New Granada and Popayan, where he witnessed dreadful things which possibly colour his account of the happenings in Peru: that account is derived from enquiry among the actors in them and some allowance must be made for the Spanish tendency to over-emphasis. The way in which these gruesome stories grow by repetition is illustrated by the fact that in a well-known English translation of Cieza the word 'some' is omitted in the passage quoted on page 201 and the translation runs, 'the Spaniards . . . cut off their heads . . .', a general statement not warranted by the original: similarly in the quotation given on page 202 the words 'others were so injured' became in translation 'the others were so injured', a very different matter. On the other hand, Cieza himself witnessed the depopulation which he deplores, the ruined buildings and the rivers, which had irrigated farms, now flowing through solitary valleys: here he is a faithful and credible witness.

In passing judgement on the Spaniards, it is well to

remember the things which Essex did in Ireland a generation later, or the horrors which fell upon the civil population of Germany during the Thirty Years' War in the following century.

EXPEDITIONS INTO THE MONTAÑA

If the Spaniards did not spare the Indians, they were not over-indulgent to themselves or to one another, particularly in the expeditions which Hernando encouraged in order to alleviate the difficulties which beset him in Cuzco after his victory at Las Salinas. His own men clamoured for the prizes of victory, demanding rewards at the expense of the Almagrists. These, who were numerous in the city, were bitterly resentful, hating their victors and longing for revenge. Hernando attempted to ease these discontents by granting licence to any captain who chose to lead out a party of Spaniards and a crowd of Indians on expeditions of 'pacification' or of fresh exploration and conquest. 'He thus at the same time rewarded his friends by giving them opportunities to distinguish and enrich themselves, and got rid of his enemies by sending them to a distance', says the contemporary historian Zárate: Hernando commanded all these captains to do no harm to the Indians, not to pillage the villages or carry off the women.

Four captains were thus commissioned to lead out their companies to different regions. One of the four was the stalwart but simple-minded Greek gunner Pedro de Candia, now a wealthy householder (*vecino*) of Cuzco, who 'forgetting that about explorations people never tell the truth and do not hesitate to lie', listened to a story told to him by an Indian girl whom he owned, that to the south-east of Cuzco there was a country called Ambaya rich in gold and silver. Stirred by this prospect, Pedro de Candia spent all that he had and borrowed more to fit out a troop of more than 300 Spaniards and a crowd of Indians; they crossed the freezing heights of the Eastern Cordillera, 'those mighty Andes where he found the road to be truly infernal'. Descending thence they plunged into dense rain-soaked forests where they had to cut their way with hatchets and knives, making about a league a day. Provisions failed, and their limbs, lacerated by thorns, swelled up as they marched through rivers, swamps and rocky wilds: 'they ate the horses which died and the few sheep (llamas) that remained . . . they traversed the forests . . . until they thought they would all die . . . they now began to hate Pedro de Candia who had brought them to such a pass by trusting to the stories of a Indian girl, and they believed that Hernando Pizarro had craftily encouraged the enterprise that they might all die'. However, after about three months they made their way back through the forest 'suffering much from hunger . . . all of them very weak and some of them sick', but without the loss of a single Spaniard: nothing is said about losses of Indians. This was the first of many expeditions, some of them unrecorded or barely mentioned, which sought rich lands supposed to lie eastwards by striving to penetrate the *montaña*, the region of dense forest stretching from the eastern spurs of the Cordillera.

When Pedro de Candia approached Cuzco on the return march, his Camp-Master, the mulato Mesa, was arrested by Hernando Pizarro on a charge of conspiracy and hanged. Villagra, afterwards one of the conquerors of Chile, narrowly escaped with his life, and the command of Pedro de Candia's men was taken

from him[1] and given to 'a captain well versed in the art
of war named Peranzures (or Pedro Anzures) who was
respected, liked and very liberal'. Peranzures was commissioned to make an entry into the country of the
Chunchos, barbarous Indians inhabiting the forest
region beyond the mountains due east of Cuzco. Hearing reports of a 'thickly-peopled country rich in gold
and silver, so that they might all return in prosperity to
Spain, many caballeros and principal men joined him.
. . . They also took the flower of the beautiful girls, few
of whom escaped being left behind dead in the forest.'

They set out over the eastern mountains at the end
of September 1538. After weeks of travel 'They had no
provisions and sustained life by eating wild herbs and
the inner part of some palm trees: sheets of rain poured
down and their clothes fell to pieces: yet they cut paths
with hatchets, and made passages with mattocks over
the rough ground for the horses to pass, and made
sloping ways down to the banks of rivers which they
crossed, and laid quantities of branches on the swamps.
The Indian attendants could not sustain life and many
died: they ate one another; and as hunger increased, the
living ate the dead. . . . It was a very great distress to see
so many die and among them many daughters of great
lords of Cuzco and noble Inca ladies.' Some of the
forest natives being captured and questioned told them
—evidently desiring to see them all perish—of a magnificent open country, very rich, at a distance of twenty-
five days' march to the east. But to advance was impossible, and Peranzures turned back, finding another
route home as best he could. 'The noise of the rain on
the thick woods was so great that they could not hear

[1] Pedro de Candia in resentment at this slight turned against the Pizarros
and in consequence came to a violent end, to be related in Chapter XXII.

one another; the sun was never seen and there was such a gloomy darkness that the land seemed more for the torment of devils than for human habitation . . . as hunger increased, they killed the horses and ate even the offal, hardly taking the pains to wash it. . . . Some Christians supporting themselves against the trees and saying "Is there, perchance, anyone who will give me a little maize?" died. Others said, "Were we not worthy to fill ourselves with the bread which in Spain is given to the dogs?" and so saying, died.' When the survivors struggled back, some six months after their departure, to their starting point, where a brother of Peranzures came to meet them with succour and food, 'They were so disfigured and discoloured that none recognised them: 143 Spaniards had died and more than 4000 Indians, men and women: they had killed and eaten 220 horses'.

Less disastrous was the expedition in the far north led by Alonso de Alvarado, who, notwithstanding his defeat at Abancay, was employed as the best of Pizarro's captains. Alvarado enforced good treatment of the Indians, and on one occasion flogged two men for stealing provisions; but with this strict discipline went inspiring leadership. When later some of his men grumbled at marching through endless forests and rivers, 'he gave out that those who wished to follow him, on certain information that he had, might do so; and those who were not willing might remain behind . . . all with one voice declared that they would follow him'.

Alonso de Alvarado founded the city of Chachapoyas, now the capital of a Peruvian province, on the extreme limit of the Inca empire, thirty leagues north-east of Cajamarca. Hearing of 'rich countries beyond the river of Moyobamba', he pushed on through the mountains and sent forty infantry to explore the 'great and rough forest where horses could not pass': this party travelled more than forty days, 'eating no bread or meat, nothing but yuca and water: of water there was too much, both falling from the skies and in the many rivers which they continually passed . . . they found nothing useful, only forests and rivers and ravines full of thickets'. In one night a river rose so high with floods of rain that 'if our Lord God had not created there tall and thickly growing trees into which they climbed, they would all have been drowned'. Undeterred by this report, Alvarado himself led seventy men into the forest and reached the great river Huallaga which flows northwards into the Marañon (the Upper Amazon). 'He had news that fifteen days' journey beyond the river after passing a great and rough forest, one came to a level country, where there was a great lake, upon the banks of which lived a noble of Inca lineage named Ancallas, besides others who were very great and rich', a tale which seems to be a version of the more elaborate story of El Dorado. Alvarado found nothing but forests and rivers; 'but he felt certain that when they had passed the forest in front of them, they would reach a good land where all would be satisfied'. Being recalled by news of an Indian rising round his newly founded city of Chachapoyas, Alvarado left his brother with orders to build a boat and cross the river: this was done, and 'they tried in many directions to cross the forests and mountains that were before them and they found no road nor way of passing . . . this land of Moyobamba is unhealthy, and it rains most of the year; it is full of foul places, of great mountains and rough forests and rivers great and small'. The attempt to penetrate the *montaña* was abandoned, but the city of Chachapoyas remained and the Spanish power was pushed as far as the Inca dominion had prevailed.

Another expedition under one Mercadillo attempted to penetrate the eastern forests to the south of the way followed by Alvarado. But the commander in this case proved to be shifty, disagreeable and obstinate. When he insisted on advancing through the forests against the universal opinion of the company, his own captains arrested and fettered him. 'They drew up a statement of the oaths he had taken and of other things which concerned the Holy Inquisition: they then returned to Jauja.'

Thus the forests, mountains, rivers and swamps which had withstood the steady expanding pressure of the Inca empire (but for some unsubstantial admissions of vassalage or of amity) baffled also the efforts of the Spaniards to penetrate the supposed secrets of the greatest forest in the world and to find wealth, fertility and dominion in the heart of the continent. In the following century Christian missionaries of the religious orders, principally Jesuits, travelled through the woods and embarked upon the streams to win the tribes of forest and river by other means and with other aims; but much of the forest remains unknown to white men to-day. These early expeditions have here been briefly told not for any grave historical import, but, since they fall within the period assigned to this book and since vivid records remain concerning them, they may serve as examples of countless Spanish expeditions through the unknown lands of both American continents.

These journeys over the eastern Andes cannot be compared in extent with Cortes' march across Yucatan or Almagro's expedition to Chile or that of Gonzalo Pizarro to the Valley of Cinnamon or that which De Soto led through the forests of the Mississippi; but it is not amiss to trace the endeavours of these pre-Elizabethan *caballeros* who had never heard of tropical outfits and with invincible hardihood travelled over snowy heights and through dense torrid forests leading their horses and clad, some of them at least, in coats of mail.

CHAPTER XVII

SETTLEMENT

Since it is a country of very high mountains, it is very cold on the heights; and since it is in a climate so hot by Nature, in the valleys it is fire.

LA GASCA

ON receiving news of the victory at Las Salinas, Pizarro set out from Lima for Cuzco; but halted over two months at Jauja, delayed by the disturbed state of the country but probably also by the wish to avoid direct concern in the fate of Almagro. He was visited at Jauja by Almagro's young half-caste son Diego, who was travelling under escort to Lima, a youth of about eighteen years, described by one who knew him as tall and good-looking, an accomplished horseman and well educated, resembling his father rather than his Indian mother, but dark in complexion and almost beardless. Pizarro greeted the young Almagro warmly, assured him that his father should suffer nothing and promised to receive the youth as a son in his own house at Lima. Continuing at last his journey to Cuzco in July 1538, Pizarro was met by the news that Almagro was dead. He showed decent emotion; but in a country where Indian runners carried news with astonishing speed and where Indian rumour flew like magic (sometimes attributed by the Spaniards to satanic oracles), his previous ignorance must have been calculated, and Hernando's omission to consult his brother must have been politic reticence: it was clearly the Governor's duty to keep himself informed of what passed in the capital of his dominions: it is, however, fair to add that Hernando openly showed an ungrateful contempt for his illiterate and baseborn half-brother, and the Marquis seems to have been not quite at ease in dealing with Hernando, whom he twice despatched on missions to Spain.

The Marquis rode into Cuzco in state wearing the rich robe sent to him by the conqueror of New Spain. Both his brothers were absent in the south; for every man who could be spared was needed to quell insurrections in the country about Lake Titicaca and in the province of Charcas lying farther south—regions which had been tranquil provinces of the Inca empire and had been traversed in peace by Almagro's Chilian expedition: now they were all up in arms. So extensive and difficult a country, much of it lying 12,000 feet above sea-level, gave much trouble; and Hernando, who had followed his brother Gonzalo to collect gold and silver for conveyance to Spain, was obliged first to aid him in the reconquest of the land. But the work was done: Gonzalo, having held the government of Charcas for some months and having received a rich *encomienda* of Indian vassals in that country, left Diego de Rojas, afterwards a famous pioneer of southern conquest, in command; and in order to hold the country, the city of La Plata[1] (now Sucre) was founded, so called from the rich silver mines in the neighbourhood (1539): the name has nothing to do with the River Plate.

[1] Nomenclature is here confusing. The native name of the city, often used by the Spaniards, was Chuquisaca: the Audiencia which was established in the city twenty-five years later was usually known as the Audiencia of Charcas. The city in the later chapters of this volume will be called Chuquisaca, to avoid confusion.

For nearly two years (1538–40) the Marquis made
Cuzco his headquarters, labouring to restore peace to
the country. He made a progress through the recently
conquered or reconquered southern provinces, visiting
both Spanish settlements and Indian villages. More
pressing were the raids of the Inca Manco, who, according to Spanish report, impaled his white prisoners
and cut off the hands and noses of any whom he caught
of their native auxiliaries. Pizarro tried negotiation,
which was apparently welcomed by Manco: but two
negro servants, bearing rich gifts from the Marquis to
the Inca, were killed with their Indian attendants by
Manco's men. Pizarro took a savage revenge. He had
in his power a favourite wife of Manco: she was stripped,
tied to a tree, beaten by Cañari guardsmen and shot
with arrows. The outrage has an exact parallel, except
for the cruel details, in the Carlist war of 1833–39, with
the difference that in the later case the victim was a
Spanish matron (mother of the Carlist chief Cabrera)
shot by Spaniards. Pizarro now sent his brother Gonzalo, fresh from the reconquest of Charcas, against the
Inca. After two months of inconclusive campaigning
against Manco's men among rocks and crags, it was
determined to secure the country by founding a city at
Guamanga (now Ayacucho) midway between Cuzco
and Lima: twenty-four householders were settled there
with a garrison of forty men; but, as in all similar cases,
this little community received the full privileges of a
república or self-governing municipality, with jurisdiction over a wide district extending to the civic territory of Lima on one side and of Cuzco on the other.
It should be added that the degree of authority exercised by the *cabildos* in these cities depended very much
on the Deputy-Governor (sometimes for convenience

called Governor), who held military command in the municipal district and had the right of presiding in the *cabildo*. About the same time (late in 1539 or early in 1540) Pizarro founded or refounded the city of Arequipa in a beautiful and productive region about 7000 feet above sea-level, sixty leagues to the south-west of Cuzco and accessible from a port on the Pacific coast. He also entrusted to various captains the care of the more remote provinces with the task of extending the dominions which he had conquered and of making fresh settlements, a work facilitated by the frequent arrival of men from Spain attracted by the fame of conquest and of treasure. Pedro de Valdivia, Camp-Master at the battle of Las Salinas, was despatched to the conquest of Chile—a long task which demands separate narrative. Pizarro's brothers were not neglected: Gonzalo was appointed Governor of Quito; Hernando was despatched on a mission to Spain which may be narrated here.

Hernando, having gathered sufficient treasure at Cuzco and having conveyed it 125 leagues over the mountains to Lima and Callao, set out for Spain. Before his departure he warned his brother to beware of the men of Chile and never to allow ten of them to meet together, a warning which the Marquis lightly put aside. Hernando avoided the direct route by the Isthmus lest the Audiencia of Panama, which claimed judicial authority over all the newly conquered regions, should arrest him for enquiry into the death of Almagro: accordingly he made a long circuitous journey by Tehuantepec and New Spain, where the Viceroy Mendoza, deciding after brief delay that he had no authority to detain the traveller and his rich convoy, allowed him to pass through the country and embark for Spain. But Almagro's friends were before him at Court, accusing him not only of the Adelantado's death, but also of having caused long wars, fatal insurrections and the death of many Spaniards by releasing the Inca Manco (page 182): one of the Almagrists challenged him to mortal duel, but suddenly died before the day of combat. Hernando, the bearer of rich treasure, was at first cordially received, but was soon placed under arrest in his own house at Madrid; he was then imprisoned in the massive castle of La Mota at Medina del Campo, treated sometimes with rigour, 'seeing neither sun nor moon', sometimes evidently with considerable relaxation of his confinement, for he was allowed to marry his niece, daughter of his brother Francisco by an Inca princess, a child of Huayna Capac. After twenty-two years he was released and lived to a great age—a hundred years, it was said—one of the few survivors of scenes as extraordinary and sensational as any recorded in the history of the world. His part in these things was not forgotten; for his grandson, who united the blood of the Spanish conquerors with the imperial lineage of the Inca monarchs, was ennobled with the title of Marqués de la Conquista.

VACA DE CASTRO

But the tumults in Peru and the death of Almagro evidently called for further action than the arrest of his slayer: accordingly the Emperor appointed one Vaca de Castro, a lawyer who held high judicial office in Spain, to be President of the Audiencia of Panama, with orders to pass on thence to Peru and hold an enquiry into recent events. He also carried a secret royal decree which appointed him Governor of Peru in the event of Pizarro's death. Vaca de Castro, after long tossing on the Atlantic, reached Panama in January 1541: after presiding for three months in the Audiencia there, he embarked in March for Peru. Had he sailed to Callao, his coming might have averted great disasters; but driven about in the Pacific by violent tempests and by the unskilfulness of pilots, he rashly decided, after accomplishing barely one-third of the voyage, to land at Buenaventura, a coast settlement consisting of a few huts, and to travel thence by land. Carried from the landing-place at Buenaventura by Indian tracks over some of the most rough and dangerous country to be found even in the Andes, where several of his companions perished, he did not reach Popayan, still more than 200 leagues from Lima, until August 1541, fully five months after his departure from Panama and two years after the death of Almagro. A student and a scholar, used to a sedentary life, he arrived infirm, sick and exhausted by fatigues which might have tried a tough campaigner, to be faced by yet greater trials; for strange things had happened in those two years. It may be remarked that in his movements Vaca de Castro showed a thoroughly Spanish disinclination to haste; but on the other hand the cautious sagacity and insight into character which guide his later handling of affairs are the marks of an experienced lawyer.

CHAPTER XVIII

QUITO AND POPAYAN

THE conquerors of the Inca empire never rested: for any enterprising captain with a few scores of men might win another Peru. Before their first conquests had been secured by establishing little groups of householders in widely separated cities, they were pushing their arms beyond the Equator northwards, far into the temperate zone along the Pacific coast of Chile to the south, and across the plains of the River Plate south-eastward; while successive *entradas* spent themselves in crossing the eastern mountains and striving to penetrate the secrets of the forests beyond.

The Spanish conquest of the kingdom of Quito, which was the first of these movements, a conquest undertaken immediately after the first successes in Peru and accordingly almost simultaneous with the Peruvian enterprise, has been incidentally mentioned in Chapters IX and XIII, but it demands brief consecutive narrative. The equatorial kingdom of Quito (now Ecuador) differs in character from the Peruvian lands to the south. The great mountain highway of the Incas passed northwards from Cajamarca through Tumebamba to Quito (a city planted almost upon the Equator), traversing in its northern part a plateau or rather a valley about thirty miles wide enclosed between the famous 'avenue of volcanoes', more than twenty peaks facing one another as it were in two ranks, many of them rising far above the snow line, the gigantic Chimborazo (20,500 feet) and the conical detached peak of Cotopaxi (19,600 feet) towering above the lesser peaks. The climatic contrast between the temperate uplands or icy heights and the low-lying coast is more marked than in Peru, for the narrow, rainless coastal strip of Peru here gives place to a broad coastal region covered in great part (with some arid patches) by steaming tropical forests with many swamps and winding rivers: thus the journey from the temperate uplands and rarified air of Quito to the denser air and hot-house swampy surroundings of Guayaquil—only cleansed from pestilence in our own day—was even more dangerous to the traveller than in Peru, and was fatal to almost all the natives compelled to make that journey.

In October 1533, a month before Pizarro entered Cuzco, Belalcazar, commander at San Miguel, having been invited by emissaries from the Cañari tribe to deliver them from the tyranny of Rumiñavi and finding his numbers increased by arrivals from Panama and Nicaragua, set out to the conquest of Quito with 200 footmen and 80 horse, besides the usual crowd of Indian attendants. His enterprise differs from others in that from the outset he met with an organised resistance from an experienced general, Rumiñavi, commanding an army of regular native soldiers; and although Rumiñavi never had more than 12,000 men (according to the exaggerated Spanish estimate), these were more formidable than the uncounted hordes which met the Spaniards elsewhere. The Spanish invaders received much aid from some of the inhabitants, not only from the Cañaris but also from a chieftain named Cachulima, lord of a group of villages about Riobamba, who declared against Rumiñavi and aided the Spaniards throughout. Cachulima received baptism and a Spanish name and, through the granting of a petition from Belalcazar to Charles V, was exempted from tribute and confirmed in his lordship, where he and his descendants held sway for a century and a half afterwards.

Rumiñavi showed skill in the choice of ground and in plans of combat, but was foiled in great part by the eager activity of Cañari spies and guides, who led the Spaniards through by-paths, avoiding the pitfalls laid for horses. Yet the Spaniards suffered much in three fights, in the third of which they were certainly not victorious and after the fight were in imminent danger, expecting a fresh attack at dawn: a terrific eruption of Cotopaxi that same night saved the invaders by spreading panic among the enemy, who took the eruption for the fulfilment of one of those prophecies of disaster which were so useful to the Spaniards both in New Spain and in the Andes. Finally, in a campaign of three or four months the horses, muskets and fighting qualities of the invaders were too much for Rumiñavi, who fled to a remote mountain refuge, setting fire to the capital in his retreat and, according to Spanish report, carrying off much treasure after burying the rest. Belalcazar entered the ruined capital about the end of 1533 but chose as the provisional seat of government Riobamba, a place seated among friendly Indians. On Whitsunday 1534, some eight months after his arrival in the country, he made his triumphant entry into the city of Quito, which had been, in part at least, hastily restored in Spanish fashion by Indian labour. Two months later, having placed himself and his troops under the command of Almagro, he took part in the dramatic episode related in Chapter IX, whereby the conqueror of Guatemala was frustrated in his designs upon Quito. Almagro and Alvarado rode away together to meet Pizarro at Pachacamac, and Belalcazar remained as Deputy-Governor under the authority of Pizarro to complete the conquest of the kingdom of Quito.

Having entered the country in the character of a deliverer, Belalcazar observed at first a certain moderation; but he proved to be a strange deliverer, for his lieutenant Ampudia pursued an exasperated search for the undiscoverable and possibly non-existent treasure of Atahualpa by means of torture, burning alive and forcing the natives to inordinate labour in destroying sepulchres and palaces to detect possible hiding-places: they were then compelled to rebuild what had been destroyed by Rumiñavi and by Ampudia himself. Moreover, Belalcazar's moderation was short-lived; 'he killed many in Quito', says the historian with significant brevity. A friar who accompanied Belalcazar, Fray Marcos de Niza (Friar Mark of Nice), after repeatedly protesting in vain against these enormities, left Quito in disgust, returned to New Spain and afterwards wrote a *History of the Conquest of Quito* in which he denounced the excesses committed or permitted by Belalcazar; his book is only known to the present writer through citations from it by Velasco in his *History of Quito*, published in 1789.

It is evident that the Inca system was not yet complete or uniform in the kingdom of Quito, for some months were spent in the piecemeal subjugation of tribes differing much in customs and character before the necessary outlet to the sea was secured by the foundation of the city and port of Guayaquil, with the regular nomination of alcaldes and *regidores* and of a

Deputy-Governor, a middle-aged and not very active person named Daza. Another maritime city farther north, Puerto Viejo, was established after dispute between rival founders had been settled by Pizarro, whose superior authority, remote though it was, received recognition throughout Quito. The history of Guayaquil illustrates the vicissitudes of the conquest and in part also the causes of those vicissitudes: the natives soon rose and slew these 'citizens' who took their goods and their women, only the commander Daza with five others escaping. Belalcazar had much trouble in re-establishing the place and only succeeded in doing so, according to one probable account, by undertaking that the new settlers should be accompanied by Christian women. The place was deserted a second time owing to the need of every able-bodied man in the south to cope with the revolt of the Inca Manco. When that trouble passed, Pizarro himself sent Francisco de Orellana—afterwards a famous name —to be the third founder of Guayaquil in 1537.

By that time Belalcazar, leaving a deputy in Quito, and taking with him many Spaniards who could ill be spared as well as thousands of Indians who never returned home, had departed on an independent career of conquest far beyond the northern limits of the Inca empire into the country of Popayan, now the southern part of the republic of Colombia. Here the Andes spread out northward into three great mountain-chains between which flow, separated by the midmost chain, the parallel streams of two great rivers, the Cauca and the Magdalena, to unite finally in their northward course to the Caribbean Sea. Travel in this region was indescribably difficult: the difficulty of access from the Pacific coast may be judged by a sentence from Andagoya, who took that route a year later: 'The country is so rugged that many dogs, not being able to go on with the men, returned to the sea'. By a movement which seemed to set the laws of geography at defiance, the astonishing impetus of the Peruvian enterprise, which had started for the remote and unknown south, was returning as it were upon its own tracks and pushing in the reverse direction northwards through lands which might seem more accessible from the shores long since discovered by Columbus and his successors.

The region conveniently known by the name of the chief Popayan, who ruled a larger territory than his neighbours, was untouched by the Inca sway and possessed no unity, no cities, no made roads; but it yielded gold. The tribes, mostly addicted to cannibalism and inter-tribal warfare, living independently in separate valleys under little chiefs, could offer no resistance to horsemen, musketeers, archers and troops of great savage dogs: when the intruders, their horses and their swine consumed the crops, often trampling and wasting what they did not use, the bewildered inhabitants ceased to till the ground: the result was famine, universal cannibalism of the most revolting kind and destructive pestilence. The conquering or devastating progress northwards of Belalcazar and his lieutenants is marked by the foundation of the city of Popayan in 1536, and somewhat later (in 1537) the city of Cali, twenty-two leagues farther north in a fertile and beautiful part of the Cauca valley. Leaving deputies in these places, Belalcazar himself, with 200 foot, 100 horse and a crowd of Indians, both men and women, set out northeastwards, having news—this time true and authentic news—that thus he might reach the city of a great king rich in the precious metals, ruler of a settled people.

Already before his departure on this new enterprise Belalcazar had ceased to send reports to Lima or sent only shifty apologies; he was evidently taking advantage of the wars and civil wars in Peru in order to shake off allegiance to Pizarro and win a separate government for himself: Pizarro, fully occupied by his dispute with Almagro—it was the end of 1537—sent for Lorenzo de Aldana, the hidalgo mentioned on page 117, and, appealing to his ancestral loyalty and zeal, charged him to go to Quito, apply remedies to the notorious tyranny and depopulation and send Belalcazar under arrest to Lima. Aldana accomplished his charge faithfully and with singular success. His authority, as conferred by the Marquis, was recognised by the deputies left in command by Belalcazar, who were now confirmed in their commands by Aldana. He introduced order into the administration of Quito and took measures to protect the natives. He then advanced slowly northwards into the province of Popayan, reducing the chieftains, who were all in revolt, to submission mostly by peaceful persuasion and by inculcating the folly of resistance. He caused maize to be carried by Indian porters from the rich lands of Cali, untouched by famine, in order to relieve the starving people of Popayan, thereby earning the blessing of Spaniards and natives alike.

At Cali a striking incident occurred. Some of Aldana's men, walking outside the city, were surprised to hear exclamations in their own language and to see a group of bearded men approaching. These were a party who had left Cartagena more than a year earlier, 345 in number—'the most noble and knightly company that had ever set out from Tierra Firme': they had traversed mountains and forests, had fought with savage tribes and had lost ninety-two of their number, besides many horses as well as negroes and Indians of both sexes by hardship, sickness, hunger and combat. They now unexpectedly found food, refreshment and a welcome in a settlement of their own countrymen: all the new-comers joined Aldana's forces, deserting their own commander, the licentiate Vadillo. One of the company was the historian Cieza de Leon, who has left a vivid account of these events and remarks that this was the first expedition which found a way (other than the Isthmus, he means) from the Atlantic Ocean to the South Sea.

It was the duty of every commander in those early days to extend occupation and found Spanish settlements (*poblar*). Accordingly, besides sending captains upon the rough work of exploring the rain-soaked forests of the Pacific coastal region (the Choco) and the mountainous country on both sides of the Cauca, Aldana commissioned one Jorge Robledo, an experienced captain, to lead 100 men northwards, to found a city and win the surrounding country. Robledo justified the choice and deserves a notable place among Spanish Conquistadores for his activity in this remote off-shoot of Peruvian conquest. By his skill, valour, liberality[1] and pleasant ways, he won the affectionate loyalty of his men, one of whom, Cieza, relates their doings—an exciting story of strange adventures among cannibal warrior tribes, all of them possessing gold. Some tribes fought against the Spaniards among their native crags and woods; others welcomed the aid of these powerful strangers in attacking some enemy

[1] One instance of this liberality is worth recording: Robledo's interpreters were three Indian women, Barbola, Antonia and Catalina. 'As the captain knew', says Cieza, 'that I was curious to know secrets of the Indians, he gave Catalina to me that I might learn them more easily.'

tribe where victory meant indiscriminate slaughter to provide a banquet and a store of food, the favourite victims being young children, to the horror of the Christians, who denounced in vain these proceedings of their Indian allies.

Two cities were duly founded, Anzerma and (some months later) Cartago, forty leagues to the north of Cali, in the heart of the modern republic of Colombia—a notable achievement which marks the extreme northern limit of Peruvian conquest; for here, a second time, the Christians were astonished at meeting white men coming from Cartagena and from the north, who had been sent in pursuit of Vadillo but now passed under the command of Robledo.

The tribes about the new city of Anzerma were seemingly pacified 'although at first there had been some punishments, cutting off hands and noses'. But obedience was doubtful: and Cieza (like Balboa and Cortes on earlier occasions) was warned 'in great secrecy, by an Indian girl who belonged to me', that the neighbouring chiefs meant to attack the city in the absence of Robledo on a tour of inspection: 'we were all under arms night and day awaiting the enemy, but . . . after giving us some bad nights they dispersed and went each one to his own land'.

Robledo himself led his men far to the north of his newly founded cities among tribes of strange names and habits whom he endeavoured to win by persuasion or force: in one part 'the natives, in order not to be wounded by swords and torn to pieces by dogs, agreed to receive the Spaniards in their province, supplying them with provisions' and bringing gifts of gold. In other parts there was fighting, after which any Spanish captive, unless killed at once, was impaled or tortured to death before being devoured. In one region all the other tribes, as in some fantastic fairy-tale, lived in perpetual dread of a tribe more fierce and formidable than all, the Pozos, and accordingly welcomed Spanish aid against these dreadful enemies. The captain Robledo having been severely wounded by the Pozos, two of his officers determined on revenge. 'The Indians of Carrapa and Picara were delighted at seeing that their dreaded enemies were in such straits and that the valiant Spaniards were preparing with such determination to kill them: all the Indians brought strong cords to bind those whom they might take.' A thousand of the Pozos, men, women and many children, took refuge on a high rock with store of provisions; their Indian enemies surrounded the base of the rock, while the Spaniards, mounting higher, let loose the dogs 'which were so fierce that with two bites of their cruel teeth they laid open the unhappy wretches to the entrails; it was no small grief to see that for defending their land from those who came to take it away, they were treated in such a manner. And the tender children, terrified at the noise, running hither and thither to escape . . . were torn in pieces by the dogs . . . and if they escaped from this peril they fell into a worse, into the power of their neighbours of Carrapa and Picara, who killed all the women, beautiful or ugly, young or old; and taking the children by the feet they dashed their heads against the rocks and at once, like dragons, biting at them ate them raw; they killed most of the men whom they took: the rest they carried away with hands strongly bound.' Cieza adds that it may be believed it was in retribution for this sin that the two Spanish officers were afterwards killed and eaten by natives in that same district.

One of his tasks, the arrest of Belalcazar, Aldana was

unable to accomplish: the culprit was out of reach or perhaps had been discreetly allowed to pass out of reach. Belalcazar, eager to emulate the achievements of Cortes and Pizarro, was on the march for the rich kingdom of Bogotá; he travelled slowly, accompanied as he was by a great herd of swine, finding his way over the great unknown heights of the Central Cordillera, penetrating dense trackless forests, searching for food as he went and often fighting with hostile Indians— among them a tribe using poisoned arrows, which were fatal to all the wounded. About the beginning of 1539 he reached the fertile valley of Neiva upon the upper Magdalena, where he made a long halt to rest his men and to choose a site for a city to be founded later. Here, to his bitter chagrin, he heard of other Spaniards in the neighbourhood: advancing slowly towards the object of his quest—now only forty-five leagues distant—he was met after some days by a party of his country- men, armed only with lances and much-used swords and wearing home-made garments of bright-coloured cotton: they were commanded by Hernán Pérez de Quesada, brother to the conqueror of Bogota. The rest of the story is told in Chapter XXV—how three rival Spanish captains met at Bogota and agreed to carry the question between them to Spain. Belalcazar, presenting his suit at Court, was appointed by the Crown to be Governor not of Bogota, as he had hoped, but of Popa- yan, the province which had been conquered by him and which was now constituted into a separate govern- ment. His subsequent fate may be briefly told. After Belalcazar had enjoyed his government of Popayan for a few years, Robledo, acting under superior authority, encroached upon that government: thereupon Belal- cazar caused Robledo to be treacherously murdered:

for this crime he was condemned to death by the judge sent to enquire into his administration (Juez de Residencia). Belalcazar appealed against the sentence and died at Cartagena at an advanced age, on the way to Spain for trial.

Aldana returned from Cali and Popayan to Quito, and towards the end of 1540 handed over the command of that kingdom to Gonzalo Pizarro, having effected a transformation in the government in the space of some two years.

CHAPTER XIX

THE LAND OF CINNAMON AND THE RIVER OF THE AMAZONS

The early expeditions into the great valley of the River of Amazons are perhaps the most romantic episodes in the history of Spanish discovery.   C. R. MARKHAM

The Amazon slopes of Ecuador are the least adapted to tribal growth and savage prosperity owing to the exuberant vegetation, extremely hot moist climate, insect pests and vast swarms of bats.
                                              G. E. CHURCH

The first of what may be called the giant expeditions.
                                              V. T. HARLOW

THE last quotation justifies the insertion here of a narrative diverging from the main theme. The expedition of Gonzalo Pizarro into the equatorial forests has a prominent place in the Spanish historians: it is part of the biography of a famous Conquistador and it illustrates the general character of Spanish exploration; it is also one of the few expeditions which have been described by the commander himself. Moreover, the circumstances of Orellana's voyage down the Amazon involve a question of historical justice.

In 1539 the Marquis, hoping to establish his brother in a permanent command of dignity and profit, appointed Gonzalo to be Governor of the Kingdom of Quito, with orders to lead an expedition eastwards to the Land of Cinnamon and the country of El Dorado—

the Gilded King. The Spaniards had found in the woods
eastward of Quito a tree bearing fragrant leaves and
nuts which was said to abound in the interior forests,
and eager hopes were aroused of opening a spice trade
which should be wholly Spanish and independent of the
Moluccas. But a stronger lure was the report of teeming
gold and silver to be found somewhere beyond the
forests. Gonzalo himself reported to the King that his
aim was 'The Province of Cinnamon and the Lake of
the Gilded King (El Dorado)'. The origin of the
legend or tale of the Gilded King is discussed by Dr.
V. T. Harlow in his edition of Raleigh's *Discovery of
Guiana* (Argonaut Press, 1928): Padre Simón, the
historian of the Spanish Main, says that the inventor
of the title 'El Dorado'—a thoroughly characteristic
Spanish nickname resembling the popular titles of
Spanish kings, El Sabio, El Bravo, El Emplazado, El
Cruel, El Impotente—was Belalcazar, who like many
men of his stamp, seems to have had a pretty wit. He
and his men had been told in 1536 by an Indian from
Bogota about the king who once a year, after being
anointed with gum and sprinkled with gold dust, was
rowed out, attended by his nobles, to an island in a lake
and there plunged into the water, a living statue of gold,
while an attendant multitude on the banks celebrated
this solemn sacrificial ceremony with music and song.

Oviedo, who talked later with many members of
Gonzalo's expedition, says, 'Gonzalo Pizarro determined to go and seek the cinnamon and also a great
prince whom they call El Dorado. . . . The Indians
report that this great lord every morning is first
anointed with some fragrant gum or liquor and is then
sprinkled from head to foot with gold dust as fine as
salt': he goes about all day gleaming like a piece of

polished gold, and every evening the gold dust is washed off, scattered and lost. Oviedo remarks that this dress does not impede the wearer's movements nor obscure the fair symmetry of his person, of which that prince is very proud: and the historian adds, 'I should prefer the sweepings of that lord's chamber to the great smeltings of gold in Peru or in any part of the world'. Oviedo's mockery was not shared by his countrymen: they listened eagerly to explorers of the forest who brought back Indian tales of 'great provinces in a level country, full of many Indians who possessed great riches, for they all went adorned with gold and jewels, and there was no forest or mountain'.

Gonzalo Pizarro, after considerable fighting with insurgent Indians on his march from Cuzco, was received as Governor of Quito in December 1540. Three months were spent in ordering the affairs of that kingdom, in sending succour to the scanty Spanish settlements and in preparations for the expedition in search of a richer Peru beyond the eastern mountains, preparations which cost him—so he tells the King—50,000 *castellanos*, in great part borrowed. At the end of February 1541 an advance party started eastwards. A little later, leaving a deputy in the capital and sending orders to Orellana to follow with thirty men from the port of Guayaquil—probably seamen, bringing implements for shipbuilding—Gonzalo set out in quest of gold, spices, glory and dominion with about 210 Spaniards, horse and foot; 4000 Indians, men and women; 4000 or 5000 swine; about 1000 dogs and a great flock of llamas both for food and to carry burdens: a rear-guard followed later under a capable commander. Eighteen months later, in September 1542, after his return to Quito, Gonzalo dictated his letter to the King, a brief and almost bald report, which may be supplemented by the narrative of Cieza de Leon; but Cieza is to be followed with caution, for his story is already encrusted with travellers' tales, which gather more thickly round the later narratives. This is inevitable except in the record of a responsible leader: after a nightmare, lasting for months, of starvation, sleeplessness and exhaustion, it is doubtful whether any two accounts, told verbally by others, would agree.

The movement, first over mountainous footpaths and then through pathless forest, of this long train of men, women and animals—animals which had to be fed on the way and some of them daily slaughtered for food—was of necessity slow. In the passage of the Eastern Cordillera many of the Indians died of cold. From the heights the train descended through broken country, bridging many rivers and cutting their way through dense forest with woodmen's knives (*machetes*) until they came to an inhabited valley named Zumaque where food was plentiful, having travelled sixty leagues from Quito by a devious route. From here a party was sent back with food to meet Orellana, who, when he overtook the expedition at a later stage, was appointed second-in-command. At Zumaque there was a long halt—a time of incessant rain, dismissed by Gonzalo in three words—*Las aguas cargaban*, 'The rains were troublesome'. Leaving the main body, Gonzalo took eighty men without horses, owing to the rough ground, and spent two months exploring the forest 'with much labour and hunger'. Finding scattered specimens of the 'cinnamon tree' and wishing to find where it grew in abundance, 'I took measures to inform myself', he says: Cieza relates with disgust that these measures were extreme and fatal torture of forest Indians. He failed to get from these unhappy people news of what did not exist: but thenceforth he always got the information he wanted—that rich lands free from forest and full of powerful lords were to be found farther on, at fifteen days' journey or at ten days' journey, but always farther on. Finding nothing but forest—which here extends for 2000 miles eastwards—he rejoined the main body: at this point he reports to the King that the cinnamon tree (apart from the question of scarcity or abundance) was worthless. But there were still hopes of the 'rich lands'; accordingly the Camp-Master Ribera was sent out with fifty men to renew the quest: he returned in a fortnight with news of a great river.

This river was the Coca, which flows in a south-easterly direction into the Napo, a great tributary of the Amazon. The whole body then travelled eastward to the river, to a land 'full of swamps and creeks': they probably reached the Coca some time in November 1541, seven or eight months after their start from Quito. On the river-bank they found people clothed and living in villages under chiefs. Then, as now, the only paths through the forest were the rivers, and anything like rudimentary civilised life was only possible on the river-banks. The Spaniards crossed the river to the eastern bank in eighteen canoes, 'taking all precautions, for there were often 100 or 150 hostile canoes with boatmen so expert that no one could hurt them'. This is all that Gonzalo says of what must have been a striking scene, the eighteen dug-out canoes, seized from their owners, passing backwards and forwards during several days to convey the men and baggage, the horses swimming, and a swarm of hostile canoes darting about and avoiding bolts and bullets. Cieza's less authoritative account says nothing of this: 'They arrived where the river formed narrows', he says, 'where they made a bridge and so passed over': and in later writers the bridge-building across lofty crags '200 fathoms high' over a deep torrential gorge becomes a romantic and sensational story, possibly with some truth. 'The Coca river', says Colonel Church, 'may be penetrated (navigated in boats) as far up as its middle course, where it is jammed between two mountain walls in a deep canyon along which it dashes over high falls and numerous reefs.' Gonzalo's remark, 'I took charge of the affairs of war; Orellana looked after the Indian guides', suggests that possibly he simply ordered Orellana to build a bridge, being himself occupied in leading his men through a hostile country where agile and invisible enemies lurked in the woods.

Having come to navigable water lower down, he determined to build a vessel to carry the baggage and the sick and to pass from bank to bank in search of food. Most of the Indian attendants were now dead, 'because the land was hot', says Gonzalo with eloquent brevity: it was the usual fate of people transported from the temperate heights to the steaming forests. The herds of swine and llamas were all gone, and the Spaniards were now living on the country or rather starving. Orellana superintended the shipbuilding, allotting to every man the amount of timber to be brought and searching for iron through the company. Gonzalo writes that his own intention was to reach the North Sea, unless he could find 'a good land for settlement'. The remark shows that there must have been talk between Gonzalo and his lieutenant Orellana about reaching the Atlantic; for when Gonzalo dictated this report, nobody knew what had become of Orellana or whether he was alive or dead.

Exploring parties sent out from both banks of the river found nothing but swamps, pools, creeks and impenetrable woods: hunger was pressing: down-stream before them was an uninhabited and foodless country; but their Indian guides were supposed to tell them by signs that farther down there was a great and powerful river flowing past villages where food was plentiful. Accordingly Orellana, 'to serve your Majesty and for love of me', proposed to take the vessel down-stream and bring back supplies; he promised to return within twelve days: Gonzalo agreed and, so he says, ordered Orellana not to go beyond the confluence of the two rivers. This order not to pass the confluence is hardly consistent with the order that Orellana should descend the river until he should find food. Gonzalo probably means that in case of emergency the confluence was to be a meeting-place. It looks as if reasonable discretion had been left to Orellana, for no one knew how far off the confluence was or at what distance food could be found.

Just after Christmas 1541 Orellana departed with the vessel and two canoes, taking with him fifty-seven men and all the baggage, including most of the muskets and crossbows. Sailing swiftly with the current, the little fleet was soon out of sight.

Gonzalo with the rest of the company waited long, starving; and no returning boat appeared: attempts to travel down-stream along the bank were baffled by impassable morasses. Exploring parties sent out by land and also in five canoes, 'which I took by miracle', returned without news and without supplies. Then Gonzalo himself took seven men in the five canoes, paddled obviously by Indians pressed into the service. On the same day they reached the place 'where the river joined a greater river' (Napo); here they found knife-slashes cut on the trees by Orellana's men, but nothing more. They turned their course up the new stream and at last—ten leagues up-stream, says Cieza—they came to a great plantation of the root called yuca, planted by an Indian tribe and abandoned through defeat in some intertribal war. Falling upon their knees and giving thanks, they loaded their five canoes with yuca and returned to the spot where their companions had been living for many days on herbs, nuts and 'unwholesome vermin'.

All now declared that they would rather die than go farther: escape from the hellish wilderness was their one thought. Accordingly they re-crossed the river (the Coca) to the western or right bank, passing and re-passing in the five canoes during a week and losing several horses. Thence, abandoning the river Coca, they traversed the forest to the yuca plantation on the bank of the Napo. Here they encamped for a week, grating the roots into meal and baking cassava bread, 'more savoury to them than the crusty loaves of Utrera'. Thence they followed the river up-stream (probably the Napo, possibly one of its northern tributaries), some wearing brogues cut from saddles, but most of them barefooted and almost naked; a few travelled in canoes while the rest hacked their way through thorns and thickets along the bank, their numbers thinned by exhaustion, exposure to constant rain and dysentery. Beyond the last Indian village there was a foodless land to be crossed; they pushed on loaded with all the yuca they could carry, often wading knee-deep and sometimes waist-deep and bridging many streams. 'The Napo,' says Colonel Church, 'before it reaches the plains, receives a great number of small streams from impenetrable, saturated and much broken mountainous districts, where the dense and varied vegetation seems to fight for every square foot of ground.' In this last stage before reaching inhabited villages, they consumed the eighty remaining horses, having already eaten 1000 dogs. A remark made by one historian (Gomara) and repeated by another (Garcilaso) that the Spaniards felt like eating (*estuvieron por comer*) the bodies of the dead, has given rise, through an error of translation, to an unfounded story of cannibalism—another example of the way in which grisly tales become more grisly in transmission.

At last, in August 1542, the survivors entered the city of Quito, less than half of those who had set out eighteen months earlier; they carried nothing but their swords and (adds Gonzalo with a touch of humour) a pilgrim's staff in the hands of each man. Of the 4000 Indians none returned. Gonzalo estimates the distance traversed at 270 leagues on the outward march and a greater distance on the return. It should be noted that the expedition did not penetrate far towards the centre of the continent: the distance traversed was due to months spent in exploring the forests which might be regarded as connected with the kingdom of Quito. Gonzalo's design to navigate the Amazon, in case that exploration should prove fruitless, and to reach the Atlantic was frustrated by Orellana's departure.

In September 1542, a month or so after Gonzalo's return to Quito, Orellana and his companions—except eleven who were left dead in the Amazonian forests—reached the island of Cubagua, off the Pearl Coast, after one of the most extraordinary voyages in the history of exploration. The story told by later historians is that after rapidly sailing down-stream for some days

Orellana declared it would be impossible to return, vehemently overruled the scruples of his companions, marooning in the forest a cavalier who protested against this desertion, and violently threatening a priest named Carbajal who joined in the protest. The priest Carbajal has left a narrative, incorporated in Oviedo's History, which tells a different story. Rowing with the stream, says Carbajal, they travelled 200 leagues in eight days, suffering extreme hunger; on the eighth day they heard the beating of drums, and next day reached an Indian village where food was plentiful and the natives received them with friendly hospitality. Orellana then ordered the boat and canoes to be loaded with food for conveyance back to Gonzalo's camp: but some seamen in the company declared that it was impossible to return in time to succour Gonzalo's men; and accordingly Orellana, after offering in vain large rewards to any who would take back the canoes with food to the camp, reluctantly yielded to the urgent insistence of all his men that they should abandon Gonzalo and sail down-stream to the North Sea (the Atlantic).

There is extant a petition or rather a 'requirement', dated 4 January 1542, drawn up by a notary and signed by the 'Caballeros, Hidalgos and priests' in Orellana's company, forty-nine in number, the signature of Padre Carbajal heading the list: they demand, on behalf of God and the King, that Orellana shall desist from his determination to ascend the river to Gonzalo's camp, since the seamen declared it to be impossible. Orellana, in a written reply dated on the following day, accedes to this demand on condition that they shall remain two or three months in that place and build a vessel which may serve Gonzalo Pizarro if he should join them there; and if he should not come, may be of service to themselves. Whether or how far the requirement was instigated by Orellana himself it is impossible to say; but evidently he cannot be accused of crushing the protests of loyal men. On the other hand, since Gonzalo with his five canoes succeeded in mounting the Napo to the yuca plantations and in stemming the current of the Coca on the return journey, it would seem equally possible for Orellana to send canoes, paddled by friendly Indians, back to Gonzalo's camp. Cieza is non-committal; 'Orellana', he says, 'stating some justifications, continued his way'. Oviedo, who gives Carbajal's narrative in full but not the requirement nor Orellana's reply, which were evidently unknown to him, adds his own opinion formed after questioning Orellana and his men: 'Orellana was unable to return . . . so he gave me to understand; but others say that he could have returned if he had wished, to the place where Gonzalo remained: and that is what I believe'. Father Carbajal, who was the first to sign the requirement, makes the best case he can for a commander whose resource and determination enabled him to accomplish the feat of navigating for some 3000 miles the unknown and difficult waters of the greatest river in the world down to the Atlantic Ocean. Carbajal duly records the wonders which have astonished many later travellers. The details of that pioneer voyage and the fable of the Amazons or tribe of warrior women lie outside the limits of this volume. It may be briefly said that, halting for fifty days in a friendly place, they built a larger vessel: in August 1542, seven months after parting from Gonzalo, they reached the great gulf formed by the mouth of the river, which a famous explorer, Diego de Ordaz, had in vain attempted to penetrate from the Atlantic ten years earlier. Having reached the wide estuary, Orellana and his men put out into unknown seas in their two home-made river-boats. Following the coast north-westward, they came after a month of navigation to the island of Cubagua, where they were welcomed by the Spanish pearl-fishers. Three months later, in December 1542, Orellana and a dozen of his men, on their way to Spain, came to the city of Santo Domingo, where the historian Oviedo talked with them and recorded the names of fifty-four men who were the first Europeans to navigate the great river.

Orellana, having returned to Spain, persuaded the authorities that his action had been righteous and necessary; accordingly he was appointed Governor of the land he had discovered. 'Publishing more things than he had seen', says Cieza; 'trumpeting through Spain the Amazons whom he never saw', says Oviedo, he set sail with a fine fleet and more than 400 men: touching at the Cape Verde Islands, he lost many of them there by sickness and desertion. With the rest he arrived at one of the mouths of the Amazon. There he died and also most of his men: the few survivors 'came afterwards in miserable condition to this our island Española', says Oviedo. The greater part of the lands traversed by Orellana passed into the hands of the Portuguese.

When Gonzalo Pizarro was struggling back to Quito in the final stages of his expedition, he dreamt one night, says Cieza, that a dragon plucked out his heart and tore it to pieces with its cruel teeth. He sent for one of his men 'who was held to be half an astrologer', and asked for an interpretation: the man is said to have replied that Gonzalo would find dead the thing that he most loved. When Gonzalo reached Quito, he learned that his brother the Marquis had been murdered a year earlier, that the young Diego Almagro had been proclaimed Governor of Peru and had occupied Cuzco, that a royal judge named Vaca de Castro sent out from Spain had spent some months in Quito, had announced his own appointment as Governor and had moved to the south to attack the young Almagro. These events and the civil strife which followed may seem hardly to fall within the story of the conquest of Peru. But that story cannot exclude the destiny of the conquerors, the use or abuse which they made of victory and the completion of the conquest by the establishment of regular government. Prescott shows a true historical intuition in devoting to these events one of his three volumes: those readers who turn to that masterpiece will find that this story, the epilogue of the conquest, holds the attention for its intrinsic character and intense personal interest. Here it can only be briefly told in the next three chapters how three royal magistrates in succession came out from Spain to deal with the affairs of Peru in the course of nine years (1541–49)—first a lawyer, Vaca de Castro; then a soldier, Blasco Núñez de la Vela; then a priest, Pedro de la Gasca. The next chapter deals with the things which passed in Lima during the earlier part of Gonzalo's absence in the 'Land of Cinnamon'.

NOTE.—Prescott described Garcilaso as a 'credulous gossip'; yet Garcilaso's account of Gonzalo's expedition has obtained such a vogue that some observation seems needful. At the date of the expedition Garcilaso was an infant of a few months: he lived at Cuzco till the age of twenty and spent the rest of his life in Spain. This account, written in Spain sixty-five years after the event and after forty-five years' absence from the Indies, was based, as he tells us, on Zarate and Gomara and on information given by members of the expedition. Under these conditions such information was not likely to be accurate, and Garcilaso goes far astray from fact and even from possibility.

Gonzalo's expedition is the prologue to the search for El Dorado, renewed by a succession of adventurers throughout the rest of the sixteenth century and never wholly abandoned until the end of the eighteenth century. Those successive attempts are briefly traced, for the first time with any completeness, by Dr. V. T. Harlow in his edition of Raleigh's *Discoverie of the large and bewtiful Empire of Guiana*. The strangest and most sensational part of the search for El Dorado, namely the story of the tyrant Aguirre, has been narrated by Robert Southey and also in a translation from Padre Simon by W. Bollaert, published by the Hakluyt Society.

CHAPTER XX

PIZARRO, 1540–1541

The patient endurer of wearisome calamities, the resolute discoverer of long-hidden lands, the stern conqueror of a powerful nation.

HELPS

IN the early part of 1540 the Marquis, fatigued by labour and travel, returned after two years' absence to his house at Lima to watch over the growth of the city, to care for the administration of the great empire which he had subjugated, and to foster trade, communication, and the cultivation of European grains and fruits. But there was one danger which Pizarro ignored, that is to say the discontent of Almagro's followers throughout the country and particularly in Lima itself, whither many of them came from all parts. In Cuzco, after Almagro's death, Hernando had tried to conciliate some of them by gifts of *encomiendas*; they indignantly refused any favours at the hands of the slayer of their chief: and now in Lima 'the men of Chile', as they were called, complained—with the exaggeration usual in an aggrieved faction—that they were passed over in all appointments of honour and profit and that *encomiendas* were granted to Pizarro's friends and not to them.

Another cause of general dissatisfaction, not only among the men of Chile, was the influence enjoyed by Pizarro's secretary Picado: the Marquis, unable to read or write—accomplishments superfluous in a conqueror but desirable in the ruler of an empire—left the conduct of business, with singular want of discernment in one who had proved himself a great leader of men, to the secretary, who at the foot of every document wrote the Governor's name between two lines traced by the hand of Pizarro. The secretary, a clever, unscrupulous and insolent jack-in-office, used for his own purposes of profit and of favouritism his position as the power behind the throne in the distribution of patronage. He even dared to inflict an outrageous insult on the Almagrists by riding ostentatiously before Don Diego's house wearing a cloak covered with little golden figs—an intolerable affront, in itself provocative of bloodshed. Diego Almagro, a handsome and spirited youth, trained in all the exercises of a cavalier, after living for a time as a guest of the Marquis, was now lodged in his own house, which became the meeting-place of the discontented party, among whom the chief was Juan de Herrada (or de Rada), who had brought to Almagro in Chile the royal order appointing him Governor of New Toledo, had been a faithful servant of the Adelantado and now became the confidential adviser, a violent and injudicious adviser, of the young Diego. The poverty of these partisans has been probably exaggerated: but many of those who came from other parts found themselves destitute in Lima, and it was said, with that mocking over-statement which Spaniards love, that a dozen of them had but one cloak for the twelve and could only walk out one at a time.

More than a year passed in seeming quietude, while the Governor devoted himself to his peaceful tasks; but in addition to poverty, idleness and resentment there was uneasy anxiety among the men of Chile at the news that the Emperor had appointed a judge, Vaca de Castro, to visit Peru and hold an enquiry: news came later that the judge was in Panama and about to sail for Peru. At first the Almagrists hoped that the judge would favour them and avenge the death of their chief: then it was rumoured that Vaca de Castro had been bribed and was all for Pizarro. The Marquis was warned of danger to his life; he contemned the warning and walked out daily, attended by one unarmed page, to superintend new buildings in the city which he had made. A strange silence was noticed among the Indians, and native women whispered to their Spanish lords that the death of the Marquis was to be about the festival time of St. John Baptist's Day, 24 June 1541 —always held to be an auspicious day among Spaniards. 'Indian gossip', exclaimed Pizarro when he heard of it: however, before St. John's Day he sent for Herrada, who found the Governor in his garden examining some young orange trees. 'What is this they tell me', said the Marquis, 'that you are buying arms to kill me?' Herrada replied that he had bought defensive armour because the Marquis had been buying lances: Pizarro explained in answer that, going out to hunt and finding his servants had not a lance among them, he had told them to buy one and they had bought four—a thoroughly Spanish incident which has the ring of truth. The two parted amicably, the Marquis plucking some oranges with his own hand, the first oranges ever grown in Peru, and giving them to his visitor. The whole scene indicates Pizarro's belief that his work was done and peace achieved; but Herrada, returning to Don Diego's house, was met by thirty of his friends, uneasy and anxious for his safety.

A day or two later the Marquis was sitting at supper with his three children in the house of his half-brother Martin de Alcantara, when a man, muffled up to avoid recognition (it was after dark), knocked at the door. It was a priest, who whispered to the Marquis that the men of Chile planned to kill him on the following Sunday, 26 June, on his way home from Mass: the Marquis returned to table pensive and ate no more; he consented to hear Mass on the Sunday in his own house: but, although he gave half-hearted directions, which were never carried out, for the arrest of some suspects, he was still incredulous.

On the Sunday, having heard Mass at home, he dined at noon; and after dinner was sitting in the customary afternoon *tertulia* with a score of friends, when a page rushed in crying, 'Arm! for the men of Chile are coming to kill my master'. Already Herrada with about twenty followers was crossing the two courtyards, for the strong street-door stood open. About six of the Governor's guests stood by him—possibly all who had any arms—while the rest hid themselves or escaped through a window. Pizarro called to his friend Chaves to secure the door of the large outer room where they sat; but Chaves half opened it to parley with the intruders: he was killed at once and his body tumbled down the stairs. Pizarro passed to an inner room to arm himself; but unable in the hurry to buckle on his cuirass, he seized his sword and went to the aid of his brother Martin de Alcantara, who faced the assailants at the door of the inner room. 'The aged Governor', says Cieza, who was no friend to Pizarro, 'with his intrepid vigour did not allow imperishable fame to detract from the great valour with which his person was adorned. So spirited and stout of heart was he that

I believe, if he had been in an open field, before dying at the hand of his enemies he would have taken vengeance on them himself.'

The assassins, unable to come to close quarters, thrust forward one of their own number, who fell by Pizarro's sword. They then burst into the room: Martin de Alcantara, repeatedly wounded, fell. Pizarro's two pages, taking their places beside their master, died defending him. The Marquis killed two of his assailants, but received a thrust in the throat and fell: tracing a cross with his finger on the ground and kissing it, he died, 'that Captain who had never wearied of discovering kingdoms and conquering provinces and had grown old in the service of the King'.

CHAPTER XXI

THE WAR OF CHUPAS, 1541–1542

I have compassion not only for these two companions Francisco
Pizarro and Diego de Almagro, whom at one time I knew as poor men
and afterwards saw raised up in titles, lordships and great riches; I also
have very great compassion for the many Christian sinners who after
them and through them have been lost.   OVIEDO

'THE tyrant is dead' shouted the assassins through
the agitated and bewildered city. The men of
Chile, surprisingly numerous and including several
notable captains, gathered round them crying 'Long
live the King and justice in the Kingdom'. There was
no resistance; it was a typical South American revolution: the streets of Lima and of other Spanish American
capitals have since witnessed many such scenes. The
young half-caste Diego Almagro, who was raised up as
a figure-head (*cabeza de lobo*) while Herrada directed
everything, was proclaimed Governor of Peru: the
cabildo of Lima, the body responsible for meeting any
emergency, was forced to agree by the simple process
of turning out dissentient town councillors and nominating others. The usual measures followed: seizure of
funds and not only public funds; arrests, executions;
requisitioning of horses, arms and stores; forging of
weapons and even of muskets; appointment of captains
and arming of men, as vagabonds came to the city from
all parts 'in order to rob and live at their pleasure'. To
extort revelation of some supposed hidden treasure of

Pizarro, the secretary Picado suffered 'very fierce torments' on the rack before he was beheaded. Many fled the city, some of whom were killed by Indians, among them Valverde, the friar who had accompanied the conquest, now Bishop of Cuzco; he embarked in a small vessel hoping to join Vaca de Castro and was killed with all his companions by the natives of the island of Puna. Herrada sent messengers to every city to claim recognition of Don Diego as Governor, a claim which the *cabildos* perforce accepted for the time, but only for the time. Some months passed in these preparations before 500 well-equipped men, including 300 horse, marched out from the city to the inevitable war.

For the counter-revolution, as in all such cases, was soon moving. News came to Lima that Alonso de Alvarado, Governor of Chachapoyas in the far northwest, had 'raised his banner for the King' and had invited Vaca de Castro to his camp; that Vaca de Castro, reaching Popayan six weeks after Pizarro's death, had been welcomed as Governor by Belalcazar; that he was advancing to Quito; that he had published the royal decree which appointed him Governor in succession to the Marquis and had sent letters claiming the allegiance of all the cities: indeed Don Diego and his troops were hardly out of sight when the city of Lima declared for the King and for Vaca de Castro.

In Cuzco, where the Almagrists were numerous, the *cabildo* at first recognised Don Diego as Governor, but the friends of Pizarro soon got together, led by one Tordoya, who, riding home from a day's hawking, was met by the news of Pizarro's death: thereupon, exclaiming that it was time for war and not for sport, he wrung the neck of a favourite falcon which sat upon his wrist. Through him messengers were sent to overtake Pedro

Alvarez Holguin, who was leading another expedition into the country of the Chunchos but turned back on receiving the news. Another messenger was despatched to the city of Chuquisaca, which declared for the King: Peranzures (Pedro Anzures), the Governor of the city, was exploring and conquering to the south: he was recalled and hurried to Cuzco with a few troops: another contingent came from Arequipa, sixty leagues distant, and chose as their captain Garcilaso de la Vega, father of the historian; and so by fifties and by scores the loyal men came together until above 300 men were assembled at Cuzco under Holguin, who was accepted as leader. The next step was to unite with the troops of Alonso de Alvarado, far away in Chachapoyas, and to avoid the stronger army of Don Diego which was moving from Lima to Jauja to intercept and separate the two royalist commanders, Holguin and Alvarado. Don Diego's march was delayed by the fatal sickness of his Captain-General Herrada; he might still have intercepted Holguin, but was led astray by a cunning ruse:[1] Holguin slipped past him and reached the fertile and beautiful region of Huaraz, abounding in food, by 'amazing marches', as Mr. Means, with knowledge of the ground, remarks; but indeed the remark applies equally to all the movements of troops through the mountain regions during these civil wars. Alvarado

---

[1] The ruse is too characteristic to be omitted. Holguin sent out a raiding party, which captured three of Don Diego's men; Holguin hanged two of them and released the third after giving him confidential details of the intended operations against Don Diego and promising him a large reward if he would suborn part of Don Diego's troops. When the released prisoner returned announcing that his two companions had been hanged, Don Diego naturally suspected something, put the man to the torture and elicited the misleading information which Holguin wished him to swallow. It is evident that the Conquistadores, callous as they were to the sufferings of Indians, were not very tender to one another.

meantime had moved south-eastward from Chachapoyas and the two little armies encamped within a
day's march of one another, in amicable communication but impatiently awaiting for four months the
arrival of Vaca de Castro before they should unite. Vaca
de Castro at last joined them in June 1542 and assumed the command of the united force, appeasing
with tactful diplomacy the inevitable jealousies of the
captains. The army then moved slowly southwards
to Jauja, while Vaca de Castro visited Lima to recruit
men and raise funds, partly by loans and contributions,
partly by confiscating enemy property.

Meantime Don Diego had occupied Cuzco (evacu-
ated by Holguin), and had there spent some months
arming and preparing. The gunner Pedro de Candia,
who had joined the Almagrists in anger at the slight
which had been put upon him,[1] superintended the
forging of cannon and the making of muskets by some
Levantine mechanics: corselets and helmets were
forged from a mixture of copper and silver; but there
were many desertions to the other side, and Don Diego
lost his three best captains. Herrada, the inspirer of the
whole adventure, died worn out by long campaigning.
The disastrous experiment of a dual command followed:
one of the two captains stabbed the other in a trifling
quarrel, and the slayer, falling under suspicion, fell at
the hands of Don Diego himself.

The Inca Manco, hating the Pizarros, sent to Don
Diego a supply of weapons and armour taken from
Spanish warriors in the great revolt of 1536 and in
later raids, but sent no troops. On the other hand the
Inca Paulu, Manco's rival, who had been attached
to the Almagrists ever since the expedition to Chile,

[1] See page 205.

preceded Don Diego's northward march from Cuzco with a body of Indian auxiliaries to arrange for the provision of food and porters, thereby probably mitigating considerably the burden which fell upon his countrymen, for 'it would be an endless matter', says Cieza, 'to describe all the evils and hurts, insults and robberies, vexations and ill-treatments which the natives endured with these disturbances, since in civil wars and tumults the soldiers are accustomed to robbery and gain and to living freely; if they were corrected they mutinied, passing to the opposite side or abandoning the army. In a way they are to be excused, the land being so rough and so wanting in animals that many went on foot for want of horses; and there are deserts where, for the very great cold, it is well to carry tents as well as provisions; and if this were done with moderation, I should not condemn the service of the Indians, but if a man needed a pig, he took twenty; and if he wanted four Indians, he took twelve—and there were many who brought with them their concubines, carried in hammocks by the poor Indians.'

After some futile attempts at negotiation the two armies met near Guamanga on 18 September 1542, and fought among the ravines and mountain spurs of Chupas, 9500 feet above sea-level; 'and it was a notable thing', says Herrera, 'to see those hills covered with women and men, natives of the country, followers of the camps; some lamenting to see their masters in this terrible pass, wailing and shedding many tears, while others rejoiced, taking it as a vengeance for their wrongs and their lost liberty'.

The royalist army of 700 men was slightly more numerous and better commanded; the Almagrists were stronger in artillery and better equipped. Holguin, conspicuous in a rich cloak worn over his armour, was struck down at the first onset, waving his men onwards. The royalist infantry was led by Francisco de Carbajal, a veteran of forty years' service in European wars, now aged seventy-five but able to fight, march and jest with the young men; he was notable for his great bulk, his skill and valour in war, his incisive humour, his strong common sense and, later, the callous brutality which earned him the nickname of 'The Demon of the Andes'. Carbajal led his men into battle by a defile which for a time protected them; and when they hesitated before the artillery, he threw off his armour, calling out, 'I am as big a target as any two of you, yet they do not hit me', and advanced followed by all his men. The Almagrist artillery was badly served and Don Diego, suspecting treachery in Pedro de Candia (one of the thirteen who had stood by Pizarro at Gorgona), ran him through the body; he then himself pointed a gun which struck down several of the enemy. This combat 'of brothers against brothers, of friends against friends' was fought, as always in civil strife, with great ferocity, the white badges of Almagro mingling with the red badges of Vaca de Castro. At last thirty horse, kept as a reserve or as a guard for his person by Vaca de Castro, entered the fight and decided the issue. When the day was lost several of Don Diego's men rushed upon the enemy crying 'I am such-an-one who killed the Marquis', preferring to die sword in hand rather than on the gallows. Of the two armies, above one-fifth fell in the fight or in the pursuit, and that night almost all the wounded died of cold, stripped by marauding Indians and exposed to the bitter night frosts. Next day Vaca de Castro entered Guamanga where he 'executed justice' on some thirty prisoners: about twenty others were later put to death.

After arranging for the disbandment of both armies by finding employment for captains and men, Vaca de Castro moved to Cuzco and entered the city in martial array, thus impressing upon the populace the victory of King and law.

Don Diego had fled from the battlefield meaning to take refuge with the Inca Manco, but had been persuaded to visit Cuzco by a companion who wished to visit a mistress in the city: on attempting to leave the place he had been pursued and arrested. He was condemned to death for rebellion and submitted to the headman's stroke 'with a generous spirit', suffering, at his own request, on the same spot where his father's body had been decapitated: he died a Catholic Christian.

Vaca de Castro fixed his residence in Cuzco, still officially the capital of Peru. In the administration of government and justice he exercised tact and wisdom, striving to alleviate the condition of the natives. The captains who had served the King were rewarded partly by *encomiendas* taken from the vanquished or formed by the division of excessively large grants, partly by sending captains out on fresh expeditions; wherein 'he acted like the wise physician who by bleeding treats the ailments of plethoric bodies, lest they be suffocated with fullness'. The most notable of these *entradas* was that which descended southwards from the great plateau into the wooded valleys of Salta and pushed as far as the river Plate, a movement to be narrated in a later chapter (Chapter XXVI).

In dealing with Gonzalo Pizarro, the Governor was remarkably discreet. Gonzalo, after his return from the 'Valley of Cinnamon', travelled from Quito to Lima, talking big and declaring that he ought to be Governor in succession to the Marquis: having been summoned to Cuzco by the Governor, he got into communication with his adherents in the city. Vaca de Castro was on his guard and required Gonzalo to retire to his *encomiendas* in the far south. One day Gonzalo approached to speak to Vaca de Castro in the street, whereupon the Governor ordered his guard to stand aside, remarking, 'Where Don Gonzalo Pizarro is, I am safe and need no other guard'. The flattered chieftain retired with a good grace to the city of Chuquisaca, where he had 'more income than is possessed in Spain by the Archbishop of Toledo and the Count of Benavente'. His princely revenues, the power of his name and his just reputation as a captain remained a danger to the state.

Vaca de Castro was accused of using his opportunities to enrich himself and also of undue ostentation. But he had given peace to the country and had laboured to introduce a more settled order. He was not allowed time to prove the results of his government, for in a few months news came that he was superseded by a viceroy charged with the task of introducing into Peru the ordinances known as the 'New Laws for the Indies'. These laws mark an epoch in the life of the Spanish empire: for they indicate that the empire had reached a certain degree of stability, and they were a notable effort to solve the difficult problem concerning the government of the subjugated population.

CHAPTER XXII

THE NEW LAWS FOR THE INDIES, 1544–1549

We desire that the Indians be treated as our vassals of the Crown of
Castile, since they are so.   CHARLES V

THE Catholic sovereigns and their successor had
long been exercised about the rights of the Indians
and had promulgated various edicts forbidding slavery
(with certain exceptions) and prohibiting or limiting
forced labour. Moved by the pleadings of Las Casas,
who was at Court in 1542, Charles V appointed a Commission to examine the whole matter and especially the
question of the continuance or suppression of the *encomiendas*, which had usually been granted to the Conquistadores, as the reward of their services, for two
lives—that of the recipient and that of his heir; indeed
many had been induced to marry by this assurance that
thus widows and children would not be left destitute.
By advice of the Commission certain royal ordinances
were published in Madrid and were proclaimed to the
sound of the trumpet in December 1542 in Seville,
which was in a sense the mother-city of the New
World. These 'New Laws for the Indies', as concerning
Peru, are well summarised by Zarate, who accompanied
the Viceroy as Inspector of Finances and wrote a history of these events. It was ordered, says Zarate, 'that
no Indian should be forced to the mines or the pearl
fishery and that they should not be loaded with burdens,

except in those parts where it could not be avoided, and then with payment for their labour; and that the poll-tax (*tributo*) payable to the Spaniards should be assessed; and that the *encomiendas* upon the death of their present owners should pass to the Crown; and that all *encomiendas* and *repartimientos* (two words for the same thing) held by bishops, monasteries and hospitals or by those who have been governors or deputy-governors should be taken away and also those held by His Majesty's officials, who may not retain them even by resigning their offices; and particularly that in the province of Peru *encomiendas* should be taken from all those who were guilty in the disturbances of Don Francisco Pizarro and Don Diego Almagro'. With this last Ordinance, adds Zarate, 'it was clear that no one in Peru could keep an *encomienda* of Indians; because there was not a single Spaniard who had not been concerned in one of these two parties more passionately than if his own life and property had been at stake'.

It may be said here that when these Ordinances reached Mexico, although the last and most stringent clause did not there apply, the *visitador* sent thither by the Crown to enforce them consented after consultation with the Viceroy Mendoza that, in order to avert revolution and the ruin of the Spanish settlements, their operation should be suspended, the Viceroy assuming a dispensing power which was frequently exercised throughout the history of the Spanish empire and which was necessary owing to the great distance of the Mother Country. But in Peru the case was different, for a Viceroy was sent thither for the express purpose of enforcing the New Laws with the assistance of four magistrates (*oidores*) who were to constitute an Audiencia, to sit as a supreme tribunal and administrative council in Lima, henceforth to be the capital of Peru.

NUÑEZ DE LA VELA, 1544–1545

The person chosen as Viceroy, Blasco Nuñez de la Vela, was a middle-aged soldier, Inspector of the Royal Guard, a man who had served the Crown faithfully in various employments. In his position as head of a government he proved to be an overbearing, tactless and obstinate martinet, violent in temper and dictatorial in method. Arriving at Nombre de Dios in January 1544, he seized, notwithstanding the alarmed protests of the four *oidores*, a shipload of silver consigned by its owners to Spain, declaring that it was the product of slave labour. At Panama, overriding all protest, he ordered that some 300 Peruvian slaves who had been brought thither by their masters should be sent back to their homes: some hid themselves rather than go; others died on the way to Peru or perished of hunger. Leaving the *oidores* at Panama to follow later and assuming unjustifiably an undivided authority, the Viceroy landed at Tumbez in March 1544, to travel slowly to Lima. As he passed, he proclaimed everywhere the freedom of the Indians: already travellers found no food or service in the *tambos*, the post-houses on the roads. Agitation and consternation accompanied and preceded him everywhere, the settlers crying out against robbery and ruin, the municipalities issuing protests and even talking of resistance. Yet in May 1544 the Viceroy was received in Lima with loyal ceremony and lodged in the palace of Pizarro. Admitting the inexpediency of the New Laws, he undertook to forward to Madrid a petition for their modification, but meantime insisted on rigid obedience. The opposition of the *oidores*, when they arrived, and the universal discontent stirred him to an almost demented exasperation. An estimable citizen, accused of a menacing affront to the Viceroy, was only saved from execution by urgent public petitions. Vaca de Castro, who travelled from Cuzco to Lima to make his submission to the Viceroy, was arrested, then released, and then placed on board ship to be sent a prisoner to Spain.

At last, finding it impossible to enforce the Ordinances, the Viceroy grudgingly agreed to temporary suspension, but the concession came too late and carried no conviction of sincerity. People were now leaving the city by night to join Gonzalo Pizarro in the south: a respected public official, whose nephews had departed, was summoned to the palace, taxed with complicity and, upon his denial, was stabbed by the Viceroy himself, despatched by the attendants and secretly buried (10 September 1544).

The crime angered the whole city. The Royal Audiencia determined to depose the Viceroy, sending soldiers to seize his person: the palace guards joined the assailants. The Viceroy, four months after his entry into the capital, was arrested and soon afterwards was placed on board ship in charge of one of the *oidores* to be conveyed to Panama and thence to Spain: as soon as they were at sea, the repentant magistrate knelt before the Viceroy, recanting his treason; and Blasco Nuñez, freed from arrest, landed at Tumbez to 'raise his banner for the King'. Upon the approach of the fleet, which the *oidores* had seized, he fled thence over the mountains to Quito, where he succeeded in raising 200 men.

Even before the coming of the Viceroy, trouble had been gathering in Cuzco. Gonzalo Pizarro came from his remote retreat in Charcas, possibly invited by the *cabildo* of Cuzco, which named him not only *procurador* of their city, that is to say agent or deputy to represent their views to the authorities (a proper and constitutional step), but also *procurador* of the kingdom of Peru—a step possibly justifiable when taken by the capital; but the further assumption or nomination that he should be Captain-General and in addition Chief Justice meant usurpation and rebellion.

In recounting the conflict which followed it is needless to dwell on the immoralities and the increasing horrors of prolonged civil wars, the frequent mutinies or changes of party as equity or expediency or profit seemed to point either way; the hanging or beheading of prisoners, deserters or supposed waverers; the torture or mutilation of spies, suspects or sometimes even of captured enemies. The greatest sufferers were the unfortunate Indians, the Spaniards becoming more callous through hunger, hardship and the breakdown of all law. Though the numbers engaged in the campaigns were small, even including the thousands of Indians accompanying every march, the range and the difficulties of operations extending from Chuquisaca in the south to Popayan in the north were immense. If the devious line of march be traced which was prescribed by the necessities of war and by the need of circumventing mountain masses, the distance between the two points measures about 2000 miles. From the lofty plateau of Cuzco the way led through Jauja, thence over the freezing heights of the western Cordillera to the torrid coast, through Lima and Trujillo to San Miguel or Tumbez, and thence once more over the barren and icy heights to Quito. Through great part of the way the Inca roads facilitated passage, but not everywhere: in the deserts and mountains of the north more men were lost on the march than in battle. The civil war in part took the form of a conflict between the rival capitals, Cuzco and Lima: such conflicts are frequent in the later history of South America.

In October 1544 the forces of Gonzalo approached Lima from the south. In defiance of a message from the Audiencia demanding submission, Gonzalo sent his Camp-Master Francisco de Carbajal into the city to claim obedience. The aged Carbajal, now according to his own account approaching eighty years, had urgently desired after his signal service at Chupas to retire to Spain in peace with his family and avoid the coming troubles; but failing to find passage to Panama, he reluctantly accepted Gonzalo's invitation to join the insurgent forces, remarking, 'I was unwilling to put my hand to the warp of this cloth; but things being as they are, I promise to be the principal weaver'. He kept his word. He stuck at nothing in the service of Gonzalo. The indomitable old man seemed incapable of fatigue; he could wear his armour night and day and appeared to need no sleep, only an occasional rest in a chair 'until the hand which supported his head became tired'. In battle, though indifferent to danger, he ran no risks, but was cool, watchful and cautious. 'He was so sagacious that people said he had a familiar spirit.' There were various tales about his past life; some said he was a renegade friar.

Having entered Lima with a few horse, Carbajal dragged from their beds some thirty cavaliers who had left Gonzalo's ranks; and when the Audiencia still hesitated, he hanged three of these prisoners. The argument was convincing: the Audiencia invited Gonzalo to assume the Government. At the end of October

1544, six weeks after the Viceroy's departure, Gonzalo entered the city in imposing martial array with 1200 Spaniards and several thousand Indians. An accomplished horseman, 'the best lance that ever passed into Peru', he rode at the head of his cavalry, a fine soldierly figure wearing a brocade surtout over his armour; before him was borne the banner of Castile, for throughout he protested his loyalty, hoping to be recognised as Governor of Peru by the Crown. He now took the oath before the Audiencia as 'Governor of Peru pending his Majesty's pleasure'; then riding to the Town Hall, he was ceremoniously received by the *cabildo*. His accession was celebrated for several days by banqueting, bull-fights and *juegos de cañas*; and the newly installed Governor was housed in state in the palace of the Marquis, attended by eighty halberdiers.

To complete his autocracy, he sent a captain named Bachicao, distinguished for his beauty, his valour and his cruel devilry, to seize the fleet. Bachicao sailed to Panama: at his approach a ship anchored in the harbour attempted to escape; he pursued her and brought her back with the captain and quartermaster hanging from the yards. He then occupied the city of Panama and swept away all authority except his own. The town of Nombre de Dios on the north of the Isthmus was next occupied and, by an audacious stretch of authority, was placed under a governor nominated by Gonzalo, who thus seized the entire command of the South Sea and held the gate between Europe and Peru: none could pass to or from Spain without his leave. The city of Panama and the fleet in the Pacific Ocean were later put under the command of Hinojosa, a discreet and trustworthy captain who, like many others, had joined Gonzalo's party from conviction.

But it still remained to deal with the Viceroy, who had returned from Quito and was now at San Miguel, 150 leagues north of Lima, increasing his forces and reasserting his authority. Accordingly, in March 1545, after five months spent in Lima, Gonzalo moved his armament of 600 men northwards, not much more than the Viceroy's force, but better equipped and experienced in Indian warfare. The Viceroy again retired by the difficult mountain paths 120 leagues to Quito, losing many men by the way and closely pursued. From Quito he retreated ninety leagues northwards with his few remaining men to Popayan, where Belalcazar joined his forces. Gonzalo, abandoning the pursuit at Pasto, took up his quarters in Quito.

Here news reached him of a revolt against his authority in the province of Charcas, the most remote part of his dominions. One Diego Centeno, hitherto a devoted adherent of Gonzalo, shocked by the tyranny of Gonzalo's Deputy-Governor in the city of Chuquisaca, headed a rising of the citizens, killed the despot and raised his banner for the King. To settle this trouble in the far south, Gonzalo despatched Carbajal from Quito with forty horsemen—a small force but sufficient. Before departure, Carbajal urged his master to make himself king of Peru, arguing that there was no room for half measures and no chance of royal clemency.

Gonzalo remained to face the Viceroy. By disseminating false news he induced Nuñez to approach Quito, misled him by a ruse into a futile night march and easily routed his exhausted troops (16 January 1546). The Viceroy himself was unhorsed and was beheaded on the spot by the brother of the man whom he had murdered in Lima. Carbajal being absent, there were few hangings after the victory: Belalcazar was allowed to depart for his own government with most of his troops; the rest, with the other survivors of the vanquished army, were invited to join Gonzalo's standard: some were sent to aid Valdivia in Chile; others were despatched under various captains to occupy and pacify the land. Gonzalo, now undisputed master of the whole Inca empire, stayed six months in Quito, a most unsuitable place for the seat of government, detained—so it was said—by disreputable amours. 'I left Quito after the rains', he said himself in a letter to Valdivia. Meantime he did not neglect the affairs of state: his deputy in Lima was Aldana, a moderate and fair man, who was accused of not being sufficiently rigorous in dealing with the many Limeños who disapproved Gonzalo's doings. In July 1546 Gonzalo travelled to the coast and entered Lima in a splendid procession, accompanied by four bishops and passing through decorated streets under triumphal arches amid martial music, the ringing of the church bells and the acclamations of the people to the palace of the Marquis.

Meantime Carbajal had accomplished his mission in Charcas. His passage thither from Quito was marked by hangings, extortion, forcible enlistment and marches of astonishing length, his men disciplined by his forceful personality and by the knowledge that the smallest suspicion meant hanging on the nearest tree. Almost without striking a blow he scattered the forces of Centeno, who fled to a mountain cavern where for eight months he was concealed and fed by the natives. Carbajal assumed the Government of Charcas and wrote to Gonzalo, urging him again to establish an independent throne, to grant titles of nobility and not to send *procuradores* to Spain, since the best spokesmen were pikes and muskets. He was able to add material arguments. In 1545 an Indian peasant was pursuing a llama on the side of a conical hill which rises about 1500 feet from the bleak and lofty plateau of Charcas; a small plant which he grasped in climbing was up-rooted in his hand: bright pellets were adhering to the roots: the man had discovered the richest silver mine ever known, which became a proverb for inexhaustible wealth and for above a century supplied, through the royal levy of one-fifth, the greater part of the revenue drawn from Peru by the Spanish Crown. The secret of the discovery soon became known; fortune-hunters crowded to the spot; claims were staked out; tunnels were driven into the Hill of Potosí; Indian serfs were set to labour and hundreds of free Indians worked by contract, delivering so much a day to the mine-owner and keeping the rest for themselves. It may be added that before the end of the century the largest town in the New World was the Villa Imperial of Potosi.

Carbajal threw himself into the congenial task of exploiting, much to his own profit, this new source of wealth: the royal fifth, so far as possible, was set aside, but not, as yet, for transmission to Spain; and it appeared as though a Peruvian throne might be sup-ported by revenues, drawn from this and other sources, rivalling those of any European monarch. But Gonzalo did not venture so far and based his hopes on negotia-tion with the Spanish authorities: in this he was de-ceived. But meantime the territorial sway of this base-born adventurer and the extent of his military opera-tions were unequalled in South American history until the time of Bolívar.

Pedro de la Gasca, 1546–1550

When the troubles of Blasco Nuñez became known in Spain, another official was despatched to deal with the problem of Peru. 'Since a lion had failed, a lamb was to be sent': this was a priest, Pedro de la Gasca, a man of awkward and ill-proportioned frame, uncomely countenance and unassuming appearance, but noted during five-and-twenty years past for exemplary character, quiet strong determination and capacity in dealing with affairs. Gasca only consented to undertake the task if he were granted unlimited powers, even the right of sending the Viceroy home. The Council of the Indies in perplexity referred this demand to the Emperor, then absent in Flanders, who at once granted to Gasca all the powers that he asked: he was expressly authorised to suspend the operation of the New Laws. Gasca refused a bishopric and would accept no salary and no armed accompaniment: his cassock and his breviary were enough, he said, just as Blasco Nuñez had exclaimed, 'My cloak and sword are enough'.

Only among Spaniards would the events which followed be possible or credible. In July 1546, just at the time when Gonzalo Pizarro made his triumphant entry into Lima, Gasca landed at Santa Marta on the north coast of New Granada (now Colombia) where he heard of the Viceroy's death and Gonzalo's assumption of absolute power. Thence Gasca sailed to Nombre de Dios, where Gonzalo's lieutenant readily admitted a priest coming on peaceful business, and upon seeing his commission stamped with the royal seal, recognised him as Governor and accepted the King's pardon.

About three months later Aldana arrived at Panama, having been despatched by Gonzalo on a mission to the authorities in Spain. Aldana went no farther than the Isthmus, convinced that loyalty to the Crown meant submission to Gasca. To persuade Hinojosa, who commanded twenty-two ships anchored at Panama, was not so easy; but finally in November 1546 by peaceful and diplomatic means Gasca won over the fleet and gained the command of the sea: 'he who is master of the sea', says Zarate, 'on all that coast holds the land as his own'. Gasca now proceeded to raise funds and troops, and at last, in February 1547, having spent half a year in cautiously securing his position, he sent Aldana, formerly Gonzalo's deputy in Lima, to sail southwards to Peru with four ships. The way had been prepared by disseminating proclamations and by a letter from Gasca to Gonzalo offering pardon on condition of submission.

Aldana met with a ready welcome as the forerunner of Gasca. Gonzalo, his power slipping from his hands, left Lima leading an array of 1000 men, 'as fine troops as any to be found in Italy': soon he had only 500; the deserters were making their way by Aldana's orders to Cajamarca, there to await the coming of Gasca. Gonzalo retired to Arequipa and resolved to escape to Chile, abandoning Peru; but the way was barred by Centeno, now up in arms again with a force double that of Gonzalo. The armies of Gonzalo and of Centeno met on the shores of Lake Titicaca, and owing to the skilful handling of the musketeers by Carbajal, the troops of Centeno were routed in the bloody battle of Huarina (26 October 1547). Pizarro, once more victorious, abandoned his intention of retiring to Chile and occupied Cuzco, resolute now to retain or recover Peru.

Gasca, who was now encamped at Jauja, had relied upon assurances that the defeat of Gonzalo was a certainty and was not yet ready to fight. Five months were spent in resting and refreshing his men and in gathering reinforcements. During those months of respite Carbajal, as Camp-Master in Cuzco, was indefatigable in providing for the needs of Gonzalo's army: day and night he was to be seen going about the city on his big reddish-coloured mule, calling to the soldiers as he passed, 'What you can do to-day, do not leave till tomorrow'. And if he was asked when he ate or slept, he replied, 'To those who choose to work, there is plenty of time for everything'.

Early in March 1548 La Gasca with his army of 2000 men, the largest force of Spaniards yet assembled in Peru, moved southwards towards Cuzco. A month later, after anxious delays from the bitter cold of the heights and the passage of rivers where the rope bridges were broken, his scouting parties were exchanging friendly or abusive remarks with parties sent out from Cuzco. Upon the nearer approach of Gasca, Gonzalo, who was daily losing men by desertion, marched out to meet the royal army and encamped at Sacsahuana (or Xaquixaguana), five leagues from the city: as he was arming next morning in his tent, his page was killed at his side by a cannon-shot. When Carbajal saw the opposing array, he exclaimed, 'Either the devil or Pedro de Valdivia is there'. He guessed right; Valdivia, a veteran of Italy like himself, was there, having come to Peru to offer his services to Gasca and also to recruit men for the Chilian enterprise. As Gonzalo led his army slowly forward, seeking the advantage of the ground, Garcilaso de la Vega, father of the historian, left the ranks on some pretext, rode across to the opposing army accompanied or followed by several other cavaliers, and was welcomed with an embrace by La Gasca: then whole squadrons followed. There was no battle; Gonzalo's army melted away in desertion or flight and he broke his lance upon fugitives from his own troops. Finally he gave up his sword to an officer and was led a prisoner to the presence of Gasca. Carbajal attempted to escape, but his horse with its corpulent rider was bogged in a swamp and he was led by Valdivia to the presence of Gasca, men whom he had injured or insulted crowding round him to kill him and Carbajal asking for death at their hands.

On the same day a tribunal was set up. Gonzalo was condemned to be beheaded and Carbajal to be quartered.[1] 'Killing is enough' remarked the old man when the sentence was announced. Next day the sentences were carried out; of the five brothers who had set out from Estremadura eighteen years earlier to the conquest of a great empire one survived, a prisoner in a Spanish fortress. It may be questioned whether such a family history would be possible in any European nation except that of the Spaniards.

Eight or nine others were executed at the same time. On the following day the victorious army, marching into Cuzco, was received with general acclamation. A tribunal was set up in the city and rigorous justice was done; for Gasca, though anything but a hard man, saw that leniency to armed rebellion would be dangerous. Many of the rebels were executed; other were flogged or sent to the galleys or banished from Peru: an amnesty upon all criminal charges was granted to those who had

---

[1] Gasca in his official Report simply says, 'Carbajal was quartered', as do some other accounts; but three contemporary historians say that he was executed by hanging or beheading before the quartering.

served the King during the recent campaign; honourable employment was found for ambitious or turbulent spirits by sending them on various expeditions, among them an expedition despatched to the region of Tucumán towards the river Plate under Núñez del Prado, one of the captains who had passed from Gonzalo's ranks to the royal army before Sacsahuana: Valdivia departed for his Government, taking many men with him to Chile. Others were sent to push forward the confines of the conquered land in frontier garrisons and in frequent *entradas*.

The *encomiendas* of all the guilty were confiscated and served, together with the many *encomiendas* which had become vacant through death, to reward the loyal. It was impossible to satisfy every clamorous applicant; but Gasca, withdrawing with one or two advisers to a distant retreat, devoted three months to the task, assigning the vacant *encomiendas* to those distinguished by signal service and requiring these beneficiaries to contribute to a fund for the reward of the soldiery.

This difficult task accomplished, Gasca travelled to Lima, where he was met by the whole population and entered the city preceded by dancers, who symbolised in their gay dresses the several cities of Peru. For fifteen months he presided in the Audiencia labouring at the reform of the administration. His Report to the Crown concerning the ill-treatment of the natives confirms the passages quoted above from Cieza de Leon: the 'tribute' or poll-tax to be paid by the Indians (the only tax levied from them) was now fixed by him at a moderate amount: it was found impossible to abolish forced labour entirely; but this also was limited and carefully regulated. The administration of justice and of finance was also improved; and peace was celebrated by the foundation of the city of Nuestra Señora de la Paz near the southern shore of Lake Titicaca, now the capital of the republic of Bolivia. About three years after his arrival, in December 1549, Gasca handed over the administration to the Audiencia and embarked for Spain amid general regret, refusing rich gifts offered to him both by the neighbouring Indian chiefs and by the Spanish inhabitants, but carrying large treasure for the Crown, derived in great part from the royal fifth levied on the silver of Potosi and the other mines of Charcas. He received a grateful welcome in the Peninsula and spent the remaining seventeen years of his life—until his death at the age of seventy-three—as Bishop first of Plasencia and then of Siguenza.

About twenty months after Gasca's departure Antonio de Mendoza, having served fifteen years as Viceroy of New Spain, arrived in Lima to rule as Viceroy of Peru. With this establishment of regular government, which endured for nearly three centuries under a long succession of viceroys and *oidores*, the stormy history of the Conquest of Peru ends. It is true that some two years later another rebellion broke out, known as the rebellion of Girón, provoked by the question of Indian labour; but this outbreak was not an undoing of the conquest, nor were the regular forces of government overthrown by it: thus it may be regarded rather as a troublesome episode in the early history of Peru, henceforth the richest among the many dominions of the Crown of Spain.

CHAPTER XXIII

CHILE, 1540–1558

The Kingdom of Chile is like the sheath of a sword, narrow and long. It has on one side the South Sea, and on the other side the snowy Cordillera which skirts the whole country. The land is of such good airs and so wholesome that no man has been seen to fall sick there.

MARMOLEJO

In breadth from East to West Chile may have a hundred miles at the widest.

ERCILLA

'MY desire is to discover and settle lands for your Majesty in order to leave memory and fame of myself.' So wrote Pedro de Valdivia to the King: nor did he fail in his desire. Hitherto Spanish conquest had been confined to the Tropics: Valdivia pushed it far into the Southern Temperate Zone, and in this new advance he displayed not only invincible determination and signal powers of leadership but also the ready ingenuity and resource (not always over-scrupulous) of an old campaigner, besides certain everyday human qualities (not always entirely respectable) which make him one of the most entertaining and familiar figures among the Conquistadores.

Pedro de Valdivia, a veteran of the Italian wars, Camp-Master at the battle of Las Salinas, being 'a man of lofty thoughts', obtained from Pizarro in April 1539 a commission to win the Kingdom of Chile as Lieutenant of the Marquis. There were two obstacles at the outset: Almagro's expedition had given Chile such a

272

bad name that 'all fled from it as from the plague and many sane men thought I was insane'; moreover every leader of an expedition had to do all at his own expense, and Valdivia was not rich: but a wealthy merchant came to his aid, and after due preparation he set out from Cuzco in January 1540 with about 150 Spaniards horse and foot, 1000 Indians, a drove of swine and a number of mares. His work thenceforth is told in his own letters to the King, to the Council of the Indies and to Hernando Pizarro (whom he mistakenly believed to be high in favour at Court), and also in a brief straight-forward history by Marmolejo, a soldier who served throughout the conquest. The famous narrative poem by Ercilla, *La Araucana*, is a document of great value concerning the character of Chilian warfare and the later phases of the conquest; but Ercilla, a cavalier of noble birth who had been a page at the marriage of Prince Philip with Mary Tudor, went out to Chile after Valdivia's death and narrates Valdivia's own work briefly and with many omissions. The story has been made accessible to English readers by Mr. Cunning-hame Graham in his book *Pedro de Valdivia, Conqueror of Chile*, in which the five more important letters of Valdivia appear translated into English.

Warned by Almagro's former experience of the mountains, Valdivia took the coast road: 'I was eleven months on the road . . . on account of the trouble of foraging; for they hid the food so that the devil himself could not have found it'; so he writes. Having at last reached the habitable land of northern Chile, he slowly travelled through the country for 100 leagues from Copiapo southwards, and after careful examination, chose a site admirably suited for a city in a beautiful valley some fifteen leagues from a convenient harbour (afterwards called Valparaiso) in latitude $33\frac{1}{2}°$ south—the climate of Southern Europe. Here in February 1541 he traced out the rectangular streets and the central plaza, with the sites for church, town-hall and prison, assigning to each householder a building site within the city and also allotting in *encomiendas* the Indians inhabiting a given district. Setting up the *rollo* or 'tree of justice' in the centre of the plaza, he swore upon the cross of his sword to defend the city of 'Santiago del Nuevo Extremo' as a *caballero hijodalgo*. He then expounded to the Indians that His Majesty had sent him to settle (*poblar*) the land and make the Indians serve the Christians and 'that we would persevere for ever, and that Almagro had been beheaded for turning back (a politic and convenient version of that event), accordingly that they must make houses for Santa Maria and for the Christians who were with me and for me . . . and they made wooden houses thatched with straw according to the plan which I gave them'. Such was the germ of a great and beautiful city, capital to-day of the republic of Chile.

Finding that the natives, instigated by emissaries from the Inca Manco, were wasting their own country in order to starve out the intruders, Valdivia, from the 'abundant harvest of a fertile land', laid in supplies for two years 'in order that if anything happened, the soldier might have his two meals a day, for that is how war is made'. Things soon happened: the Indians talked of killing the Christians 'as the son of Almagro had killed the great Lord (Pizarro) at Pachacamac'. Some Indians under torture confirmed the news, a month before the event. Thereupon, since Valdivia's commission as lieutenant had lapsed with the supposed death of his commander, the town council summoned

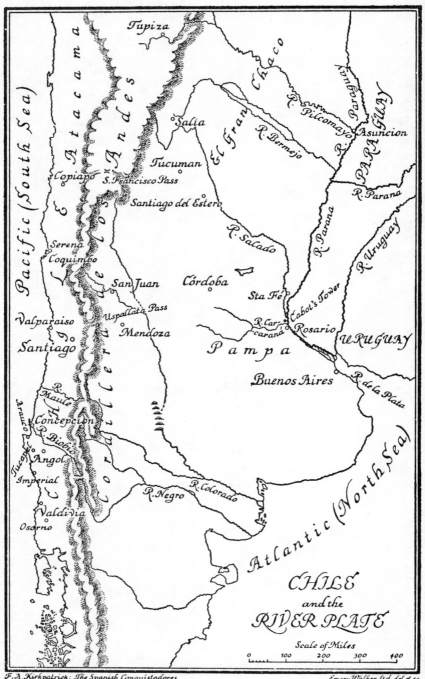

CHILE
and the
RIVER PLATE

Scale of Miles
0   100   200   300   400

the chief householders to a *cabildo abierto*, an open
assembly of the citizens or town meeting, a popular
medieval Spanish institution already obsolete in the
Peninsula but revived in America by the wise local
initiative of the Conquistadores. Since the city did not
yet possess a town-bell, the citizens were summoned
by the sound of a sheep's bell: this civic assembly in the
capital appointed Pedro de Valdivia to be Captain-
General and Governor of the kingdom of Chile pending
the King's pleasure; after a decent show of reluctance
Valdivia accepted the charge, as Cortes had done at
Vera Cruz twenty years earlier.

But the news of Pizarro's death, although premature,
stirred up trouble among the Spaniards themselves.
Valdivia, leaving an able and resourceful captain
named Monroy in command at Santiago, had departed
for the coast to the spot where now stands the great
port of Valparaiso, in order to build a ship for communication with Peru—for from that day to this the
most convenient route between the two countries has
been by sea; he was recalled to Santiago by a message
from Monroy that a conspiracy with murderous intent
was on foot among the Almagrist faction. The Governor
rode back to the capital and hanged five ringleaders,
'dissimulating with the rest, on account of my need of
men'. The detachment which had been left at the coast,
carelessly neglecting precautions, was cut off by hostile Indians, only two men escaping to Santiago.

The incident both proved and stimulated the hatred
which animated the native population: this hatred soon
flamed out perilously. Half a year after the foundation
of Santiago, while Valdivia with the bulk of the force
was absent on a foraging or pacifying expedition, the
Indians in force assailed the capital: the garrison of

fifty men defended themselves in a fenced-in precinct which formed a kind of fort within the city: the chaplain, Padre Lobo, proved himself 'a very wolf' in fight: a woman named Inez Suárez, Valdivia's mistress, who had borne all the hardships of the expedition, was no less conspicuous; by her suggestion and in part by her hand seven native chiefs held as hostages in the city were beheaded and the heads thrown among the assailants to cause dismay. The incident is no myth: Valdivia himself relates it with eulogy in the formal document whereby he granted an *encomienda* to Inez in reward for this signal service which, so he declares, saved the lives of the garrison, since if the captive chiefs had escaped, all the Spaniards must have perished: only he does not mention the hurling of the severed heads at the assailants, a detail which is entirely probable. Finally, Monroy with the thirty horsemen sallied out and put the Indians to flight with slaughter; but all the Spaniards were wounded and four were killed, as well as twenty-three horses; and the city of thatched wooden huts was burnt with all that it contained. Valdivia, recalled by a messenger, found 'not one post standing: we had nothing but our arms and the old rags which we wore in fight . . . a little maize, two handfuls of wheat, two little sows and a boar and one cock and hen. . . . We rebuilt the city' (he simply adds) 'and I set to work to sow and breed . . . and in the first year we reaped eighteen bushels of wheat.' To seek relief for their destitution, Valdivia now despatched his lieutenant Monroy to Peru with five horsemen carrying all the gold which could be got together. To make it conveniently portable, he had the gold made into swordhilts, two drinking-cups and six pairs of stirrups: the existing iron stirrups were forged into horseshoes and nails; for iron, unknown to the natives, was the most scarce commodity in the New World. For two years nothing was heard of Monroy, two years of starvation and strain at Santiago, half the men working and half in turn guarding the crops night and day: 'I was land-surveyor, architect, shepherd, farmer': for the first time in the history of the conquest, the Spanish conqueror was obliged to become a colonist for a time, wielding the spade and hoe with his own hands instead of living by the labour of a conquered peasantry. Valdivia notes later, as a novel curiosity, that they were obliged to put horses in the plough since they had no oxen. During the two years of Monroy's absence 'we went about like phantoms, and the Indians called us *Cupais*, which is their name for their devils (that is to say superhuman beings), because at whatever hour they tried to come upon us—for they know all about night attacks—they found us awake, armed, and, if need were, on horse-back . . . and your Majesty may know that we did not catch trout without wetting our feet, as the proverb goes'.

Meantime Monroy and his five men, riding northwards with golden stirrups, were assailed at Copiapo by Indians, instigated, as was believed, by an indianised Spaniard, a straggler from Almagro's expedition who had lived for six years among the natives and now led them against his own countrymen: four of the Spanish horsemen were killed: Monroy and one companion were saved alive as captives—by favour of an Indian chieftainess, according to a romantic story. The two captives offered to give riding lessons to the chief: after some months Monroy contrived to stab his pupil during one of these lessons, galloped away, leaving the Indian chief wounded, and escaped with his companion to Peru. Arriving at Cuzco, he was welcomed by Vaca de Castro, fresh from the victory at Chupas: when Valdivia's first success and subsequent plight were made known, funds were provided by a group of friends and a ship was despatched to Valparaiso with food, stores and twenty men; who, arriving in September 1543, found Valdivia and his men clad in skins and suffering the utmost extremity of want. Monroy himself rode into the city of Santiago three months later accompanied by sixty horsemen who had been recruited in Peru. By this succour Chile was saved and thenceforward made progress. Ships and men came at intervals from Peru, among them a Genoese pilot named Pastene. Valdivia, quick to recognise worth and fidelity, appointed Pastene his 'lieutenant by sea' and sent him to explore southwards in hopes of adding to the Emperor's dominions and to his own Government all the land as far as Magellan's Straits and the North Sea, and of opening a regular maritime route from Spain to the Pacific coast—a thing not effected until the eighteenth century. At the same time Villagra (or Villagrán) the Camp-Master, 'a noble person and a lover of war', was despatched by land to explore the south. Meantime in the opposite direction the city of Serena, so named after Valdivia's birthplace in Estremadura, was founded in 1545 in the valley of Coquimbo to secure the passage to Peru; 'and in order that the people whom I sent there might go willingly, I assigned to them Indians who were never born, in order to avoid telling the settlers that they would have to work there without Indians after their hard work here at Santiago'.

When Valdivia wrote his first reports to Spain in September 1545, things were going well. The Indians seemed to be tired of war: there were now 8000 swine descended from the two sows and one boar; from the one cock and hen chickens were 'as plentiful as grass' and an abundant harvest of wheat and maize was in prospect. But among the 200 Spaniards now settled in Chile there was some discontent: Inez Suarez used to declare openly that anyone who wanted a favour from the Governor should apply to her. More interesting, as illustrating Spanish methods of settlement, is a petition presented to the Governor by the sixty *vecinos* of Santiago in 1546: they complain that the Indians allotted to them in *encomienda* were too few; that the territory assigned to the city, which had been supposed to be eighty leagues in length, was in fact only thirty-six leagues in length and fourteen in breadth; that the native population was less than had been supposed and had been diminished by war; that some *encomiendas* consisted of only a hundred Indians, some of fifty, and some of no more than thirty, not enough to maintain a man with horse and arms; that there were *vecinos* in Peru who individually possessed 2000 Indians and were lords of a territory larger than the whole jurisdiction of the city of Santiago. Valdivia acceded to the petition by enlarging the territory of the city and by reducing the number of *encomenderos* from sixty to thirty-two, thus increasing the number of Indians in each *encomienda*: 'and to the man from whom I have taken a hundred Indians I will give a thousand at fifty leagues from this city'. Among the thirty-two enriched *encomenderos* who remained were Inez Suarez and Padre Lobo. There is no evidence how far the promise to the twenty-eight dispossessed was fulfilled; they were bitterly discontented, but the reform was carried out without disturbance.

In September 1547 the faithful Pastene, who had

been despatched on a mission to Peru, returned to Valparaiso, bringing a reinforcement of twenty men together with the news of Gonzalo's usurpation and the arrival of Gasca. Valdivia, notwithstanding his friendship with the Pizarros, at once resolved to offer his services to Gasca—not only an act of loyalty but a prudent political move. At sailing from Valparaiso he committed a colossal practical joke: he gave out that all who chose might depart in the ship to Peru with their savings. Ten or twelve men went on board with all the gold that they possessed: Valdivia invited them ashore to a banquet, and then rowed out to the ship and sailed away with the gold, leaving the owners behind and also leaving orders to Villagra, his deputy in the Government, to repay the property of which a careful inventory was taken. One of the unfortunate men went mad; another, who was a trumpeter, after playing in mockery a popular tune, broke his instrument 'in order that he might have no treasure left', a truly Spanish and romantic gesture, which resembles the story told three centuries later of the poet Espronceda that on approaching Lisbon by sea he threw into the water the only two pesetas which he possessed, since it was unseemly to enter so great a capital with so small a sum in his pocket.

Valdivia joined Gasca in February 1548 with about ten horsemen; for, so far from being able to bring help, he hoped to recruit men for Chile: but Gasca declared (so says Valdivia) that his arrival was as welcome 'as if it were 800 men', and in fact, he entrusted to the veteran Valdivia a great part in the ordering of his host. Moreover, after the victory of Sacsahuana, he confirmed Valdivia in the post of Governor of Chile, his government to extend to 41° south and 100 leagues inland from the coast: this last provision justified Valdivia in claiming that the land east of the Andes, now part of the Argentine Republic, belonged to the Government of Chile, although in fact he successfully pushed his claim to the east far beyond the 100-league limit. Valdivia had actually set out on his return to Chile, when he was summoned to Lima by Gasca to answer charges brought against him by some of the men despoiled of their gold at Valparaiso, who had contrived to follow their despoiler to Peru. After a searching enquiry, of which the written *proceso* still exists, he was allowed to return to his Government, but with an admonition to pay his debts in Chile, to allow all who chose to leave the country, to be just in granting *encomiendas* and to sever his relations with Inez Suarez, who was to leave the country unless she were married within a certain time. It may here be said by way of anticipation that the lady chose the alternative of marriage and became the spouse of a captain named Quiroga, who, twenty-six years later, after the death of his wife, became Governor of Chile. Valdivia himself was joined in due course by the wife whom he had left behind in Spain some ten years earlier.

Returning to Chile in the early part of 1549 with ninety men, Valdivia found the city of Serena in ruins and its forty-three inhabitants slain in a serious Indian revolt which had spread over northern Chile. But recovery was swift. This revolt had already been quelled by Villagra; and in August 1549 Serena was refounded by a stalwart and imperious captain named Aguirre, who became, under the authority of Valdivia, Governor of a l northern Chile and of the valleys beyond the Andes, now part of Argentina. The next three years, 1550–53, were a time of confident advance, of the founding of cities and apparently of proud success, not only in Chile proper but also beyond the Andes; for Villagra, returning from a recruiting journey to Peru, took the road of Tucuman southward: he found that a rival captain, Nuñez del Prado, despatched by Gasca from Peru, had founded a city afterwards known as Santiago del Estero, the oldest city in the Argentine Republic: Villagra, by mere superiority of numbers, asserted his authority over the interloper (as he regarded Prado to be) and allowed him to remain in command of the new city as a subordinate of Valdivia. Continuing his march southwards, Villagra reached the neighbourhood of the present city of Mendoza; thence he made his way by the Indian track, as yet untrodden by white men, over the Pass of Uspallata, 12,000 feet high and blocked by snow for half the year, which later became the regular route between Chile and Argentina; and after this astonishing circuitous march he finally joined his chief at Santiago.

The land from which Almagro had turned back in disappointment Valdivia finds to be abundant, wholesome, rich and fertile. In a succession of campaigns Spanish dominion was pushed southward and secured by the foundation of forts and of cities. Valdivia's description of one fort may serve as an example of all: it consisted of a wall eleven feet high and about five feet thick constructed of adobes, large sun-baked bricks. The fort therefore evidently was an enclosed space containing quarters built for the tiny garrison; the whole surrounded by a wall, rude indeed but to all appearance easily defensible by Spanish warriors against attack by barbarians on foot, armed with primitive weapons and unused to fortifications of any kind. On the north bank of the river Biobio, the widest of the many short rivers which traverse the land from the Andes to the Pacific, a fort was built, and here in October 1550 the city of Concepción was founded, which was to become the capital of the South and the rival of Santiago, and after the usual custom Indians were allotted to the *vecinos* of the new city. During the following eighteen months four other cities were founded farther south, including Imperial on the coast and Valdivia in a beautiful wooded country on a river providing a convenient harbour at its mouth two leagues distant. Valdivia writes to the King that by the navigation of Magellan's Strait 'your Majesty will have all this land and South Sea, and will have in your hands all the Spice Trade'. When early in 1553 a ship penetrated the Strait from the Pacific although without reaching the Atlantic, Valdivia believed that he was within sight of adding to the Emperor's dominions and to his own government all the southern part of the continent from Ocean to Ocean. With a discretion rare among the Conquistadores, he forbade gold-mining at first in these new cities: tillage and cattle-breeding were to precede the precarious business of searching for the precious metals.

Nevertheless the discovery in 1552 of rich gold-washings in a river near Concepcion dazzled the conqueror of Chile. 'Now I begin to be a lord', he exclaimed, and declared that he hoped to sail to Spain carrying gold by way of Magellan's Strait and so 'to unite the East and West'. There were now 1000 Spaniards in Chile, distributed among six cities, three harbours and various forts—a small number, one might think, to hold 1000 miles of conquered country; but it must be remembered that the little groups of Spaniards were everywhere accompanied by Indian servants and auxiliaries, many of them brought from Peru, who usually served their masters faithfully and delighted in the pursuit and slaughter after victory, for by long tradition under the Incas the bond between captor and captive, between master and servant, was regarded as something almost sacrosanct: one conqueror remarks that going to war without Indian auxiliaries was like hunting deer without dogs; moreover the horses, now much increased in number, were still a monstrous terror to the natives. As the Spanish arms advanced southwards, there were frequent combats and no defeats; after one victory (the battle of Andalien) Valdivia cut off the right hands and noses of 400 prisoners and so sent them home, after expounding to them that this was the penalty of rebellion. To use an expressive Spanish phrase, the chastisement proved to be *contraproducente*. The warlike tribes of the South, hating these forts and cities, refusing to be treated as vassals or to be subjected to forced labour, began to compose their differences and unite against the Christian invader. Three southern forts were built by Valdivia at a distance of eight leagues from one another, named Arauco, Tucapel and Puren; but they were precariously held by small Spanish garrisons in a country seething with revolt. In December 1553, the early summer, Valdivia set out from Concepcion for Tucapel with forty cavalry to pacify the land, ordering the commander of Puren to meet him with fourteen horse. He found the fort of Tucapel in ruins; advancing to chastise these audacious rebels, he found the severed arm of a white man lying in his path. Warned by his Indian servant to turn back, he refused, never having known defeat.

But now, for the first time in the history of these Spanish conquests, the defenders of their country were learning how to avail themselves of their great numbers.

As the native chieftains were sitting in a circle holding the customary debate before fighting, a young Indian named Lautaro, who had served Valdivia as groom and had escaped to his own people, rose and addressed them: 'The Christians are mortal like us and so are their horses; and the horses soon tire in hot weather (it was Christmas-time, midsummer). Valdivia himself is no more than a man.' He then gave the simple advice, that besides taking every advantage of ground difficult for cavalry, they should form reserves; not only one but several. A dozen squadrons were to be formed one behind the other: the first squadron, when broken, was to retire and reform behind all the others. Thus the Spanish cavalry would be exhausted by successive combats with an endless succession of squadrons; and when the horses should be well tired, he (Lautaro), who understood horses, would give the signal for a mass attack: meantime the Indians of the neighbourhood must be warned to cut off every path of retreat for the Spaniards. The plan succeeded; the forty horsemen, first hampered by rough and swampy ground and then worn out by a succession of combats, were overwhelmed and destroyed. Valdivia himself, being well mounted, might perhaps have escaped, but would not desert his chaplain who rode with him; both were made prisoners and taken to the Indian camp, Valdivia being dragged rather than led, for he had become corpulent: there they were done to death. The fourteen men who had been ordered to support him fell into an Indian ambush: only the captain escaped, wounded, together with his negro servant.

Thus the strange duel between the Spanish Governor and his former groom ended apparently with the victory of the young Indian: the death of Valdivia looked like the fall of the keystone from an arch not yet compacted: Villagra the Camp-Master, taking over the command in the south, suffered another defeat two months later at the hands of Lautaro, who advanced triumphantly northwards; terrified, the inhabitants of Concepcion fled to Santiago, abandoning their city to destruction; yet with characteristic Spanish tenacity the cities of Imperial and even the city of Valdivia in the far south held out, nor was the recently conquered southern land ever wholly lost. Some of the people of Concepcion returned to restore their ruined homes; a second time they were obliged to flee to the capital before Indian assault, leaving their dead behind them: yet the tiny garrisons of Imperial and Valdivia still held their posts during three years of struggle, doubt and disaster. Disaster was inevitable, for Chile was without a recognised government. A country without a firm government cannot make war; and in Chile the government was disputed. The imperious and self-willed Aguirre, holding Serena and all the North, repudiated the authority of Villagra who was attempting to govern the South. Alderete the treasurer, an upright man of affairs who played no spectacular part in the conquest but was Valdivia's right-hand man in the conduct of government, had been designated by Valdivia as his successor in case of emergency; but Alderete was absent on a mission to Spain. The Audiencia of Lima (for at the time the vice-regal throne of Peru was vacant) authorised the *cabildos* of Chile to rule the country; the result of this thoroughly constitutional and apparently prudent arrangement was a brief and totally ineffective essay at a kind of parliamentary government, deputies from the cities assembling in the capital and sitting in consultation with the *cabildo* of Santiago: that was not the way to make war. Finally Villagra was recognised as Governor *ad interim* by the Audiencia of Lima (but not by Aguirre); and in April 1557 he won a decisive victory over Lautaro, who fell in fight. Alderete, having been appointed Governor of Chile by the Crown, died on his way from Spain and was buried on an island in the Pacific, as is recorded by his companion the soldier-poet-historian Ercilla. Thereupon the recently arrived Viceroy of Peru, Andrés Hurtado de Mendoza, appointed his young son García Hurtado de Mendoza, who was barely twenty years of age but already experienced in Italian warfare, to be Governor of Chile.

Hitherto the Conquistadores had been left to do their work mainly at their own expense; but the Viceroy now equipped an expedition for his son at the expense of the Treasury of Lima: a fleet of ships was despatched to Chile carrying 300 men, with horses, munitions and stores. The new Governor entered the city of Serena, lodged in Aguirre's house, and summoned Villagra thither from Santiago; he then arrested the two rival captains and sent them by sea to Peru. On meeting his rival on ship-board Villagra remarked, 'yesterday there was no room for us two in a great kingdom; to-day we both find room within a few planks'. The two captains on arriving under arrest at Lima were welcomed with honour by the Viceroy and were allowed a limited freedom. Villagra later succeeded Garcia Hurtado de Mendoza as Governor of Chile by royal nomination and ruled there until his death in 1563. Aguirre was allowed to return to northern Chile and to the country which is now north-western Argentina, there to pursue a picturesque and active career.

The young Garcia Hurtado, arriving in Chile early in 1557, caused bitter resentment by his haughty arrogance and by his open preference for the men who had accompanied him from Peru, even insulting the men of Chile by opprobrious allusions to their parentage (Villagra, it may be remarked, only bore his mother's name). But the captains and the troops under his command did their work well under most difficult conditions. The insurgent Indians, led by the valiant and aged Caupolican, who had obtained the chieftainship by the test of carrying a heavy beam upon his shoulders for a longer time than any other competitor for command, attacked Garcia near Concepcion. Acting upon the defensive—for the cavalry had not yet arrived—the Spaniards repelled the attack victoriously. In the course of the skirmishing which followed Garcia cut off both hands of a captive and sent him away with a message that he would treat in the same way all who resisted, but that those who submitted might have peace. The Indians, so far from being intimidated by this example, were roused to fury: in November 1557 they again attacked the Spanish army as it advanced southwards, the unfortunate man holding out before his comrades his mutilated limbs and urging them to avert a like fate by valour in fight. Their valour was vain against horses, crossbows, muskets and cannon more powerful than any yet seen in these wars: many were killed; 700 prisoners were taken and ten captive chiefs were hanged. Next the Governor fell upon the Indians when they were helplessly prostrated in one of their customary drinking bouts and slaughtered them. The resistance of the natives, although never completely quenched for nearly three centuries, died down, partly owing to the ravages of smallpox, and the young Governor signalised his victory by the foundation of the city of Osorno early in 1558 some twenty leagues to the south of Valdivia. Three years later (1561–62), by command of the Governor, men crossed the Cordillera by passes 12,000 feet high to found the cities of Mendoza—so named from the Governor's surname—and San Juan, thus creating to the east of the Andes a province which under the name of Cuyo[1] formed part of Chile for two centuries and was governed from Santiago, although cut off from that capital by snowbound heights during half the year.

Throughout the long subsequent period of Spanish domination the Kingdom or Captaincy–General of Chile required soldiers from Peru and money from the treasury of Lima to meet the needs of the incessant or intermittent Araucanian war: but the foundation of Osorno marks the close of the work of the Conquistadores. The Kingdom of Chile had taken form and passed under regular government. As the Chilian historian Amunátegui remarks: 'The work of Valdivia remained standing, and although it was still to suffer serious shocks, possessed in itself sufficient strength to resist them'.

[1] On the other hand, the more remote province of Tucuman was separated from Chile by royal decree in 1563.

CHAPTER XXIV

THE SPANISH MAIN

Where there is a store of gold, it is in effect needless to remember other commodities for trade. RALEIGH

That bait which increases hunger the more it is consumed.

CASTELLANOS

THE conquest of half the New World cannot be narrated in chronological order, for several movements were in progress in various regions at the same time, as groups of Spaniards attempted to penetrate the land from different points in quest of new and richer realms. Thus, since the various phases of the Conquest range themselves not into sequence of time but into geographical grouping, it has been thought well to treat consecutively as one great movement the whole story of Peruvian conquest, including its developments northward through Quito and southward through Chile before turning to trace the doings of Spaniards during the same years in the northern regions of South America fringed by the Caribbean Sea.

By one of those odd contrasts which diversify Spanish history, at the time when a Spanish empire in North America was expanding steadily northward and while Spaniards were establishing municipalities after the Peninsular pattern in remote Andine regions, during those same years the smaller West Indian islands, within two or three days' sail of Puerto Rico, were left in primitive savagery unvisited by Europeans. So late as 1528 a troop of cannibals from Dominica descended in their war-canoes upon the coast of Puerto Rico, carried off a planter named Guzmán together with many of his negro slaves, and enjoyed two hilarious cannibal feasts on neighbouring islands. Two years later one Sedeño, a capable official of pleasant social gifts, 'desiring to leave reputation of himself and increase that of his noble lineage', obtained a commission to 'settle and pacify' the fertile and beautiful island of Trinidad. Having equipped two ships with seventy men, he landed near the present capital of the island: by barter with the natives he got food and some show of goodwill; but when there were no more hatchets or knives or scissors, he was driven out[1] and, instead of discreetly abandoning his enterprise, set up a fort garrisoned by fifty men on the neighbouring mainland of Paria—the beginning of labours which ended in his death.

Spanish activities in the adjoining mainland provinces of Paria and Cumaná were even less admirable. The Spanish pearl-fishers, a jovial company of fortune-hunters—numbering about 300 when the pearl-fishery was at its height—made their headquarters on the sterile island of Cubagua, to which firewood and even

---

[1] Forty years later another Treasurer of Puerto Rico, also bearer of a noble name, Ponce de Leon, made a second attempt on Trinidad, with the same result; and it was not until the last decade of the sixteenth century that effective Spanish settlement was made in Trinidad, as may be read in Raleigh's *Discovery of Guiana*. The smaller islands, Spanish in nothing but their reminiscent Castilian names, were left to be picked up by parties of French, Dutch and English in the following century, a story which Professor A. P. Newton tells in his book already cited on page 23. The Dutch at an even earlier date, before the close of the sixteenth century, established themselves on a coast untouched by Spanish settlement in Guiana, thus effecting the only encroachment upon the Spanish-Portuguese monopoly of the South American continent.

water had to be brought from the neighbouring mainland by people who thus made a more regular profit than
did the rapacious but careless crowd of pearl-fishers.
The pearls were obtained partly by barter from the
natives of the coast, partly by dredging with nets, but
chiefly by compelling slaves to dive and bring up the
oyster-shells: when the supply of skilled divers kidnapped from the Bahamas fell short, Spanish slavers,
regarding all these people as cannibals and therefore
legally liable to enslavement, brought slaves from the
neighbouring mainland, where quasi-friendly tribes—
whose friendship, however, was always dubious—were
readily induced by gifts of alcohol and of iron tools to
help in catching their neighbours into slavery. Slave-
trading was an industry supplementary to pearl-fishing;
for there was a constant demand for slaves in Cubagua,
since, as Castellanos remarks, 'ten died in order that
two or three might remain alive': shiploads of slaves
were also despatched from the Pearl Coast for sale in
the Great Antilles.

But if the Caribbean coast was not the scene of
heroic conquest, it was the scene of heroism of another
kind: in 1513 a few Dominican friars set up a little
monastery on the coast of Cumana and established
friendly relations with the neighbouring tribes at first:
but falling under unjust suspicion of complicity with
kidnappers of men for sale as slaves in Española, they
were killed by the indignant natives. Five years later
two monasteries, of Dominicans and of French Franciscans, were founded on the same coast, and the
friars succeeded in gaining the trust and amity of the
natives, some of whom proudly assumed Spanish
names; but in 1519 the Indians broke out in revolt
'either because of their natural wickedness', says

Gomara, 'or because they were forced to labour in the pearl-fishery': all the Spaniards caught on the mainland were killed, and the Indians, again unjustly suspecting the friars of complicity with the slavers, burnt the two convents: two Dominicans, the only Spaniards who were in the convent at the time, were killed as they were preparing for Mass on Sunday morning: most of the Franciscans contrived to escape to Cubagua, where they found the pearl-fishers embarking in needless panic for Santo Domingo, abandoning all their stores on the island. When the news of the disaster reached Santo Domingo, the Audiencia despatched an armament under one Gonzalo de Ocampo to chastise the natives, to establish a civic settlement at Cumana and to bring back slaves; for these people were now evidently 'rebels'. At this inopportune moment the philanthropic priest Bartolome de Las Casas arrived from Spain in Puerto Rico with a number of emigrant peasant farmers in order to carry out a scheme of colonisation at Cumana. He had departed for Spain three years earlier to obtain official protection for the Indians. At the Spanish Court, by force of impassioned sincerity and fervent religious zeal, he found powerful supporters, overbore the opposition of Fonseca and other Ministers, and obtained an extensive grant on the Caribbean coast, with unlimited hinterland. There was to be no forced labour, no *repartimiento* of Indians: yet with impulsive inconsistency Las Casas undertook to explore every mine and every river producing gold, to found three cities defended by fortresses and to bring into obedience to the King within three years 10,000 Indians paying tribute.

Apart from these persuasive promises and from some Quixotic trappings—fifty 'Knights of the Golden Spur' were to lead and finance the enterprise—the essential part of the design is a notable attempt to open a new phase in the expansion of Europe overseas, the phase of colonisation in the modern sense of the word. Las Casas did not, like other leaders, recruit his men by the sound of the trumpet in the streets of Seville; he sought them in the cultivated fields, for they were to be not, as heretofore, soldiers and adventurers, but farmers who should till the land with their own hands and make industrious homes for themselves in the New World. The defect of the scheme lay not in the design of establishing working farmers on trans-Atlantic land, but in the belief that a suitable field was to be found on a tropical coast inhabited by cannibal warriors whom Las Casas, never having visited Cumana, believed to be as mild and amenable as the inhabitants of the Bahamas and the northern Antilles whom he knew. Having got together a number of peasant farmers ready to accept grants in a new country in order to escape feudal obligations in Spain, Las Casas sailed in November 1520 from the Guadalquivir for Puerto Rico; there he heard of the recent tragedy and saw Ocampo's armed fleet touch at the island on the way from Santo Domingo to accomplish the task of hangings, terrorism and branding of slaves at Cumana. Since it was clearly impossible to convey peaceful emigrants to a scene of strife and slaughter, Las Casas had to look on while his men dispersed through the island of Puerto Rico beyond all possibility of reassembling them. His design, in any case impracticable 'unless his companions had been angels', was thus undone at its inception by uncontrollable circumstances; but rather than admit failure Las Casas carried loud complaints to Santo Domingo, urged the authorities there to do something, and finally sailed with a few followers for

Cumana, where he was greeted with psalms of welcome by the Franciscan friars, who had restored their convent; but neither the place nor the quality of the settlers were suitable. Most of the men deserted; and while Las Casas was absent on a mission to Santo Domingo in hopes of finding a remedy for these ills, the Indians fell upon the settlement and burnt it, convent and all. Most of the Christians contrived to escape by water, leaving some, killed by the assailants. A city founded by Ocampo a year earlier had already been abandoned.

The efforts of Las Casas to lead his countrymen into more gentle and industrious methods of settlement deserve emphasis in any history of the Conquest. The condition of Cumana when those efforts were made was no fault of his; but he cannot be excused for persisting in his efforts under impossible conditions. This devoted priest, impassioned preacher, hot-headed disputant, violent propagandist and enthusiastic philanthropist was the equal of the greatest Conquistadores in courage and determination, but he had not the qualities of a discreet and business-like commander. In the following year he joined the Dominican Order in Santo Domingo; and he left his mark on the history of the Spanish empire as a devoted missionary in Guatamala, as Bishop of Chiapa in New Spain and as the champion of Indian liberty throughout a life which was prolonged to ninety-two years.

After this second Indian revolt, a second punitive expedition was sent from Santo Domingo to Cumana under a captain named Castellón, who 'pacified' the country by the customary methods and re-established the deserted city, afterwards known as the city of Cumana, which professes to trace its history from that date (1521) and claims to be the oldest city in Spanish South America. Yet in the year 1522, thirty years after Columbus' voyage, the year which brought the definite conquest of the Aztec empire, the first continental coast discovered by the Spaniards was still the scene not so much of orderly settlement as of pearl-fishing and slave-trading. The horrors of this slave-trade are described by Benzoni, an Italian emigrant who took part in a slave-raid in 1541: a translation of his book by Rear-Admiral W. H. Smyth was published by the Hakluyt Society in 1857. Although much diminished by the decrease in the supply of pearls and also of Indian slaves, slave-hunting continued in Cumana and also in Veragua until 1542, when the 'New Laws for the Indies', by proclaiming the liberty of the natives, made the traffic a crime and put an end to it, unless possibly as a surreptitious and occasional business.

The stretch of coast from Cumana to the Isthmus, some 1300 miles measured longitudinally apart from the windings of the coast, inhabited as it was by many separate tribes, possessed no unity and offered no field for a single conquering enterprise. The only possibility was piecemeal occupation at different points on the coast, which might serve as starting-places for gradual penetration of the interior; and this was slow to come, for in general the Spaniards only made their settlements where they could be supported by the labour of a dependent native peasantry. Ojeda in his unfortunate attempt in 1509 by his aggressive pugnacity had left the natives bitterly hostile, and Pedrarias on his way to Darien in 1514 raided Santa Marta. Yet the Spaniards of Darien, in spite of mutual suspicion and of deep-seated hatred in the natives, carried on a profitable trade with the tribes beyond the Gulf of Darien, profitable among others to the historian Oviedo, who tells us that he bartered hatchets made of old barrel-hoops for gold.

In 1520 that region, still unsubdued, was divided by the Crown—on paper—into two governments, Cartagena and Santa Marta. Four years later the veteran Bastidas who had explored that coast in 1502, although now a gouty sexagenarian, obtained a royal licence to settle Santa Marta as Governor. He was carried to war in a litter, but strove to establish regular and peaceable intercourse with the nearer tribes. After a year his lieutenant Pedro de Villafuerte, resenting discipline and the control of the gold trade, conspired with others to murder Bastidas and assume the government. Entering the Governor's chamber by night, he stabbed Bastidas in his sleep. The old man, wounded but not mortally, leapt from his bed and grappled in the dark with the assassin, who fled, but revealed his identity by dropping in the scuffle a string of beads which he wore on his left wrist to guide his devotions. Finding himself detected, Villafuerte took to the woods and persuaded the Indians for a time that he was a fugitive from tyranny and an enemy of the Christians. Bastidas, appointing a deputy, departed for Cuba to be healed of his hurt, and there died. The savage surroundings, the daily peril of sickness and death, the gamble for sustenance and for gold were evidently demoralising, for Santa Marta passed through a decade of disorder, rapacity and tyranny; but the settlement was maintained and was later the starting-point of a great enterprise.

In 1528 the Audiencia of Santo Domingo, in a tardy effort to check slave-raids, sent Ampues, Factor of the Crown in the island, himself a slave-trader, but a discreet person, to make another settlement. He chose a site upon the sheltered bay of Coro about 100 miles east of the Gulf of Maracaibo. There he received a visit from an Indian chief borne in a hammock and attended by the great men of his tribe: these friendly neighbours listened to the exhortations of the white men, watched their religious ceremonies with admiration and some of them accepted baptism and new names. But in 1528 there were only two little groups of Spaniards established upon 1300 miles of coast. However, during the years when the Pizarro brothers were pursuing their enterprise southwards, in the course of the decade from 1530 to 1540, attempts were made to penetrate and conquer tropical South America from the Atlantic and the Caribbean Sea in three separate movements. Five ambitious adventurers—Ordaz, Herrera, Alfinger, Hohemut, Federmann—approached from three different points the goal which at last was reached by the Conquistador Jiménez de Quesada. It is convenient to treat first the expeditions by way of the river Orinoco, then the German expeditions which started from the neighbourhood of the Gulf of Maracaibo, and lastly in another chapter the great movement whereby Jimenez de Quesada, starting from Santa Marta, succeeded in finding another golden kingdom and winning a great name among the Conquistadores by taking the 'Great River' Magdalena as his guide through forests and over mountains to the Chibcha capital on the savanna of Bogota.

THE ORINOCO, 1531–1535

Diego de Ordaz, who had served with Cortes in the conquest of New Spain, being eager to win fame and wealth for himself, obtained a royal licence for settlement and set out from Teneriffe in November 1530 with a flag-ship and three small vessels (caravels) conveying about 500 men and thirty horses. He sailed first to the estuary of the Amazon, but the three caravels were sunk by storms or wrecked by running aground; and Ordaz, entangled among shallows off a swampy shore, turned back from the Amazon and steered northwestward with the one remaining ship to the coast of Paria, where he strengthened his diminished numbers by pressing into his service the garrison of Sedeño's fort. Having explored all the coast, he determined to penetrate the continent by way of the river Orinoco. After two months spent in building vessels for river navigation, he disappeared for a year into the wilds with 280 men, travelling against the current of the great river through a vast prairie which changes with the change of season from desert to flood, and suffering the customary trials of hunger, fights with savages, torrential rains and loss of men. An Indian guide, pointing westward, was supposed to tell of people clothed and rich in gold, whose country might be reached by travelling up the river Meta, a great affluent whose sources in the eastern spurs of the Andes are in fact not far distant from the savanna of Bogota. But 'everyone interpreted according to his desire'; and when the Indian, pointing to the south, imitated the sound of water dashing over rocks, many of his hearers declared that this meant the hammering of goldsmiths and that the rich lands lay to the south: accordingly they continued up the main stream of the Orinoco until, coming to the cataracts of Ature, they were obliged to turn back. An attempt to follow the Meta up-stream was foiled by the diminution in the depth of water with the coming of the dry season, and Ordaz returned down-stream to

Paria, having determined, according to Oviedo, to make his way overland to the 'Province of Meta'. But his violent and imperious temper—proved by an atrocious slaughter of Indians to avert or chastise a suspected conspiracy—had alienated his men; his claims caused disputes with the Spaniards of Cubagua: finally the Alcalde of Cubagua arrested him: the two disputants carried their quarrel to the Audiencia of Santo Domingo, which remitted the question to Spain: on the voyage thither Ordaz died, poisoned, according to rumour, by the Alcalde.

After an interval of disputes, mutinies, arrests and escapes at Paria—matters illustrating character but of little intrinsic interest—the Camp-Master of Ordaz, Alonso de Herrera, a man beloved by his followers although hated, with reason, by the Indians, renewed the quest, resolute this time to travel westward. Accordingly, having embarked upon the Orinoco and having reached the mouth of the river Meta, he chose the Meta as his road. For a month his men pushed up-stream from the confluence, sometimes wading up to their waists as they towed the boats or struggling along the bank through thickets and rocks, faint from hunger. During part of the rainy season they encamped among floods, their soaked and verminous clothes falling to pieces. Longing to return, they were released in a way they did not wish—by a poisoned arrow which slew their commander: the survivors returned down-stream to Paria eighteen months after their departure. The Orinoco, third of the great South American rivers, was the last of the three to yield its secrets; and the country traversed by its countless tributaries remained little known until the Spanish missionaries of later generations established their posts and gathered their Indian neophytes into villages, as may be read in Humboldt's *Travels in the Equinoctial Regions of South America*.

Other captains, among them Sedeño, who died on the road, led laborious expeditions by land in search of the 'Province of Meta'. One of these parties pushed so far westward that they met the German explorers of Venezuela. The foundation of the city of Barcelona in 1534, at a point where the plains of the Orinoco break through the hills northwards to the sea, marks an advance in the settlement of the coast, but it was not till after the mid-century and after much fighting with Indians and many deaths that there was any definite occupation of the pleasant and fertile hill country which lies inland. The city of Valencia was founded in 1553 on the margin of a lake among the hills by a group of Spaniards who were driven from a coastal settlement by the raids of French corsairs: a more decisive step was the foundation of Caracas in 1567 by Diego Losada, who had served as a captain under the Germans of Coro; he surmounted the Silla, the saddle-shaped eminence which here rises steeply from the narrow coastal strip, and in a beautiful well-watered valley beyond, about five leagues from the coast, he set up the city of Caracas which is to-day the capital of the republic of Venezuela.

It may be added that any notable progress in the Spanish settlements on the whole coast from Paria to Darien only became possible when the importation of negro slaves from Africa supplied labour for the needs of the small groups of Spaniards; for the natives of that coast, although they could be shipped to the islands as slaves, were untameable in their own country. The English slave-traders who visited that coast after 1560 found a ready sale in these towns.

VENEZUELA, 1528–1540

The conquest or attempted conquest of Venezuela is a singular affair, a commercial speculation undertaken by a firm of German merchant-bankers, the Augsburg house of Welser. The Welsers had lent to Charles a large sum to facilitate his election as Emperor: eight years later by a grant[1] from the Emperor they became proprietary lords of Venezuela—'for ever' according to the terms of the grant—with the right of nominating governors. They undertook to send at their own cost 300 men to the country, to found two towns and three fortresses and to pay the customary royal dues. The usual injunction was added about conversion and good treatment of the Indians; but another clause runs, 'I give you licence and faculty . . . to take as slaves those Indians who are rebels, after admonishing and requiring them . . . and you may take and purchase those who are (already) truly slaves, paying the usual fifth on slaves'. These merchants evidently hoped for a return on their capital in the form of gold and slaves.

They chose as Governor Ambrose Ehinger (whom the Spaniards called Micer Ambrosio Alfinger), agent of the firm in Santo Domingo, who was promoted from his desk and counting-house to be Governor and military commander of an unconquered and unexplored province, charged with the duty of providing a good return upon large capital invested. Ambrose Alfinger arrived at Coro in February 1529 with three ships and

[1] The capitulation was granted in March 1528 to two Germans, Henry Ehinger and Jerome Sayler, agents of the Welsers: two years later it was transferred to the Welsers by name.

a gay company of adventurers recruited in Spain; for although the commanders were German, all the soldiers were Spaniards. The new-comers smiled at the sunburnt and rudely clad figures who met them at landing: when they came to cut their way through thorny jungle under torrential rain, the laugh was with the *baquianos*, the seasoned veterans, who mockingly asked the *chapetones*, the raw new-comers from Europe, whether their plumed caps were a good shelter against the downpour. Ampues, the founder and first Governor of Coro, when Alfinger produced the royal order, was obliged to obey and retired with natural mortification to the three neighbouring islands which were granted to him by way of compensation or consolation.

After some months' preparation, Alfinger set out thirty leagues westwards in order to explore the vast lake of Maracaibo, traversing its waters in boats, examining the shore, sometimes skirmishing with Indians, and finally setting up on the western shore of the lake a *ranchería* or village of huts—which afterwards grew into the city of Maracaibo—to serve as a rest-camp or base. Leaving here a small garrison and the sick men, for many were prostrate with fever, he returned to Coro after a year's absence to find that he had been given up for dead and a successor had been appointed, who in turn opportunely died. Having resumed the government, he left for Santo Domingo to procure arms, stores and fresh recruits: the expenses were paid by shipping numbers of slaves, duly branded, from Coro for sale in the Antilles. At last in 1531 Alfinger set out from Coro with about 200 men and many attendant Indians; he crossed the great lake to his rest-camp and thence pushed westward over mountains not of forbidding altitude to the neighbourhood of Rio Hacha: thence he turned south following the Rio César to the valley of the Magdalena, often fighting with fierce and warlike Indians, collecting gold by barter or by force and suffering the usual straits of hunger. Padre Aguado relates with horror that one man, Alfinger's Spanish servant, used to behead any chained slave who fell by the way, since the chain was so arranged that, in order to release one slave, all those in front or behind had to be loosed and rebound: Aguado adds that the scoundrel met the violent fate which he deserved. After a march of four months Alfinger encamped at Tamalameque, some distance from the present village of that name. Thence he despatched a captain named Vascuña with thirty-five men, carrying all the gold—60,000 pesos or 600 pounds' weight—to bring provisions and recruits from Coro. Vascuña and his men—seeking a safer way of return, for they dreaded the vengeance of the tribes through which they had passed—lost themselves in a foodless and uninhabited land of jungle, swamp, rivers and lagoons. Exhausted and unable to carry the gold, for evidently their Indian porters were dead or lost, they buried the gold and 'with it their hearts' under a great tree, where it was never found by later searchers. Finally they deserted their commander Vascuña and broke up into small parties: some were driven by the torment of hunger to cannibalism, the victims being Indians. Their story only became known through the survival of one man, Francisco Martín, who became captive to Indians, gained credit as a medicine-man and on the strength of that reputation was bought by a neighbouring tribe, where he married an Indian wife and 'went native'.

Alfinger waited several months in vain for Vascuña's

return, suffering the utmost straits and sending out
exploring parties: one of these having reported that
beyond the Eastern Cordillera there were fertile and
temperate valleys, the commander, abandoning the
Magdalena valley, led his diminished and suffering
company across the mountains south-eastwards: as
they travelled over the icy wind-swept *páramos* many
Spaniards perished and few or none survived of the
naked Indians from the torrid lowlands. Yet Alfinger
still pushed southwards, advancing far to the south
of the present town of Pamplona before he turned. Had
he gone ten leagues farther, says Padre Aguado, he
would have reached the margin of the rich lands afterwards conquered by Quesada; lands of which Alfinger
must have heard, although he failed to reach them,
only preparing the way for others. Having abandoned
the quest and turned northwards, he was killed in a
skirmish with Indians at a spot which was long known
as the 'Valley of Micer Ambrosio'. His men chose leaders
to take them back to Coro: in the later part of their
march they were astonished to meet the indianised
soldier Francisco Martin, who approached them naked,
painted, wearing a feathered crown, with bow in his
hand and quiver on his shoulder: by his influence with
his adopted tribe he ensured them safe passage through
a dangerous country; and at last in November 1533,
two years and two months after their setting out, they
entered the city of Coro much diminished in number.

Alfinger's successor, George Hohemut, whom the
Spaniards called Jorge Espira (George of Speyer),
arrived at Coro in 1534 and in May of the following
year set out for the south, not following the same route
as Alfinger, but crossing the Mountains of Mérida
and travelling far into the distant southern plains, a land

of many streams which flow into the Orinoco. He heard talk, as other explorers had done, of rich lands lying beyond the mountains at the sources of the river Meta: he actually reached that river and sent scouts to examine the mountain passes to the west: they reported that the Cordillera was impassable, and accordingly the commander, having lost many men and horses from hunger, exhaustion, disease and frequent fights with Indians, turned back northwards, when he was on the brink of winning a great prize. Half the men who had set out with him from the city three years earlier returned to Coro. Two years later, in the midst of preparations for another *entrada*, Hohemut himself died.

Where he had failed, his lieutenant Federmann succeeded in the great discovery, but too late to win the prize. Federmann, a sagacious and ambitious leader who understood men, was deeply mortified at not receiving the chief command, and in the absence of his chief determined to conquer on his own account. A year after Hohemut had set out, Federmann marched southwards from Coro with 400 men, afterwards reinforced to nearly 500. He carefully avoided overtaking or meeting Hohemut, although he was traversing the same plains at the same time: he in turn, like the commander to whom he was faithless, crossed the tributaries of the Orinoco and came to the upper waters of the Meta. Undeterred by the difficulties of the mountains and braving the passage of the icy *páramos*, he reached after three years, with less than one-third of his original company, the object of his journey, the savanna of Bogota, only to find that he had been forestalled: Jimenez de Quesada, having thrust his way up the Magdalena Valley from Santa Marta, was there long before him, as will appear in the next chapter.

The very remarkable four years' journey (1541–45) of Von Hutten from Coro across the plains and its tragic ending belong to the story of the search for El Dorado and cannot find space here. German rule in Venezuela finally proved so undesirable that the 'perpetual' concession lapsed, and the province by successive steps of administrative reform passed under the rule of the Spanish Crown about 1550. The Germans, notable though they were as explorers, had done little for the development of the province; but in the decade 1550–60 some small towns came into existence in the interior of the country which they had attempted to exploit and had found unprofitable; and the whole region was securely held as part of the Spanish empire in the Indies.

CHAPTER XXV

NEW GRANADA, 1536–1539

Time, patience, alertness and caution are the trackers which search out the things most hidden and most fenced in.

JUAN DE CASTELLANOS

THE triumphs of Hernan Cortes and Francisco Pizarro have thrown into unmerited shadow the achievements of other Conquistadores, who with equal endurance, sagacity and courage overcame difficulties not less although different in kind. For English readers Mr. Cunninghame Graham has repaired this injustice in his book *The Conquest of New Granada, being the Life of Gonzalo Jiménez de Quesada* (London, 1922), a book which tells the story with intimate reality, being written with knowledge of the ground traversed by the conquerors and of the nature of their work.

After the conquest of Mexico and of Peru there still remained another opulent region strangely remote, isolated and self-contained like the fabulous empires of legend or fiction. When Cortes reached the coast of Yucatan, he was at once in touch with a civilisation which extended from Ocean to Ocean: when Pizarro reached Tumbez he was within the orbit of the vast Inca empire which stretched through thirty-five degrees of latitude. But the Chibcha people had developed an organised civic life in a limited highland region, measuring about forty-five leagues in length from north to south, and twelve or fifteen leagues in width, cut off by gigantic mountain barriers and by illimitable plains from all external contact and surrounded by tribes of whom some were naked savages and none shared much of the Chibcha culture. The land was rich in gold and emeralds and the people were expert in agriculture, pottery and the weaving of dyed cotton fabrics. Though they seldom built in stone or brick, their dwellings of wood and clay were solid and artistic structures, carpeted—at least the better sort of them—with reeds; for the climate of Bogota is temperate. The Chibchas owed their comfortable advance in the arts of life partly to the possession of salt springs which produced a luxury wanting to the neighbouring tribes and eagerly desired by them as an article of commerce, partly to the potato, a prolific and nutritive plant which responds kindly to cultivation by hand. Quesada himself reports that this 'trufle', as he calls it, yielded heavy crops, and Castellanos describes with curious particularity this strange plant with its 'scanty flowers of a dead purple colour' and its 'farinaceous roots of pleasant flavour much prized by the Indians and a delicacy even to the Spaniards'. There were no domestic animals, for the llama was unknown, and all transport, as in New Spain, was on the backs of men; but the country abounded in game. Although the two principal 'kings', Bogotá and Tunja,[1] were never quite at peace, and although there was constant guard and frequent hostility against the cannibal tribe of Panches, the people were no great fighters and were not united, every valley in that broken country having its chief who aimed at independ-

[1] It is convenient to do as the Conquistadores did and call these hereditary chiefs by the names of the valleys or districts which they ruled, writing the names as the Spaniards wrote them.

ence. Thus, whenever Bogota in successive generations attempted to subdue his less powerful neighbour
Tunja, his rear was always assailed by lesser chiefs, so
that he never was able to pursue his imperial designs.

Accordingly the main trouble of the Conquistadores
was not the subjugation of the people (although the
subjugation of a rich and populous country by 160 men
without fire-arms, their powder being ruined, is a remarkable event) but the difficulty of finding the way
to this 'cloistered circle', as Castellanos calls it 'this
treasure-casket only to be approached by roughest
ways'. These comparisons suggest that the story which
he tells almost resembles some tradition of folk-lore or
fairy-tale: a remote, hidden or dimly discerned prize
of great value, the reward of endurance, courage and
(above all) faith, sought with brave endeavour by many
knights in succession and finally won by the most
worthy. Piedrahita, the episcopal historian of these
events, expresses this feeling in exclamatory passages:
Alfinger, says the Bishop, by confusion of mind and
error of direction, twice missed 'the discovery which
Heaven reserved for another'. Espira, either from dread
of the craggy mountains or, more certainly, by the
disposition of Providence which reserved this conquest
for another, committed the same error when the gleam
(*el relámpago*) of good fortune was in sight. Federmann
declares in a letter that Alfinger eight years earlier and
Espira three years earlier could have gained the prize
'if they had had devotion'. Federmann adds that it is
'the best corner in all the Indies, even if Peru be in-
cluded'. Success was at last achieved by the destined
hero not through a series of dramatic or triumphant
strokes, but by the patient and painful overcoming of
many obstacles with great loss and suffering during

many months. Juan de Castellanos, who served as a soldier throughout the expedition and afterwards settled at Tunja as a priest, tells the story twice, first in rhymed eight-line stanzas (*octavas reales*), then in hendecasyllable blank verse stanzas: Oviedo also gives two narratives, first a short account by two of the captains in the expedition, San Martín and Lebrija, and then a narrative derived from information supplied by Quesada himself, with whom Oviedo had much talk 'when Prince Philip held his court in Madrid and Valladolid' in 1547–48. The historians who wrote in the following century, Padre Simon and Piedrahita, Bishop of Santa Marta, knew the country, and told their story well. Piedrahita uses and quotes Quesada's own history of his doings, now unfortunately lost: only his brief report survives of *encomiendas* granted to sixty-two of his men.

In 1535 Pedro de Lugo, Governor of Teneriffe, having been appointed Governor of Santa Marta, brought with him to his new capital many Spaniards and Canary Islanders and sent out, to explore the interior, his son Alonso. Finding himself beyond control, the young man made off to Santo Domingo and to Spain with all the gold he could lay hands upon, robbing with complete impartiality the natives, his father and the King: the Governor died some months later, but not before he had despatched in April 1536 an expedition of 900 men under Gonzalo Jimenez de Quesada, a man of about thirty-four years, by profession a lawyer, who had come out as magistrate of Lugo's company. The magnitude of the expedition, the carefully chosen direction and the records show that there was a definite object, not merely exploration but the conquest of a rich country known to exist somewhere in the southern mountains, although as Castellanos says (striking again the folk-lore note), the only guide was 'blind report and the echo of an ill-formed rumour'. One-third of the men with most of the baggage were embarked in five hastily built vessels to make for the mouth of the Magdalena and ascend the river to Tamalameque, there to join forces with Quesada. Meantime Quesada himself with the rest of the men and 100 horses marched overland about forty leagues to the bank of the Magdalena. The men were protected against poisoned arrows by tunics of thick quilted cotton, and a helmet of the same; the horses were draped with a sheet of the same quilted stuff, so that man and horse together must have been a monstrous and terrifying sight. The preliminary march to the river first through a waterless land and then through forests and swamps and across a broad river, often skirmishing with Indians, was a foretaste of what was to come; for the real difficulties began in the march or rather the slow struggle up-stream parallel to the flooded bank—for the season of rains, about May to October, had begun.

They reached the meeting-place, but there were no brigantines. The light vessels built for river navigation met with a gale at the river-mouth: three were driven ashore and wrecked, one with the loss of all hands, killed by Indians; the other two, much battered, returned to Santa Marta. The Governor Lugo, undismayed, after sending a party overland with a message of encouragement for Quesada, built two vessels and despatched them with the two remaining vessels of the former fleet to join Quesada, who during the long months of waiting had been slowly forcing his way up the bank, with diminishing numbers. At last three vessels, for one of the four was wrecked, overtook him, alternately sailing, rowing, punting with poles and towing from the bank. The vessels brought welcome supplies of food, which lasted for a time; they also took on board the most ailing of the sick and facilitated foraging on both sides of the river; but there was no slackening of toil for those who fought their way up the valley parallel to the stream but avoiding the flooded banks. 'Quesada saw', says Castellanos, 'his numerous troops diminished by fevers and sores from the plagues of travel, ticks, bats, mosquitoes, serpents, crocodiles, tigers (jaguars), hunger, calamities and miseries with other ills which pass description. . . . Jerónimo de Insa, captain of the *macheteros* (a corps of pioneers armed with woodmen's knives), advances breaking through thickest woods and bridging the swamps and creeks, consuming the whole torrid days in incredible labours, so that with innumerable ink the fifth part could not be told.' 'Heaven help me!' says Piedrahita a century later, 'that men of flesh should suffice to break through two hundred leagues of thickest wood with their own hands, the forest being so rough and dense that all working together could scarcely pierce through one league or two in a day. How many sicknesses prostrated men reared in gentler climates. How many died of pestilent fevers, still labouring with their hands . . . some died eaten by tigers and crocodiles, some of hunger or of thirst caused by the poisoned arrows of the barbarians.'

Eight months after leaving Santa Marta, when they were in the utmost straits of famine, the men in the vessels saw an Indian village ahead. Quesada himself pushed on in a canoe travelling all night: the village, Tora by name, was deserted, but there were fields of ripening maize: when the army arrived some days later, rations were served out, and San Martin, the ablest and most spirited of the captains, was sent up the river with one vessel to look for better land. In twenty days he returned with no good news: at Tora the bodies of the dead were daily thrown into the river, food for the crocodiles, which became so bold in attacking the living that the enfeebled men were forbidden to approach the river-bank. At last, in despair, the men petitioned through San Martin, an unwilling spokesman, that they might return to Tamalameque and there set up a city as a base for future operations. Quesada gently but firmly declined; so far from retreating he sent out San Martin a second time to explore a large affluent, the river Opón, which descends from the eastern mountains. This scouting expedition was decisive: San Martin found cakes of salt in canoes, and in some abandoned huts more salt and many robes or blankets of coloured cotton: his men returned to the camp at Tora gaily clothed 'like savages' in bright blankets and singing a rude rhyme announcing the discovery of a 'good land'. The whole expedition now left the main river, travelling up the course of the Opon to the left towards the 'good land', but meeting the same difficulties as before, dense wood, rough ground, scarcity of food, inundated land and once a dangerous flood. When the vessels reached the limit of possible navigation, it was determined to send them back to Santa Marta with the sick, 150 in number, while Quesada pushed on with the sounder men, numbering about 200. Gallegos, commander of the vessels, took leave of his chief, promising to meet him (once more as in a fairy-tale) at the same place on the same day of the same month a year later. The promise fell through, for only twenty of those who embarked reached Santa Marta; the rest perished in an ambush, into which they were led by a baptized Indian guide whom Gallegos blindly trusted. Gallegos himself, mortified and humiliated, passed to Peru, where he did good service fighting for the King.

Quesada with his 200 men pushed on skirmishing, foraging and sometimes starving through a country which, says Mr. Cunninghame Graham, can only be traversed to-day by men well armed against people using poisoned arrows. About eleven months after leaving Santa Marta, he emerged from the forest and mountains into the upland plains and valleys cultivated by a milder and more settled people, near the spot where the city of Velez was founded three years later by one of his captains. There he reviewed his troops and found that of the 900 who had set out from Santa Marta 166 remained, and also sixty-two horses preserved by a miracle of patient care and determination. Piedrahita gives the names of 137 of the men, with notes on the later history of many.[1] They were now upon the threshold of the country rich in gold and emeralds which they sought. In the adventures which follow everything seems to happen in an inconsequent and unexpected fashion, as in some story where curiosity is constantly pricked by startling surprises: these hardy survivors, who came famished, exhausted and chilled by the change of climate, restored to vigour in fifteen days by abundance of food found in raided or deserted villages and by dyed cloth of every colour except black and white, two colours which were barred by the natives as abominable; the dangerous passage of the river Suárez (so called from one of the men), where any resistance might have destroyed them all, accom-

---

[1] Piedrahita notes of one man only that he was killed in battle, not against the Chibchas, but against their cannibal enemies the Panches.

plished without a soul in sight; babies offered to satiate those bearded strangers, supposed to be devourers of human flesh; a man and a woman bound and also a deer offered for their choice of provisions; the people falling on their faces to avoid even the sight of horses; a threatening army disappearing in one night panic-stricken when two jealous stallions galloped neighing through the Indian camp; the 'Valley of Castles' with its many villages or spacious dwellings surrounded by strong stockades from which stood up at intervals painted masts with yards like those of ships; the thin sheets of gold hung close together outside the house-doors and tinkling against one another in the wind, 'sweetest melody to the Spaniards'; a succession of valleys with strange names subjugated without the loss of a single man or horse; glory, gifts and grateful alliance won by the Spaniards through helping the people against their fierce and wicked enemies the Panches, whose custom was to devour their captives on the battlefield itself; the alarm when four Spaniards suddenly went mad, then others, and finally forty men raving; their restoration to sanity and the discovery that the Indian women seized by them as servants and concubines had given them in their food a powerful intoxicant which was commonly administered to those who were to be buried alive in human sacrifice; the visit of an Indian who swam the Magdalena from the opposite unknown shore and presented to the Spaniards encamped in the valley of Neiva fourteen golden hearts, each weighing two pounds, was rewarded with beads and scarlet cloth, repeated the journey and the gift on the following day and then appeared no more; nor is it explained how he swam so weighted; the astonishing visit to the mines where emeralds were dug from the ground before their eyes; the Zipa (hereditary king or chief) of Bogota hiding with his countless treasure in a secret forest retreat which none would reveal; the King of Tunja seized as a captive in the midst of an agitated and noisy but unresisting crowd of his vassals, his treasure thrown over the palace wall and carried away by his people. These events, which, together with exploring expeditions to outlying regions, occupied many months, cannot be told in detail, but the last two, concerning Tunja and Bogota, demand fuller narrative.

In August 1537, four or five months after entering the Chibcha country, Quesada, in order not to be burdensome to his hosts, determined to attack Tunja, whom he accused of rebellion[1] against the Christians. An Indian noble, eager to avenge the death of his father at the hands of Tunja, said to be a ferocious despot, acted as guide. As the Spaniards advanced into Tunja's valley, Indian skirmishers made a show of impeding them but dared not approach the horses, and Quesada rode on, ignoring them: as he drew nearer, messengers met him offering gifts, friendship and lodging in an outlying valley. Still he rode on up to the outer of two stockades which surrounded the royal palace: his lieutenant, drawing his sword, cleft the thongs of the closed door; and Quesada, ordering the cavalry to remain without in their saddles, dismounted and entered the precinct, twelve paces wide, between the two stockades. Followed by some of his men, he passed

---

[1] Oviedo, who had this account from the lips of Quesada, remarks indignantly that Quesada, as a lawyer, ought to have known better than to accuse of rebellion one who had never yielded obedience and had a full right to kill and drive out those who against his will entered his country where he peaceably enjoyed his lordship and liberty. Oviedo elsewhere pours scorn on the unintelligible 'requisition' which was read out as a preliminary to treating Indians as rebels.

the second fence by a door which stood open and made his way through a crowd of attendants to the inner chamber where the aged and corpulent chief, stern and commanding in aspect, sat upon a low stool in motion-less dignity: some civil speeches or gestures passed between them; but when Quesada turned to give some order to his men, Tunja's attendants attempted to raise their master's bulky frame in order to carry him away to liberty: thereupon half a dozen Spaniards rushed in, thrust aside the Indians and made Tunja prisoner in the midst of a vociferous but inactive crowd of his people.[1] The soldiers then ran in to ransack the palace, and with cries of 'Peru! Peru! another Cajamarca!' threw thin sheets of gold, ornaments and jewels upon a heap which grew until two men on opposite sides of the heap could not see one another: next day the distribution was made and the royal fifth duly set apart, but the bulk of the chieftain's treasure was never found, having been thrown over the stockade in bundles of convenient weight and carried away. One bundle, abandoned by chance, was found containing 8000 pesos, eighty pounds' weight, as much as one man could conveniently carry.

The captive chief was treated with respect and was allowed the company of his nobles, attendants and women; and when, after some weeks of living at ease in the valley, the Spaniards took their leave, Tunja was released with injunctions that in future he must be a peaceable vassal of the Emperor. Eighty of Tunja's subjects, chained together, carried the booty as his guests departed to the 'conquest' of other valleys.

But the savanna of Bogota, which they called 'the

---

[1] This account, given to Oviedo by Quesada himself, differs slightly—perhaps for reasons of modesty—from another story which represents Quesada as seizing Tunja with his own hands, aided only by his lieutenant.

Valley of Castles', was what drew them most. It is true that they had occupied the plain and ransacked the 'castles' almost unresisted, finding great store of provisions and coloured cloth and much gold and emeralds: but the King still lay in his secret fortress somewhere in the woods and the mass of his treasure was out of reach. Torture now provided guides to the King's retreat: as the Spaniards approached, there was a 'battle', or rather the usual confused flight before the lances of the horsemen; the King, flying with the rest, fell by a chance thrust, to the intense chagrin of the Spaniards, anxious to secure his person and so get possession of his treasure. But a claimant appeared, the late King's cousin and general, Sagipa (a more convenient form than Saquezazipa), who though he had no legal claim, never having borne the title of Chia always held by the Heir Apparent, was recognised by Quesada; who, like the conquerors of Mexico and Peru, seized the opportunity of becoming king-maker and so master of King and people; for obviously 160 men could not hold the many valleys of that broken country except through skilful diplomacy, backed by military pressure, friendly advances and seasonable intimidation. The 'alliance' with Sagipa was clinched by effective aid in a second campaign against the ferocious Panches and by putting out of the way two rival pretenders to the throne. But after a time Sagipa was informed that the treasure of the late 're-bellious' King belonged by right to the Spaniards, and he was placed in confinement until the treasure should be produced. For about four months he played with the cupidity of his captors by promises, excuses and postponements and by a pretended show of collecting the hidden treasure. At last he was put to the torture of the cord, in vain: at a repetition of the torture he revealed nothing, probably knowing nothing. A month later he died either from 'the delicacy of his constitution' or, as Quesada himself suspected, from worse tortures inflicted without authority by the soldiers. He was the last King of Bogota: for although the titular succession was preserved for many generations, authority was in other hands, as Quesada now showed by setting up on the savanna of Bogota the town of Santa Fe, germ of the vice-regal and (later) republican capital, so named after the city which Ferdinand and Isabel set up within sight of the towers of the Alhambra. To the country he gave the name New Kingdom of Granada, after his native place. The new Santa Fe consisted merely of a dozen huts, their number representing that of the twelve Apostles: but the paucity of dwellings indicates the obvious fact that the captains, accompanied by troops of friendly Indians, were constantly engaged on detachment duty and on visits to outlying valleys.

Towards the end of 1538, having been eighteen months in the upland country and having apparently established his authority, Quesada set out on a journey for Spain to solicit an independent appointment as Governor; for his legal position was still that of lieutenant to Pedro Lugo, Governor of Santa Marta, whose death, some two years earlier, was unknown to him. But he changed his mind and turned back to Santa Fe; fortunately so, for in February 1539 startling news came that a body of about 160 Spaniards with some horses had appeared descending from the eastern mountains: it was Federmann with the survivors of his troop, who after three years' wandering in the plains had surmounted the Cordillera. They were welcomed by Quesada as a valuable addition to strength and were supplied with food and clothing; for the new-comers, exhausted, half naked, clad in skins, with a few emaciated horses, were not dangerous rivals.

But, almost at the same time, news came that, encamped in the valley of Neiva, on the upper Magdalena, some forty-five leagues from Bogota, there was another troop of Spaniards, well clothed and supplied with arms, including muskets, and accompanied by fine well-fed horses. It was Belalcazar, coming from Popayan and Cali, as was told on page 227. Quesada's brother, Hernan Perez de Quesada, was sent to meet them. He met them three days' march from the capital; and although some haughty rhodomontades passed between some of the captains, they were soon marching together amicably to Santa Fe. The 300 pregnant sows which accompanied Belalcazar's slow movements, a most valuable gift to the country, must have been a strong inducement to peace; for Quesada's men had not tasted bacon for two years and a half. Soon there were three camps on the savanna of Bogota, each of the three numbering, according to Piedrahita, exactly 163 men—another touch resembling folk-lore. There was some uneasy apprehension lest the two new arrivals should combine to unseat Quesada; but a gift of 4000 *pesos de oro* to Federmann helped to avert a breach which would have endangered the whole conquest, and it was agreed that the question of delimitation of government should be referred to Spain. Three months were spent in rest, in hunting, in feasting and in erecting the little settlement of Santa Fe into a city with alcaldes and *regidores*: and in May 1539 Quesada, leaving his brother Hernan Perez in command at Santa Fe, departed for Spain after two years spent in winning the country, apparently without losing a man or a horse in fight, except one man killed in fighting the cannibal Panches; for the loss of man or horse is always recorded in these histories, and none is here mentioned. One man known as Fat John (Juan Gordo) had been unjustly hanged on a mistaken charge of looting, for Quesada's orders were strict that the Indians should be kindly treated and won by peaceful methods; three or four had died in exploring the torrid valley of Neiva: thus Piedrahita's estimate of 163 survivors out of 166 is only two or three in excess of the fact. Evidently the fighting had not been destructive except to the Indians: but the preservation of men and horses is a striking proof of Quesada's care and capacity. In one respect his conquest was singular and indeed unique: unlike Cortes and Pizarro, he had been completely cut off from the outside world for nearly three years, including the march up the Magdalena valley. During all that time he had received no reinforcements, no weapons, munitions or provisions: he finished his work with the same men with whom he had begun it, not one more.

The three captains, rich in gold and emeralds, rode out together from Santa Fe traversing a now pacified country to the banks of the Magdalena, where a vessel had been built. They travelled to Cartagena in fourteen days and thence to Spain: Belalcazar went to Court, presented his suit and was appointed Governor of Popayan: Federmann trod the royal antechambers in vain: Quesada was strangely slow in visiting the Court and pressing his claim. His services were ignored, and Alonso de Lugo, in spite of his former misconduct, was appointed Governor of New Granada: not a happy appointment, for he proved to be anything but a benefactor to the kingdom. Thenceforth royal governors were regularly sent out, and in 1549 an Audiencia, a supreme tribunal and an administrative council, was set up in Santa Fe: proof that it was now the capital of an organised and considerable kingdom, not dependent on the Government of Panama. In the same ship with the *oidores* or magistrates of the Audiencia, Quesada returned to the country, having at last obtained some slight reward for his services; he was appointed Marshal of the New Kingdom of Granada (probably little more than an honorary military title) with the right to build a fortress of which he should be paid Governor for life —an illusory privilege which he never exercised. A more modest but more substantial appointment was that of *regidor* (town-councillor) for life with precedence of his colleagues and a salary, a post which must have meant frequent election to the important annual office of alcalde: he received also a *repartimiento* (that is to say *encomienda*) of Indians after some delay due to the discussions in Spain concerning the future legal status of the *encomienda* system. He lived to eighty years enjoying the respect and trust of the citizens and ready to serve them in any emergency, devoting his energies in later years to the search for El Dorado and charging Berrio, who married Quesada's niece (Quesada was never married), to pursue that quest 'to the utmost of his fortune and his life', as Raleigh relates.

The conquest of Bogota and its neighbourhood was the decisive step in winning for the Crown of Spain the great country which now forms the republic of Colombia; but obviously it was not the only step. In 1532 the city of Cartagena was founded by a Spanish caballero of a fine type named Pedro de Heredia; who, although like other governors he made war on all 'rebels' and sold slaves in the Antilles to provide men and munitions, won the friendship and confidence of the neighbouring tribes in the country where Ojeda had been routed and La Cosa had been slain. Heredia in 1536—the same year in which Quesada set out from Santa Marta—'sent a bold, able and valiant captain' named Francisco César on an expedition to the interior. 'For ten months Cesar travelled through a difficult country of dense forests, he and his men suffering great hardships. Their horses were without shoes and themselves so worn out that they only kept the form of men, when at last they reached a very high range of mountains called Abibe which they crossed and came to the valley of Goaca, where they fought a hard battle with the Indians . . . the Spaniards found there a temple of the devil and took 30,000 pesos from a tomb and heard that in the valley there were many more sepulchres like the one which they had found. But as Francisco Cesar had so few Spaniards with him and the horses being unshod were useless, he resolved to go back. It pleased God that by the route that had taken them nine or ten months in coming they returned in seventeen days. They came out at the city of San Sebastián, the port of Uraba, whence the news soon reached Cartegena.' So writes Cieza, one of the soldiers. Heredia was unjustly deprived of his government by a lawyer named Vadillo who had been sent out to enquire into his administration. In order to shake off the consequent odium and win credit, Vadillo himself led out a second expedition, which in 1538 reached Cali and joined the forces of Aldana, as was related in Chapter XVIII. The same chapter tells how Robledo in his progress northward met parties coming from Cartagena and founded the city of Cartago, so called in compliment to them. Cartagena with its sheltered harbour and better access to the Magdalena replaced Santa Marta as the principal port of New Granada; and it was chiefly from Cartagena, partly also from Buenaventura on the Pacific coast, that the gradual process went on of winning that rich but extremely difficult country and subjugating its many hostile tribes, a process carried on during many generations not by signal strokes of conquest but by slow and inconspicuous penetration. But the Conquistador of New Granada was Gonzalo Jimenez de Quesada.

CHAPTER XXVI

THE RIVER PLATE

The crown of the Spanish King is the orbit of the sun.

BALTASAR GRACIAN

Has Heaven reserved, in pity to the poor,
No pathless waste or undiscovered shore?
No secret island in the boundless main?
No peaceful desert yet unclaimed by Spain?

SAMUEL JOHNSON

AT the mid-sixteenth century, within sixty years of Columbus' first voyage, the wave of Spanish conquest in America had in the main spent itself. The Spanish empire, extending through sixty-seven degrees of latitude, had attained form and cohesion. Two viceroyalties had been set up holding sway over wide dominions: the lesser kingdoms and provinces were ruled by Captains-General and Governors subordinate to the Viceroys; and all the provinces were divided into districts under magistrates entitled Corregidor or Alcalde Mayor. Audiencias, which were at once judicial tribunals and administrative councils, held their sessions in the principal capitals; a chain of municipalities, each having a territorial jurisdiction extending to that of its neighbours, formed the basis of the whole fabric, and the course of trade between Spain and the Spanish kingdoms beyond the Ocean had been regulated for purposes of security and of fiscal control.

Yet one phase of conquest, the greatest of all in its late and unforeseen results, was still in its first stage; that is to say the conquest, or rather the slow and laborious occupation, in the course of two generations, of the River Plate region, with its northern forests, its western mountains and, above all, its vast plains stretching far into the South Temperate Zone—to-day one of the richest and choicest parts of the New World, marked out by fertility and climate to be the seat of a great civilisation of European type. That region was gradually penetrated from three distinct starting-points, Peru, Chile and the Atlantic coast. The natural gate to the country is the immense estuary of the second in magnitude among South American rivers. It has been already told in Chapter X how in 1516 Juan de Solis, endeavouring to pass that gate, met a tragic end. Ten years passed before the attempt of Solis was followed up by Sebastian Cabot (Gaboto in Spanish form), Venetian by birth, long domiciled in England and now in the service of Spain as successor to Solis in the office of Piloto Mayor—a better geographer than captain, says Oviedo; a judgement which is endorsed by Señor Medina in his exhaustive documentary examination of this voyage.

When, after the arrival of the *Victoria* with her cargo of cloves, a Board of Trade for spices was set up at Corunna and Loaisa sailed thence for the Moluccas, some rich merchants of Seville, eager to share this prospectively lucrative trade, contributed funds for an expedition through Magellan's Strait to the Moluccas. A royal capitulation was duly obtained with the unusual addition of a royal grant of money; and Gaboto sailed in April 1526 from the Guadalquivir with four ships and 250 men 'for the Moluccas and other islands already discovered and also in search of Tarsis, Ophir, Oriental Cathay and Cipango . . . to barter and load his ships with gold, silver, precious stones, pearls, drugs, spices, silks, brocades and other precious things'.[1] But during the voyage there was much distrustful grumbling about the command: the ships were not victualled for the long voyage to the Moluccas: accordingly, hoping to find wealth and royal favour by richer discoveries inland, Gaboto marooned four officers on a Brazilian island in order to be free from any check on his action, and sailed up the 'Rio de Solis'. A vessel which he sent up the river Uruguay was wrecked and many of the crew were killed by Indians; a small fort was built on the Uruguayan coast, but later, being found untenable, was abandoned. Gaboto continued his difficult course up the delta of the river Paraná, and at the mouth of the river Carcaraná, now known as the Río Tercero, about thirty miles to the north of the present city of Rosario, he built and garrisoned a fort. Continuing his voyage up-stream he got from the riparian Indians some objects of silver, whence the river received its second high-sounding name of Rio de la Plata, 'River of the Silver', a delusive title, for its shores yield no precious metals, though rich to-day in produce of a less precarious kind: the Indians, questioned about the silver, pointed westward and talked of the 'White King' (the Inca): the silver had in fact come from Peru and was the first specimen of the Inca treasure to reach Europe. The exploration of these immense water-ways, which lead to the innermost recesses of the continent, was an achievement preliminary to later occupation; but the spending of three

[1] The words are from Antonio de Herrera, written with a touch of satire unusual with him.

years in river navigation meant that Gaboto lingered in the vain hope of justifying his proceedings by some rich discovery. At last, having lost many men in skirmishes with Indians, he abandoned the search, passing on his way down-stream the ruins of his fort, destroyed by the Indians and all its garrison slain: the broken walls, known as Gaboto's Tower, long remained a landmark in that flat country to later explorers. Gaboto returned to Spain with half of the men who had sailed with him nearly four years earlier.

Yet his highly coloured reports, the sight of the Peruvian silver, the excitement raised by Pizarro's discoveries, the hope of finding another way to the opulent shores of the South Sea and, in addition, the rivalry of the Portuguese from Brazil, led to the despatch of one of the greatest expeditions which had yet sailed from Spain. A German soldier named Schmidel, who served throughout this enterprise, wrote an excellent account of it some years later in his own language: a translation was published by the Hakluyt Society in 1891. Pedro de Mendoza, a Gentleman of the Royal Household, a man of rank and influence, said to have been enriched by the sack of Rome although he had never held military command, was commissioned to settle the River Plate region, to found three fortresses, to cross the continent and occupy 200 leagues of the Pacific coast to the south of the grant made to Almagro in the same year. Not the Atlantic coasts, but the shores of the South Sea were in men's minds, and no one thought of obstacles in the way, 1000 miles of prairie and, beyond them, the highest mountain range in the New World.

Profuse promises and hopes brought eager recruits, among them many members of noble houses; and in August 1535 a fleet of a dozen well-equipped ships great and small, carrying 100 horses and mares as well as the army, set sail from the Guadalquivir for the river Plate. Many men deserted in the Canaries; others disappeared on the coast of Brazil and two ships turned back. Moreover a crime stained the beginning of the enterprise: Osorio, the second-in-command, having incurred the suspicious jealousy of the commander, was stabbed to death, at his command, by Juan de Ayolas, Mendoza's favourite officer, while the fleet was refitting on the coast of Brazil.

After a four months' voyage, the ships reached the great estuary, probably carrying between 1200 and 1500 men, including over 100 Germans, subjects of the Emperor. Coasting along the low inconspicuous southern shore, Mendoza chose a site for a city on the edge of the immense grassy plain which stretches thence to the Andes: within the enclosure of a mud wall huts were built of mud and thatched with reeds—for the plain yields neither stone nor timber—to form the city of Santa María de Buenos Aires. The only inhabitants of the vast plain were scanty tribes of nomadic barbarians, sheltering in rude movable huts or booths of hide, living on fish and game, raising no crops and owning no domestic animals, for neither cattle, horses nor sheep are indigenous to the country. The neighbouring Querandi Indians were friendly and for a time brought presents of game and fish, but when they wearied of feeding these strange people, the Spaniards, expecting to be supported by obedient vassals, demanded supplies; and finally, on Corpus Christi Day 1536, six months after arrival, Mendoza sent an armed force to chastise these audacious natives: the Spanish horsemen, attacking the Indian encampment, were entangled in a swamp; Mendoza's brother Diego fell by the *bolea-*

dora, the typical weapon of the Pampa, and several others were killed. The Querandis, now summoning other tribes to their aid, attacked in thousands. Fiery missiles burnt the thatched huts and some of the ships anchored near the shore; but the real enemy, within the mud wall, was starvation followed by pestilence and once at least by cannibal horrors, when the corpses of three soldiers, hanged for killing and eating a horse, provided food for famishing men. Ships sent up the river in search of food brought some relief, but not before half the searchers themselves had died of hunger. Another ship despatched to the coast of Brazil brought back some food: but these were makeshifts, and Mendoza, after leading some of his much diminished company to a site higher up the river, sailed homewards about the middle of 1537 to die on the voyage from the ailment which afflicted so many of the Conquistadores, leaving as Lieutenant-Governor the most devoted of his captains Juan de Ayolas, who had already departed up the river with orders to seek the rich regions of the west. Ayolas having sailed northward to latitude 25° S., found on the left bank of the river Paraguay a tribe of Guarani Indians living in villages and raising crops of maize, people who after brief resistance proved friendly or submissive. Here on a bluff overlooking a bay sheltered from the broad and rapid current, a stockaded fort was set up, Santa María de Asunción. Leaving a small garrison in the fort, Ayolas sailed north far into the tropics, plunged westward into the pathless forest and there perished with all his company. A year or so later the post which he had established at Asuncion was erected into a little city with alcaldes and *regidores,* the earliest permanent settlement in the River Plate and for eighty years, until 1620, capital of all that region.

Ayolas had named as his deputy Martínez Irala, who had been active in this pioneering work, a typical fighting adventurer, ambitious, self-indulgent, imperious and unscrupulous but a capable and inspiring leader. He was now elected Governor by virtue of a royal edict which recognised the need of local initiative in those distant lands by empowering the settlers to fill any vacancy pending the royal decision. Irala contrived to retain the command, with a brief stormy interval and some sanguinary faction fights, until his death in 1557, when, like a true patriarch of the young community and a true South American Dictator, he nominated his son-in-law as his successor. Irala extended his authority by war and by alliances in a succession of campaigns, pursued with varied fortune: he succeeded in taming some of the fierce fighting tribes of the north and even made some impression on the savage forest region of the Chaco beyond the river; he satisfied his loyal followers by gifts of rich *encomiendas*, encouraging them to make captives in war and to follow his own example by taking Indian concubines. In 1541 the remnant of the settlers at Buenos Aires were brought to Asuncion: 'Buenos Aires was abandoned because there was no service of Indians'. The Spanish settlers were not colonists but Conquistadores expecting to live as a dominant aristocracy supported by Indian serfs: where Indian labour was wanting, the immigrants starved.

In the following year the population of Asuncion was largely increased by the arrival of nearly 400 Spaniards led by Alvar Nuñez Cabeza de Vaca, survivor of the expedition mentioned on page 109, who had been appointed Governor by the Crown. His four months' march overland through unknown country from the coast of Brazil to Paraguay with 200 of his

men (the rest going round by water) was an extraordinary achievement, for there was no fighting with
Indians and only one man was lost, drowned in the
river by accident. But a year after his arrival this well-
intentioned Governor, who strove to introduce a more
civil administration than Irala's dictatorship, to protect
the Indians and to restore the abandoned settlement at
Buenos Aires, was arrested by Irala's followers, was
confined in a mud hut for eight months and was then
shipped to Spain as a prisoner.

Five years later settlement from the Atlantic came
into touch with Peruvian or Pacific conquest when a
party from Asuncion traversed the forests of the Chaco,
emerged upon the Peruvian plateau near Chuquisaca
and reached Cuzco on a mission to La Gasca.

Except among Spaniards, where nothing surprises,
it would be strange that for thirty-six years the only
stable settlement in the River Plate region stood in the
centre of the continent nearly 1000 miles from the sea.
Still more anomalous is the fact that the Pampa region,
which faces naturally towards the Atlantic, was in great
part penetrated by Spaniards coming from the Pacific,
some descending from the Peruvian plateau, others
even crossing the Cordillera from the west and adding
a great slice of the Pampa to the kingdom of Chile: this
double movement from Peru and from Chile is a continuation of the far-reaching enterprise of Pizarro and
Almagro, which in its last southern sweep touched the
river Plate where its lower course gives easy access to
the Atlantic. The men of Peru did as much as the men
of Paraguay to win the country: but the penetration
from the north-west, not guided by any natural feature
such as the great river, is the story of small groups of
frontiersmen in unknown lands advancing, driven back,

advancing again; living on the country wherever they went, sometimes in abundance, sometimes in misery of hunger and even of thirst; winning little or nothing for themselves—for it was no land of gold and silver or suddenly acquired wealth—but finally winning wide provinces and profitable lands for the Crown of Castile.

It has been related on page 254 how Vaca de Castro, to relieve the plethora of warriors, gave a concession for an *entrada* to the south; three associates combined as leaders, contributing all that they possessed; Diego de Rojas, who after service in Nicaragua, had proved himself a valiant and trusted captain in the wars of Peru and had recently led an *entrada* into the *montaña*; Felipe de Gutiérrez, a Gentleman of the Royal Household, an honourable man who had been Governor of Veragua and had there led a disastrous *entrada* into the savage forest, in which he had not distinguished himself as a commander; the third was Nicolás de Heredia who had fought for the young Almagro and was threatened with severe penalties but, upon the intercession of his friend Diego de Rojas, had been let off with a fine and so enabled to join this new enterprise.

They descended from the plateau of Charcas at Tupiza—about 200 men[1] with some horses and many attendant Indians—into the wooded valley of Salta and the region comprehensively but vaguely known as the Province of Tucuman, in three divisions, Rojas in chief command going first with 125 men and bearing the brunt of the early fighting with forty horse. For nearly

[1] Don Roberto Levillier in his book on the conquest of Tucuman gives the names of 121, including two women: Catalina Enciso, mistress of Gutierrez; and Maria López, who on one occasion, taking sword and shield, remained to guard some captive Indian chiefs while all the men were out fighting.

four years, 1543–46, they marched and encamped and
fought, shifting their ground frequently in search of
food but hoping somehow to find the fabled 'Trapa-
landa, the City of the Caesars', a rich and civilised city
supposed to exist somewhere in the far south—a fable
which lingered on until late in the eighteenth century.
Among the natives, who, unlike the nomads of the
Pampa, were tillers of the soil living in villages and
having some contact with the Inca culture, the Spaniards found some allies but many enemies. Rojas, dying
of a poisoned arrow—although a momentary rumour
agitated the camp that he had been poisoned by the
mistress of Gutierrez, 'La Enciso', who tended his
wound—bequeathed the command, in spite of the
rights of his two colleagues, to a spirited young soldier
named Francisco de Mendoza, who, having arrested
Gutierrez and sent him back under escort to Peru,
reached a signal goal in the history of the Conquest:
guided by the course of the river Carcarana (or Tercero), he led a party south-westward across the plain
to Gaboto's Tower and the margin of the river Plate:
here to his astonishment he was greeted in Spanish by
Indians plying their canoes on the great river, who told
him of Irala and the Spanish city of Asuncion. Finding
it impossible to travel thither northward along the
bank flooded by the summer rains, Mendoza turned
back to his main camp, having for a moment met the
stream of conquest coming from the Atlantic.

Tragedy followed: Mendoza, in revenge for some
affront, was murdered in his tent; and at last the men,
having failed to find the rich habitations which they
sought, were led back by Heredia up the steep pass to
southern Peru, where they were caught up into the
war against Gonzalo Pizarro, and their leader, with

some of his followers, perished at the hands of Carbajal, the 'Demon of the Andes'. Yet the 'men of the *entrada*', as they were always called, had done much in those four years: they had prepared the way for others through lands now forming several provinces of the Argentine Republic and had traced a path across the continent.

Their work was followed up when Nuñez del Prado, as is related on page 270, was despatched by La Gasca at the end of 1549 with orders to make a settlement (*poblar*) in the newly explored region: Prado with no more than seventy men, including some of the 'men of the *entrada*', descended into the plains and established a city which after several changes of site—for the material frame of these civic communities was at first unsubstantial—took form later as Santiago del Estero, the oldest existing city in the Argentine Republic. Hardly had he installed the civic authorities when a rival and stronger Spanish force appeared in the neighbourhood, led by the masterful Villagra on his way to Chile but deviating considerably to the east, evidently with deliberate intention. Prado was obliged to submit to the authority of Valdivia, who appointed the vigorous warrior Aguirre to rule the province of Tucuman. Aguirre, from his headquarters on the Pacific at Serena, crossed the Cordillera, pacified by force or persuasion the surrounding Indians, and firmly re-established the city of Santiago del Estero, bringing cattle, sheep and farm-seeds across the mountains from his own estate on the Pacific coast and spending his fortune on his province with noble generosity: a true South American Dictator, he mounted a cannon on his house, repudiated all authority but his own and, an anti-clerical before his time, declared that there was no pope or bishop in the country but himself. He won the natives by martial rigour and by truth: 'Heaven may fail you', he told them, 'and earth may fail you, but not my word': any rising was ruthlessly suppressed, but Aguirre never broke his word to those who submitted: thus his city became the capital of a wide district where peace was imposed or accepted.

Although the defeat and death of Valdivia at the end of 1553 and the banishment of Aguirre to Peru brought a temporary set-back, two new cities were founded, one of them named Londres in honour of Philip, King-Consort of England, and his English wife Mary Tudor: both cities perished in 1560 in a widespread Indian revolt provoked by a blow inflicted by some insolent soldier on a friendly or 'pacified' Indian chief: only Santiago del Estero, hard pressed but unvanquished, escaped fire and slaughter.

Recovery followed: in 1563 Aguirre, now an old man but still vigorous, returned as Governor of Tucuman, no longer merely Lieutenant-Governor, for Tucuman was now a distinct province separated from Chile.[1] His energy brought new vigour and also a great stride in advance through the foundation of the city of San Miguel de Tucumán in a fertile plain to the south of the present city of Tucuman. But after three years Aguirre, accused of heretical talk, was suspended from his government: he was allowed to resume it in 1569, but a year later was finally removed and spent the last five years of a long life among his family on his estate at Serena.

[1] On the other hand the men of Chile about the same time (1561–62), by the foundation of the cities of Mendoza and San Juan, created the province of Cuyo, which although geographically belonging to the Pampa or Argentine region, was regarded for two centuries as part of Chile: see page 289.

His work was continued by his successor Jerónimo de Cabrera, 'a person noble, affable, with other good qualities of a caballero', who accomplished another great step towards spanning the continent when in July 1573 he inaugurated the city of Córdoba, 300 miles south of Santiago del Estero, on the edge of the forest country, at the foot of a range of wooded hills, looking out upon the immense grassy plain which stretches thence to the Atlantic and to the Rio Negro. Two months later Cabrera led a party to the bank of the great river, not far from Gaboto's Tower, being resolved to set up a city and thus extend the Peruvian dominion to the North Sea: having reached the river, he was astonished at finding vessels manned by Spaniards moored to the bank and a horde of hostile Indians approaching them: the assailants fled at the sight of Cabrera's armed horsemen, who—so they said —thus saved the lives of their chance-met countrymen in the ships. These were a group of sixty-six Spaniards from Asuncion, of whom fifty-nine were Creoles (*criollos*), that is to say Europeans born in the country, commanded by Juan de Garay, a Biscayan captain who held office in that city and was seeking a site for a new settlement. From the deck of his ship Garay conversed with Cabrera seated in his saddle, the two captains greeting one another with a certain jealous reserve; for although the two streams of conquest from Atlantic and Pacific had met, they had also clashed: but the conflict was eventually settled in a common-sense manner, all the river region being assigned to the men of Paraguay, while the city of Cordoba received a large jurisdiction in the interior. Two months later Garay set up the city of Santa Fe, about 600 miles south of Asuncion, as a link between that city and the sea:

the neighbouring Indians were, in part at least, subdued and distributed in *encomienda* to his followers.

But the conquest was still incomplete as long as the shores of the estuary were not secured by Spanish settlement: several attempts had been made to restore Buenos Aires, among them an imposing expedition from Spain, which went to pieces through a series of disasters. The work was reserved for Juan de Garay, who sailed southwards a second time from Asuncion in 1580 upon the mission which has immortalised his name, conducting sixty Spaniards, of whom fifty were Creoles, together with 200 Guarani families. Near the site of Mendoza's ruined settlement he set up the pillar of justice in the King's name with the usual solemn ceremonies, and thus inaugurated El Puerto de Santa Maria de Buenos Aires 'necessary and convenient for the good of all this Government and that of Tucuman'. The central plaza was marked out with sites for church and town-hall: streets were traced from it at right angles upon the chess-board pattern prescribed by authority throughout the Spanish Indies; two alcaldes and ten *regidores* were nominated to constitute the *cabildo*: the sixty men became *vecinos*, every man receiving a building site within the city and land outside for tillage and pasture, undertaking in return to defend the city with horse and arms. Garay, leading his three-score armed horsemen, drove the Indians in rout and taught them to keep their distance. He then distributed sixty *encomiendas*: some of these grants, consisting of Guarani Indians living on the banks and islands of the Parana, were of some value until fatal epidemics swept away the *Indios repartidos*: other grants, consisting of the indomitable nomadic Pampa Indians, were no more than paper promises.

Returning northward after three years spent in this work, Garay was caught asleep in the wilds and killed by Indians near the city of Santa Fe which he had founded. But he had done his work and met the fate of a true backwoodsman and Conquistador, a happier end than that of his rival Cabrera, who was put to death on a trumped-up accusation by his successor in the Government of Cordoba.

The second foundation in 1580 of Buenos Aires—to-day a city of over two million inhabitants—is the culmination of conquest in Tucuman and the River Plate: indeed it is rather the result than a part of the Spanish conquest; for the settlements on the Pampa differed from most of the Spanish settlements in America in that they were true colonies, not being supported by the labour of an Indian peasantry. The *vecinos* of Buenos Aires were stock-farmers who had to look after their cattle, to find labour as best they could and to defend themselves against hostile Indians; they were colonists, just as the British settlers in North America were colonists.

With the foundation of Buenos Aires the vast semicircle of Spanish dominion in South America was complete: the line of empire, in parts broad and solid, in parts narrow but nowhere interrupted, extended from Paria westward to the Pacific, thence southward along the Andes through New Granada, Quito, Peru and Chile, eastward across the Pampa to the river Plate estuary and from the estuary nearly 1000 miles northward up the river beyond Asuncion. This line enclosed an interior frontier measuring 7000 miles, everywhere bordered by savagery, a frontier which in the nature of things could not remain immovable, as the experience of every empire shows: yet armed conquest paused before the end of the sixteenth century, and early in the following century was forbidden by royal decree, a decree which was generally obeyed. It is true that the intermittent but endless Araucanian war kept soldiers busy in the south of Chile: but defence, pacification and expansion along the immense interior frontier were chiefly effected by *conquista evangélica*, *conquista espiritual*, the work of Christian missionaries.

Upon the long northern frontier of New Spain, infested by fierce marauding tribes—Apaches, Comanches and others—conditions were different and required an administration largely military in character, in which defence, as always upon every imperial frontier, meant gradual advance of that frontier, but henceforth gradual and cautious advance under the control of established authority, no longer the *entradas* of individual adventurers seeking glory and gold: indeed the advance of Spanish authority northward through California was in great part also the work of missionaries. Thus from 1580 for more than two centuries the prevailing note of the Spanish dominion in both American continents is peace.

NOTE.—The number of Pedro de Mendoza's expedition is variously stated: Schmidel's estimate—2650—is merely a wild reminiscent guess; Oviedo, who saw the muster of the men at Seville and afterwards spoke with the crew of one of the deserting ships at Santo Domingo, says that 2000 sailed from Seville and 1500 reached Buenos Aires: the latter number is confirmed by a letter (printed by Mr. Cunninghame Graham) from a lady who accompanied her husband on the expedition; she says that 1500 reached Buenos Aires and 1000 died. A poem by one Padre Miranda (also quoted by Mr. Cunninghame Graham) says, 'Out of 2000 not 200 of us were left'; since the 200 is obviously a rhetorical round number, the 2000 need not be taken as historical. Herrera, not an original authority but a careful compiler, writes half a century later that the press to join the expedition at Seville was so great that the ships hastily put to sea with 800 men; possibly he does not include the sailors. The late M. Paul Groussac, a learned exponent of Argentine history, argues from probability, from the capacity of the ships and from the terms of Mendoza's capitulation that the number did not exceed 800. On the other hand the contemporary evidence of Oviedo and of the lady's letter cannot be ignored. The impression conveyed by the accounts is that there was big talk at Seville and frequent mention of 'Two thousand men!', that in fact a much smaller number left Seville and that considerably less than 1500 reached the river Plate.

CHAPTER XXVII

SPAIN THE PRECURSOR

*I like a plantation on a pure soil; that is where people are not dis-
planted to the end to plant in others.* FRANCIS BACON

*Our principal intention and will has always been to preserve and
augment the numbers of the Indians.* CHARLES V

IN viewing the work of Spaniards in America,
thought naturally turns to the later work of the
English farther north. Points of contrast at once occur.
Since the first permanent Spanish settlement dates
from 1493 and the first permanent English settlement
from 1607, both countries reproducing themselves in
the New World, the England so reproduced was the
England of the Stuarts and the Commonwealth, whereas
the Spain so reproduced was that of the Catholic
sovereigns and of Charles V. Spanish settlement coincided with the period of adventurous exploration:
English settlement followed the period of adventure.
When the Spanish Conquistadores are accused of inhumanity and inefficiency, this difference of time must
be remembered: all that has been said—in the first
instance by Spaniards—about that inhumanity and
inefficiency is true, but not the whole truth. It may be
noted that during the same period the English too were
pursuing conquest and colonisation—in Ireland: and
one would hesitate to claim that their work was more
efficient or more humane.

Thus the two movements differed in the world which they brought with them; they differed still more in the world which they found: the English found no Mexico, no Peru, no Bogota.

But there was also a difference of theory: 'In Spanish America', says E. G. Bourne, 'the natives from the start were regarded as the subjects of the Crown of Spain, whereas in English America they were generally treated as independent nations—friends or enemies as the case might be. . . . Daniel Denton in 1670 quaintly observes: "it hath been generally observed that where the English come to settle, a divine hand makes way for them by removing or cutting off the Indians either by wars one with another or by some raging mortal disease".' The Spaniards on the other hand constantly deplored the depopulation which they caused; they wished to rule a subjugated population. The Spaniards were conquerors who spread in little groups over a vast area: the English were colonists who made homes for themselves on the margin of the Atlantic. Yet theory and method were modified by circumstances; the Spaniards had to deal with peoples and tribes differing widely in culture, and where the natives did not fit into the Spanish scheme, they disappeared: the Pampa Indians have travelled the same road as the 'redskins' of New England and Virginia.

Spain was the precursor; the English leaders of thought and action, Hakluyt and Raleigh, repeatedly point to Spanish example. Raleigh in his *History of the World* turns aside to write: 'I cannot forbear to commend the patient virtue of the Spaniards. We seldom or never find that any nation hath endured so many misadventures and miseries as the Spaniards have done in their Indian discoveries; yet persisting in their enterprises with invincible constancy, they have annexed to their kingdom so many goodly provinces as bury the remembrance of all dangers past. Tempest and shipwrecks, famine, overthrows, mutinies, heat and cold, pestilence and all manner of diseases both old and new, together with extreme poverty and want of all things needful, have been the enemies wherewith every one of their most noble discoverers at one time or another hath encountered. Many years had passed over their heads in the search of not so many leagues; yea more than one or two have spent their labour, their wealth and their lives in search of a golden kingdom without getting further notice of it than what they had at their first setting forth; all which notwithstanding, the third and fourth and fifth undertakers have not been disheartened. Surely they are worthily rewarded with those treasuries and paradises which they enjoy; and well they deserve to hold them quietly, if they hinder not the like virtue in others, which perhaps will not be found.'

APPENDIX

I. THE SPICE TRADE

GOLD, slaves and spices were the three valuable commodities which Columbus sought and claimed to have found on reaching the Antilles. The third of these objects of trade—spices—demands brief explanation in order to elucidate many passages in this volume. Before the modern rotation of crops and cultivation of turnips provided feeding for cattle during the winter, all the beef for consumption in Northern Europe during many months was killed in November and salted: in order to add flavour to this hard diet, there was an immense and hungry demand for spices, particularly pepper and cloves. Moreover in the Middle Ages, possessing no potatoes, fewer vegetables than those grown to-day, less materials for 'second course', little rich pasture and no pedigree cattle, spices were lavishly used in every well-provided kitchen throughout the year. Besides this, tea, coffee and cocoa being unknown, sugar an expensive luxury and tolerable wine a rich man's indulgence, there was an unlimited consumption of condiments in order to add pungency to thin beer, sour wine and various home-made beverages. Moreover the shelves of every druggist's shop and the cupboard of every physician were furnished with jars of spices, whose fragrance and flavour gave confidence both to practitioner and to patient that they possessed powerful medicinal virtues. In the narrow unsavoury streets of medieval cities, cramped within a binding circle of walls, often visited by infectious fevers and occasionally by plague, strong perfumes were a constant necessity, both for personal comfort and as a supposed guard against pestilence. Accordingly throughout Northern Europe, particularly in England, Germany and the Netherlands, there was an immense demand for pepper, cloves, cinnamon, mace, nutmeg, ginger, benzoin, galanga, cardamom, cassia, aloes and aloe-wood, incense, camphor, sandalwood, aromatic products of the southern and eastern Asiatic lands, the islands of the Indian Ocean and the Malay Archipelago.

In the ages following the fall of Rome the wealth of Constantinople was largely due to the trade in spices gathered from Oriental lands to the shores of the Bosphorus and distributed thence with great profit throughout Europe. Venice, succeeding Constantinople as emporium for the spice trade, 'held the gorgeous East in fee': in the Indian Ocean, Arab traders carried their cargoes of spice either to the Persian Gulf, thence to be conveyed many weeks' journey overland by caravan to Levantine ports, or else sailed up the Red Sea to Suez: thence the spices were borne by trains of camels to Alexandria, where Venetian ships awaited them.

This costly mode of transport greatly increased the price of the goods. Accordingly the Portuguese discovery of an uninterrupted sea route round the Cape of Good Hope to India and the East Indies at the beginning of the sixteenth century was nothing less than a commercial revolution. When news reached Venice that Portuguese ships had sailed to India and back to Lisbon, the city of the Lagoons was filled with dismay. Lisbon displaced Venice as the distributing centre for the spice trade and soon became the busiest port in Western Europe. Two-thirds of the cargoes brought by the Portuguese carracks from the East consisted of pepper, which could be found in India and Ceylon: but cloves—a more rare and precious product which loves a tropical insular climate—had to be sought more than 3000 miles farther to the east in a group of islands, the Moluccas, lying close to the Equator. The capture of the city of Malacca in 1511 brought the Portuguese nearer to what they sought: but they were determined to make themselves masters of the Moluccas and of a monopolised trade in cloves. The Spaniards cherished the same ambition and also desired generally to open up a direct maritime trade in spices independent of the Portuguese. This desire—this anxious view fixed upon the Far East—colours the whole history of the Spanish conquest in America. The rivalry between the two Peninsular nations for the Spice Trade is briefly told in Chapters X and XI.

II. MONEY

During the period of the conquest there was little or no coined money in the Spanish Indies. In Peru there was none, except rude disks forged by the conquerors, until a mint was founded at Lima in 1565. Coin was scarce in the Peninsula, where payments were often made by cutting off pieces from a gold chain; nor did Spain send gold and silver to the Indies. Thus throughout the Conquest payments were made by weight, and scales or steel-yards were carried everywhere. The unit of weight was the *castellano*, more commonly called *peso de oro* ('piece of gold' or rather 'weight of gold') and often simply *peso*, which, as the context shows, always means the *peso de oro* (*castellano*), not to be confused with the later silver *peso* or dollar (*peso de a ocho* or 'piece of eight') of about half the value. The *castellano* or *peso de oro* had been a coin, containing one-hundredth part of a pound weight of fine gold (the Spanish pound = 1·014 lb. avoirdupois). When the *castellano* ceased to be coined in 1497, it still remained the unit of weight in payment: that the Conquistadores consciously thought of the *castellano* as a weight appears from such frequent phrases as 'fourteen golden hearts which weighed 2700 *castellanos*'. Thus all payments were weighed out in bars of gold or in golden vessels and ornaments or else in equivalent weights of silver. Jerez, Pizarro's secretary, writes: 'The *peso de oro* is as much as a *castellano*: each *peso* is commonly sold for 450 *maravedis*'.[1]

The *castellano*, containing about one-sixth of an ounce of gold, was nearly equal to two-fifths of a pre-war sovereign (eight shillings) or two pre-war U.S. dollars. But its buying value is difficult to estimate: in Spain about 1500 the *castellano* probably went as far as £5 or £6 pre-war: fifty years later it was

[1] The *maravedi* was a measure of value derived from an obsolete coin, 60 *maravedis* being rather more than a shilling pre-war. This again makes the *castellano* nearly equal to eight shillings or two dollars, pre-war. Philip II, somewhat later, claimed two dollars as the equivalent of the *castellano* in the payment of royal dues.

worth much less—perhaps £4—owing to the influx of precious metals from America. But in the Indies its value varied greatly and diminished with distance from Spain and consequent scarcity of European goods, with the emergencies of war and with any sudden access of treasure. The careless lavishness of the soldiers and the difficulty of cutting off small sums from bars of gold tended to high prices. Jerez, after describing the treasure of Atahualpa, writes: 'The usual price of a horse was 2500 *pesos*, and they could not be had at that price . . . a pair of boots or of breeches cost 30 or 40 *pesos*, a cloak 100 or 120, a sword 40 or 50. . . . I gave for half an ounce of damaged saffron, 12 *pesos* . . . a debtor would give a lump of gold without weighing it, careless whether it were double the debt; and debtors went from house to house with an Indian loaded with gold, seeking their creditors.' Obviously these prices were not normal: but normality is difficult to find in the doings of the Conquistadores.

A mint was established in Mexico in 1535 and a few years later was coining the silver *peso* or dollar, which became the monetary unit in New Spain about the middle of the sixteenth century, and later (with some exceptions) in Peru also.

III. ENCOMIENDAS

In these pages the technical term *encomienda*, 'a trust or charge or feudal fief', has been generally used, rather than the more usual synonym, *repartimiento de Indios* or simply *repartimiento*, 'an allotment of Indians'. *Repartimiento* is an everyday term for any distribution—of land, houses, food, gifts, detachments of troops, anything. Like our word 'allotment', it may mean either the act of assigning or the thing assigned; and in this latter sense it is used as a convenient synonym for the technical term *encomienda* which implied the obligation of defending and instructing the Indians and of serving the King with horse and arms. In the royal decree of 1509 which sanctions the system, the words *repartir*, 'to allot Indians', and *encomendar*, 'to entrust as a charge', occur in the same paragraph: *repartir encomiendas—repartimiento de encomiendas* are familiar phrases. Indeed Velasco, the official geographer, in his statistical survey of the Indies

(c. 1574), never uses the term *encomienda*: for example, he writes, 'Cartago . . . is a city of seventeen *encomenderos* . . . there are 4500 tributary Indians *repartidos* in as many *repartimientos* as there are *encomenderos*'.

The *encomienda* was not a landed estate and had nothing to do with ownership of land: the *encomendero* was lord of a district or village or group of villages whose inhabitants owed to him the same services which otherwise would have been due to the Crown; but he did not own the soil of his territorial fief: indeed in parts where a territorial grant was inconvenient, the *encomienda* consisted of an Indian chief and his tribe. After the Conquest, from 1552 onwards, the Crown attempted to reform the *encomiendas* by forbidding the *encomenderos* to exact any other service than the payment of the poll-tax.

IV. Audiencia

On page 43 the term *Audiencia* ('Supreme Court') is used by anticipation. The four *oidores* who ruled in Santo Domingo from 1511 did not receive that full official title until 1526. As conquest advanced, every capital had its *Audiencia*, consisting of trained lawyers sent from Spain. Having an uninterrupted life and holding supreme power during any vacancy, the *Audiencia* exercised a stable and consistent authority in its advisory and administrative functions, as also in its judicial decisions. It was, like every tribunal which has to interpret law, in some degree a legislative body—the more so owing to the distance from Spain and slow communication with the Council of the Indies.

INDEX

ABOUT THE AUTHOR

F. A. KIRKPATRICK is Emeritus Reader
in Spanish at the University of Cambridge.
He is the author of
History of the Argentine Republic
and is a contributor to the
Cambridge Modern History.